Su e Sketch

Presented by Ume Aoki

Room 201

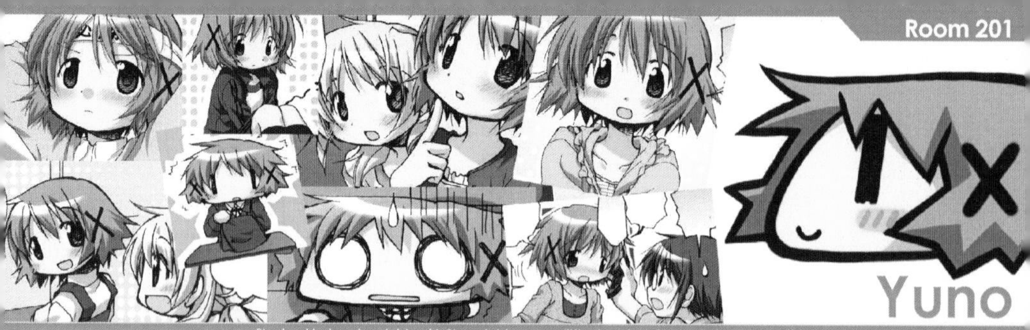

Yuno

She is a kind and amiable girl. She might seem a little slow, but she works hard in anything she does. She likes cute things.

Room 202

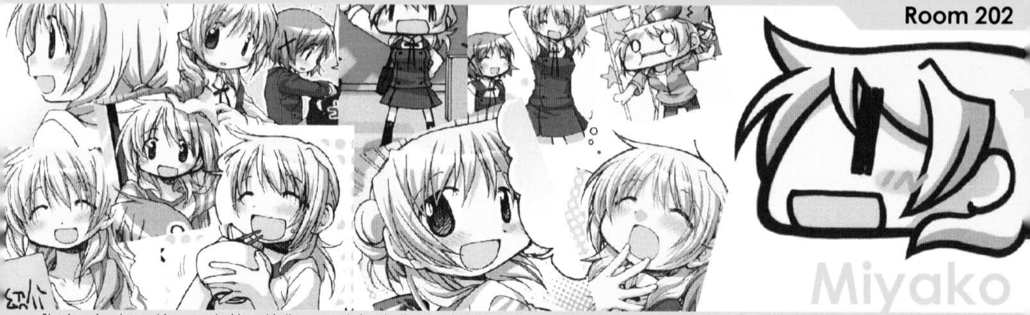

Miyako

She is a simple and innocent girl and is the group's inspiration (er, troublemaker?). She is always on budget and hungry. Surprisingly, she does well in school!

Character Profiles

Sunshine Sketch 4

She is a gentle and caring big sister type. She is good at cooking and has a sweet tooth. She is always worried about her weight.

Hiro

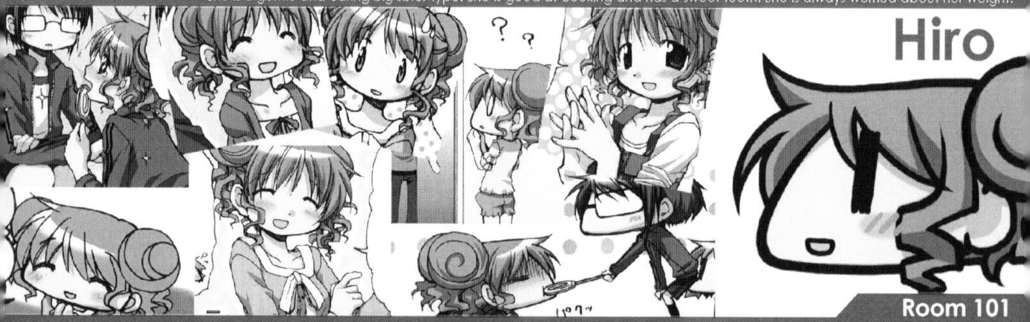

Room 101

She is a novelist. She seems to have a lot of experience with love, but actually she reads most of what she knows. She is a slender, beautiful, and talented girl.

Sae

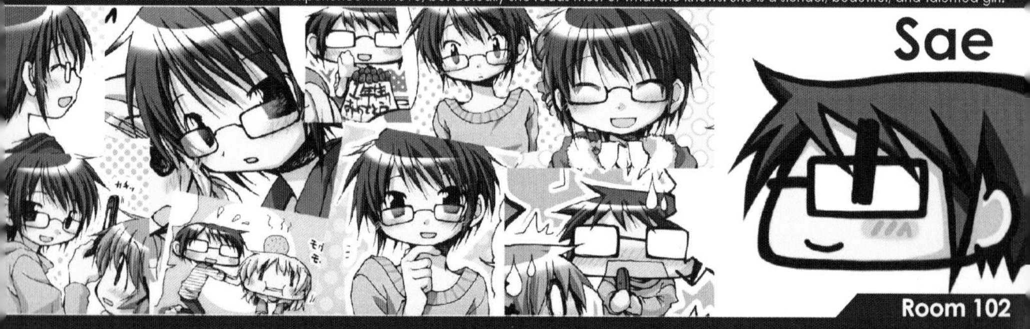

Room 102

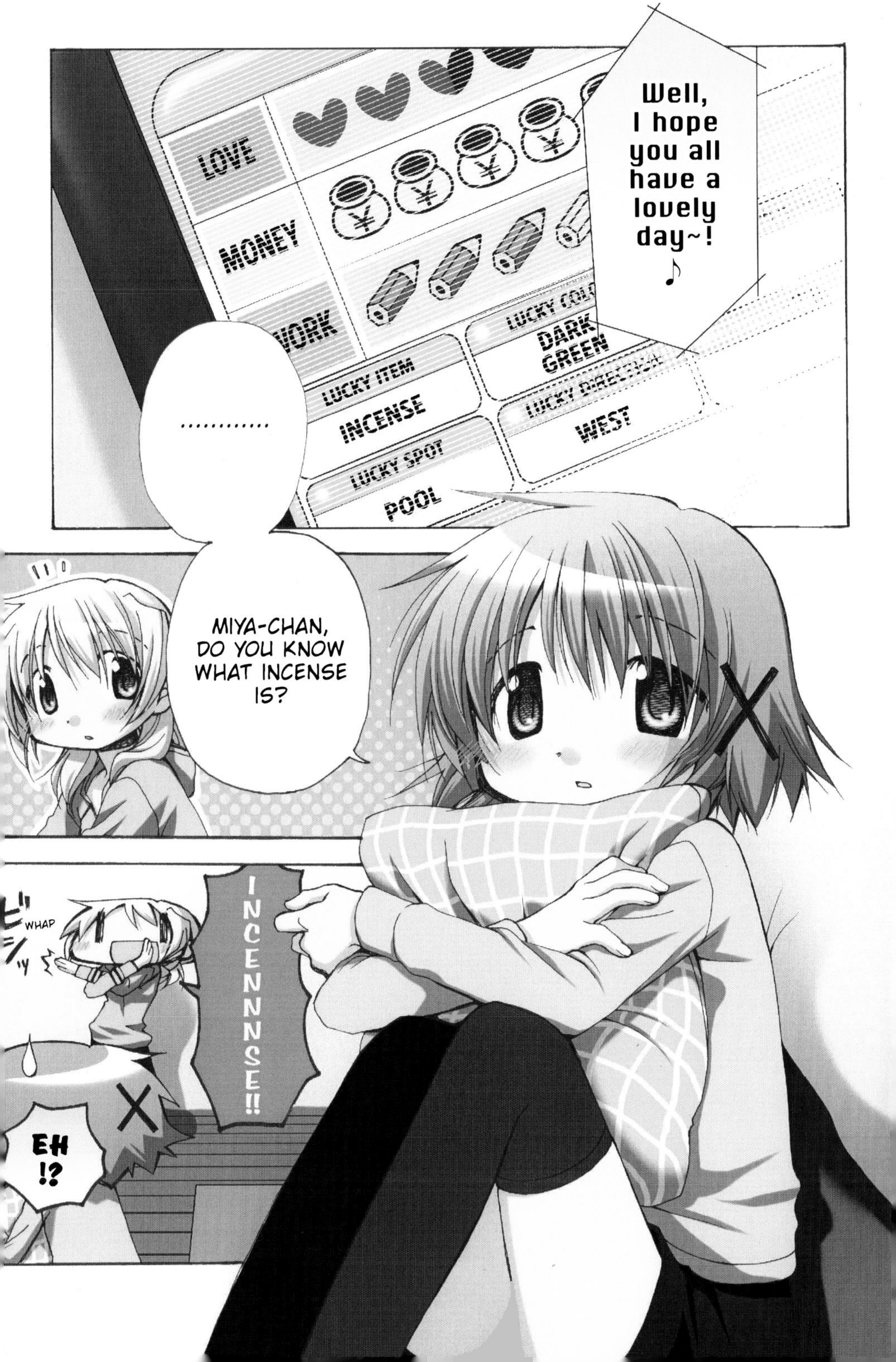
Well, I hope you all have a lovely day~! ♪
LOVE
MONEY
WORK
DARK GREEN
LUCKY ITEM
INCENSE
WEST
LUCKY SPOT
POOL
....
MIYA-CHAN, DO YOU KNOW WHAT INCENSE IS?
INCENNNSE!!
WHAP
EH!?

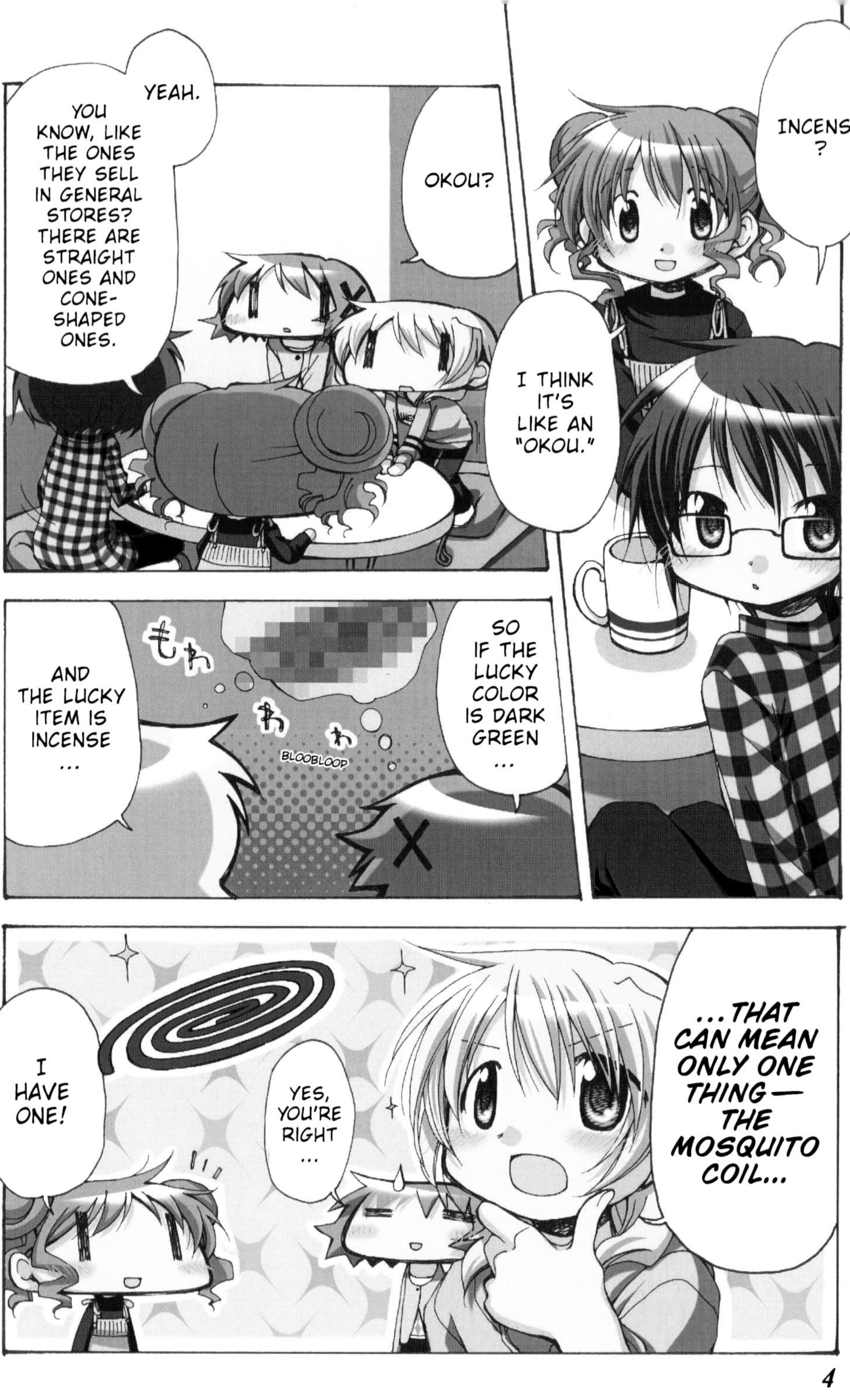

INCENSE?
I THINK IT'S LIKE AN "OKOU."
OKOU?
YEAH. YOU KNOW, LIKE THE ONES THEY SELL IN GENERAL STORES? THERE ARE STRAIGHT ONES AND CONE-SHAPED ONES.
SO IF THE LUCKY COLOR IS DARK GREEN...
もわわわ
BLOOBLOOP
AND THE LUCKY ITEM IS INCENSE...
...THAT CAN MEAN ONLY ONE THING—THE MOSQUITO COIL...
YES, YOU'RE RIGHT...
I HAVE ONE!

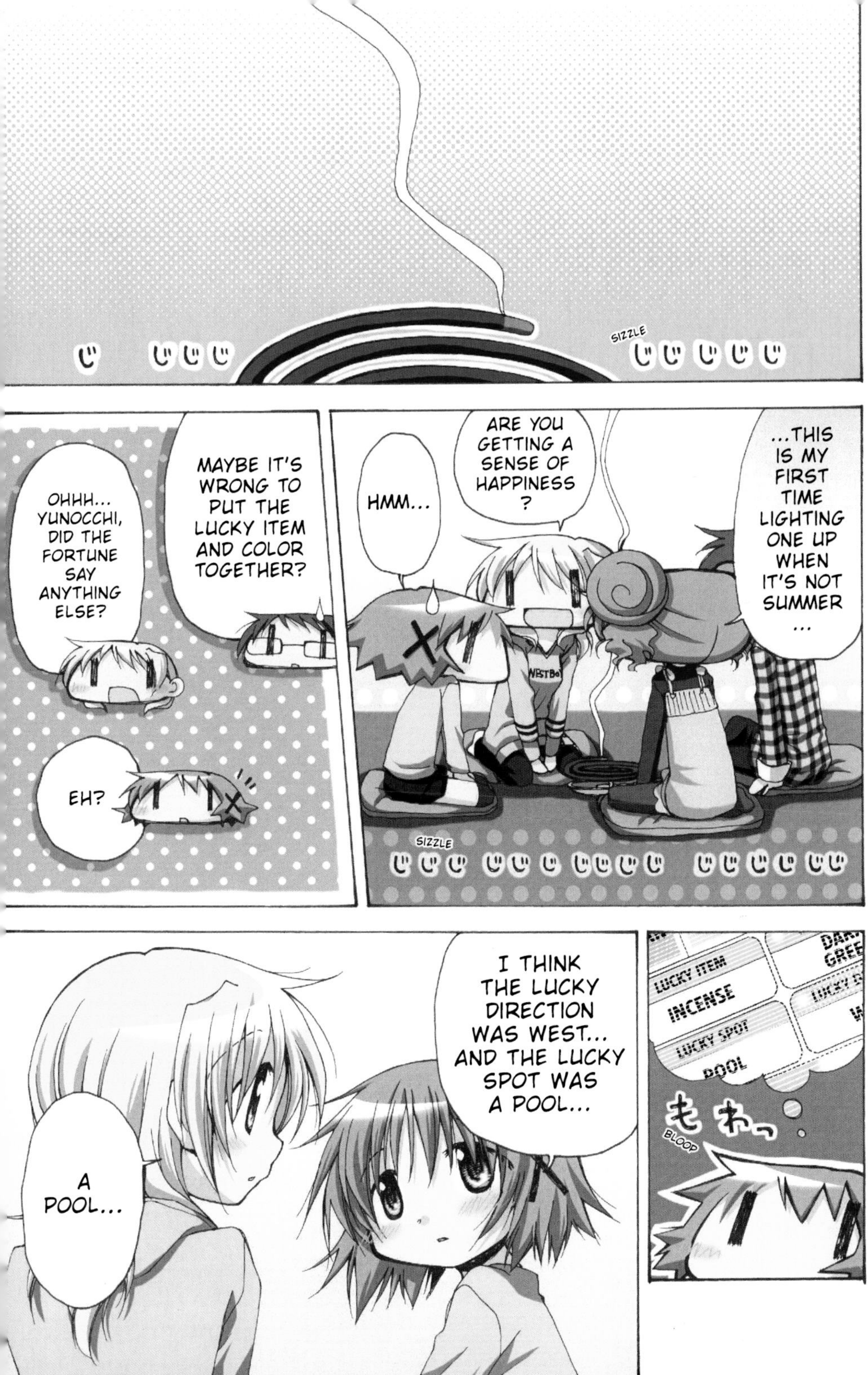
SIZZLE
じじじじじ
じ じじじ
...THIS IS MY FIRST TIME LIGHTING ONE UP WHEN IT'S NOT SUMMER...
ARE YOU GETTING A SENSE OF HAPPINESS?
HMM...
SIZZLE
じじじ じじじ じじじじ じじじじ じじ
MAYBE IT'S WRONG TO PUT THE LUCKY ITEM AND COLOR TOGETHER?
OHHH... YUNOCCHI, DID THE FORTUNE SAY ANYTHING ELSE?
EH?
LUCKY ITEM
INCENSE
LUCKY SPOT
POOL
もわっ
BLOOP
I THINK THE LUCKY DIRECTION WAS WEST... AND THE LUCKY SPOT WAS A POOL...
A POOL...

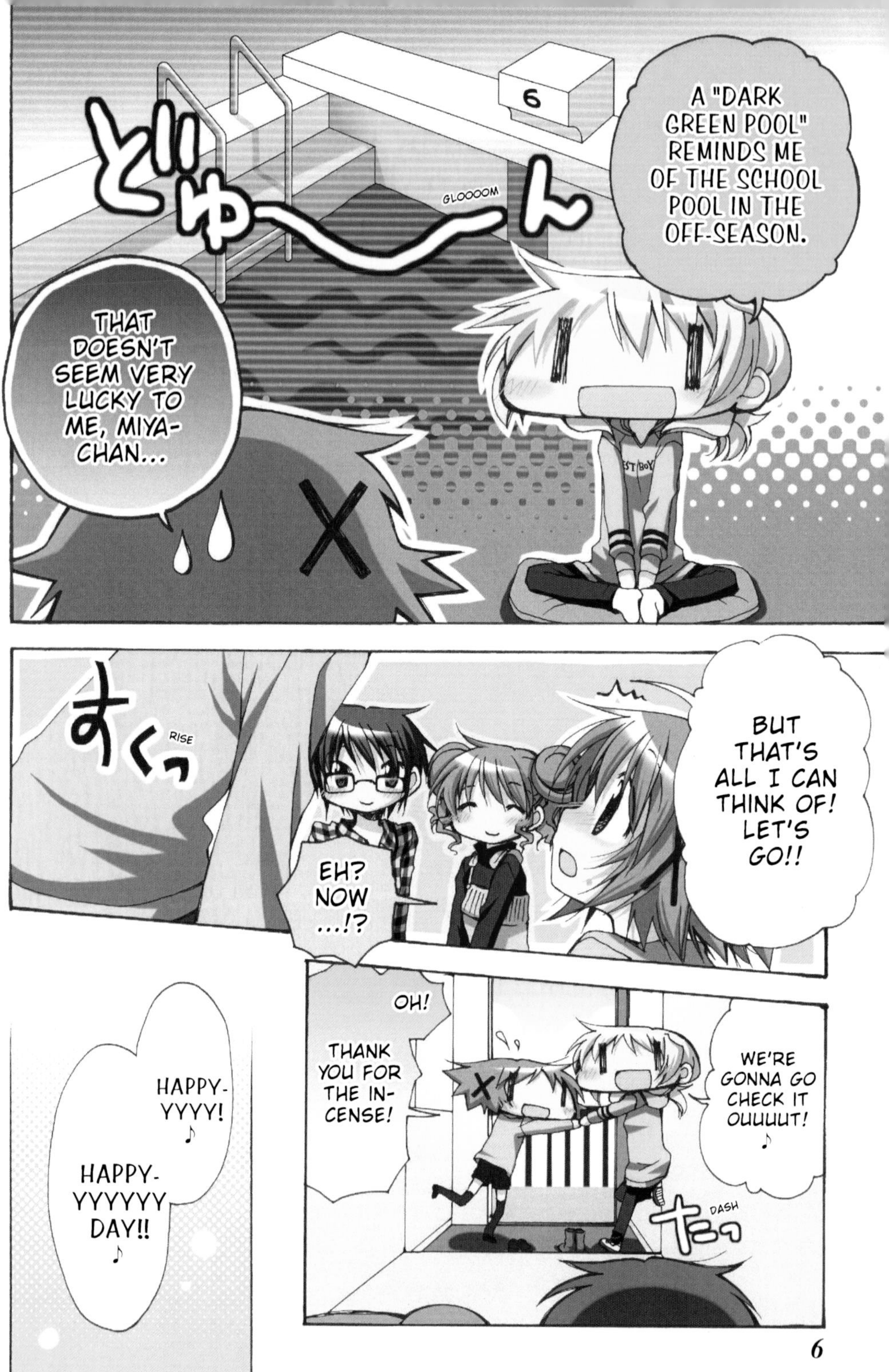
A "DARK GREEN POOL" REMINDS ME OF THE SCHOOL POOL IN THE OFF-SEASON.
どゅ～～ん
GLOOOOM
THAT DOESN'T SEEM VERY LUCKY TO ME, MIYA-CHAN...
BUT THAT'S ALL I CAN THINK OF! LET'S GO!!
EH? NOW ...!?
すくっ
RISE
WE'RE GONNA GO CHECK IT OUUUUT! ♪
OH!
THANK YOU FOR THE IN-CENSE!
たっ
DASH
HAPPY-YYYY! ♪
HAPPY-YYYYYY DAY!! ♪

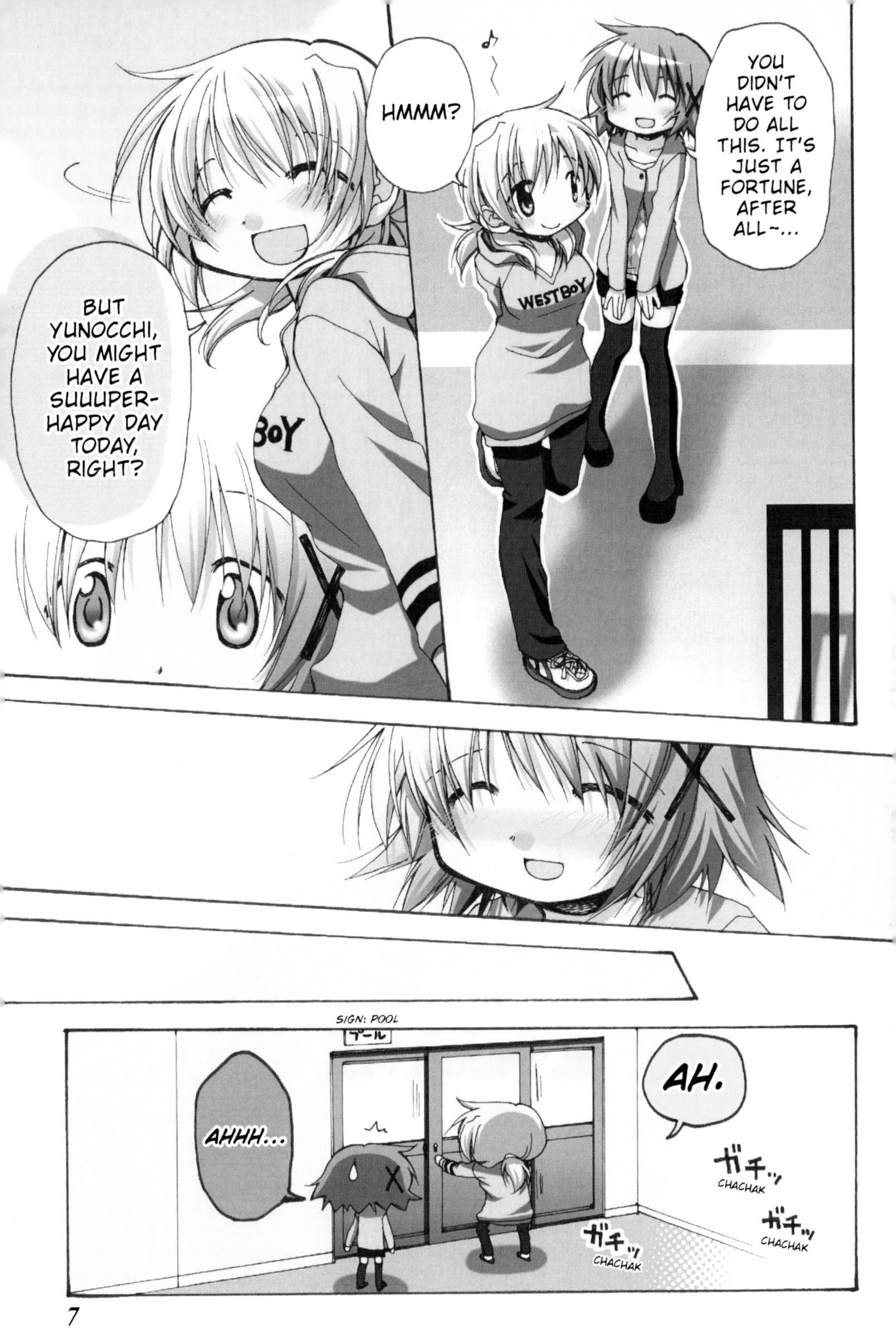
YOU DIDN'T HAVE TO DO ALL THIS. IT'S JUST A FORTUNE, AFTER ALL~...
HMMM?
BUT YUNOCCHI, YOU MIGHT HAVE A SUUUPER-HAPPY DAY TODAY, RIGHT?
WESTBOY
SIGN: POOL
プール
AH.
ガチッ
CHACHAK
ガチッ
CHACHAK
ガチッ
CHACHAK
AHHH...

~ TABLE OF CONTENTS ~

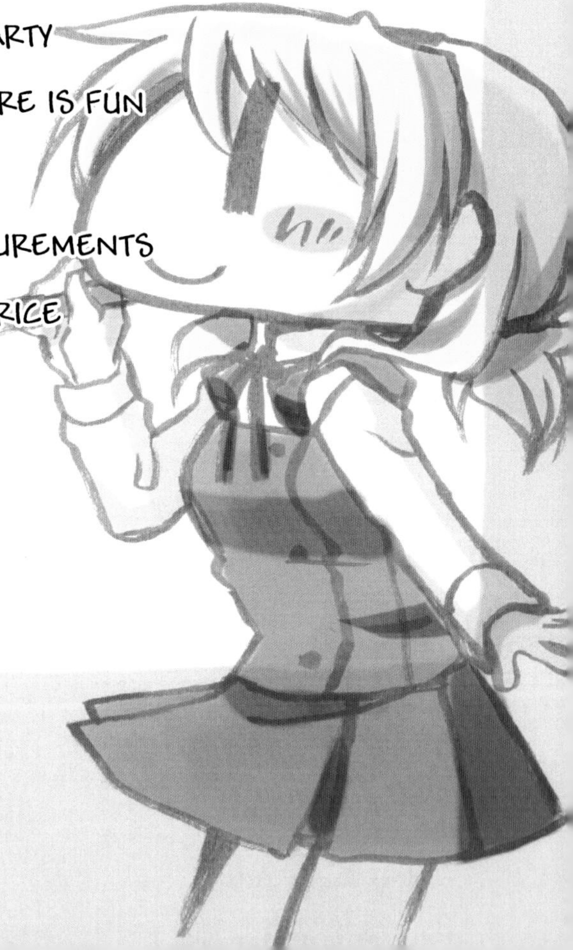

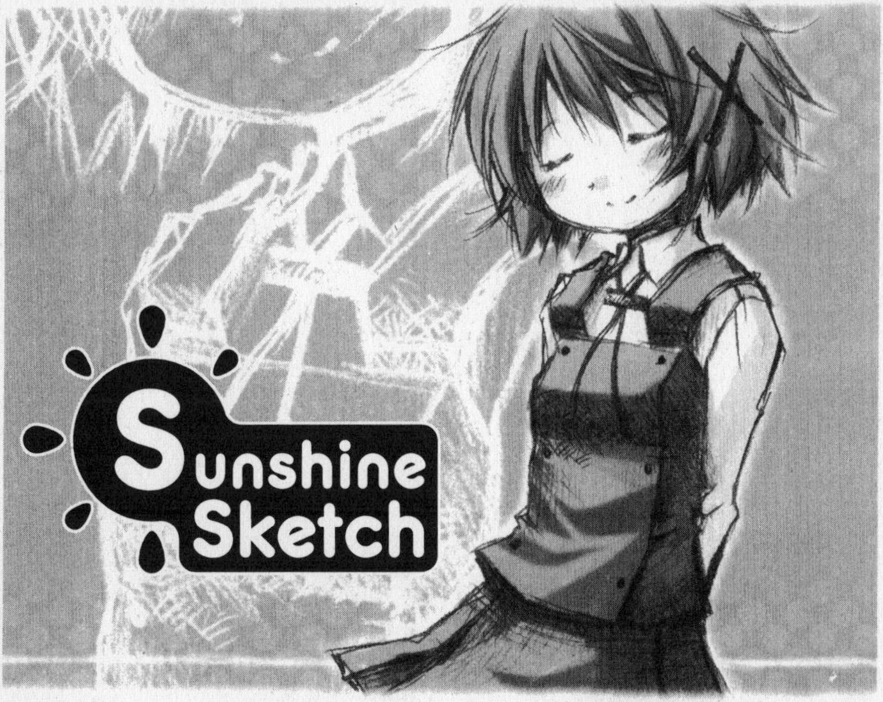
Sunshine
Sketch

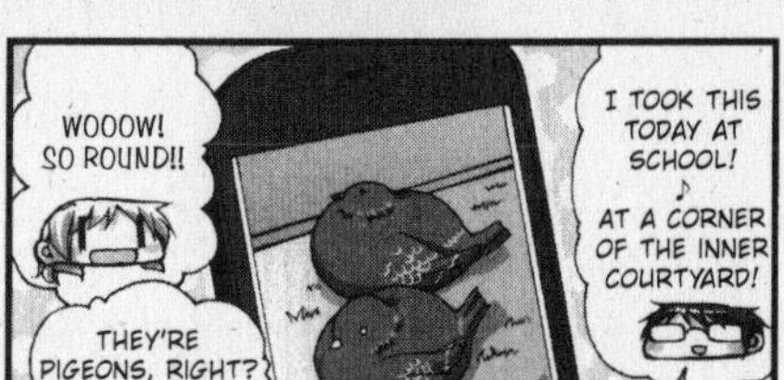
I TOOK THIS TODAY AT SCHOOL! ♪ AT A CORNER OF THE INNER COURTYARD!
WOOOW! SO ROUND!!
THEY'RE PIGEONS, RIGHT? THEY'RE TUCKING THEIR NECKS IN BECAUSE THEY'RE COLD! HOW CUTE! ♡

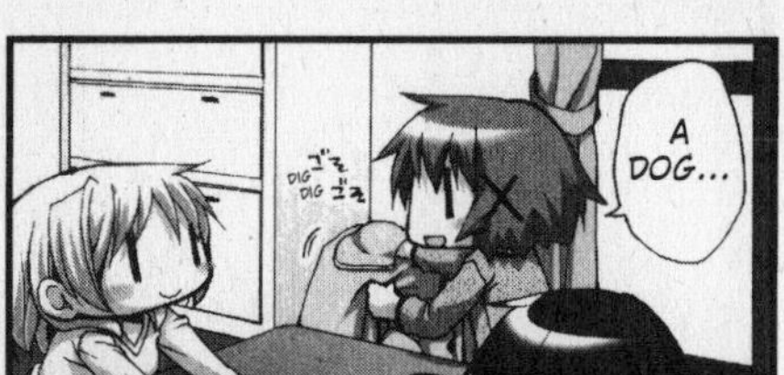
A DOG...
DIG DIG

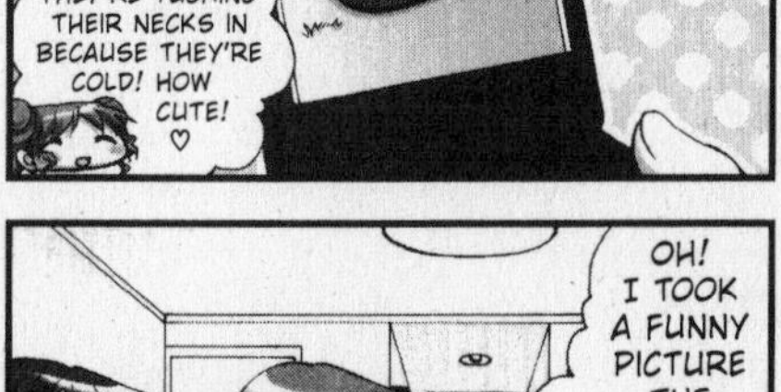
OH! I TOOK A FUNNY PICTURE THE OTHER DAY TOO! ♪
SEE, THIS DOG ...
DIG DIG

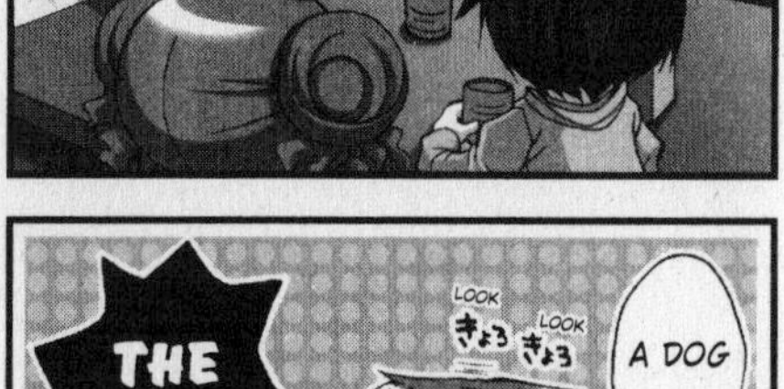
A DOG ......
LOOK LOOK
THE DOG WHAT !?

WHERE

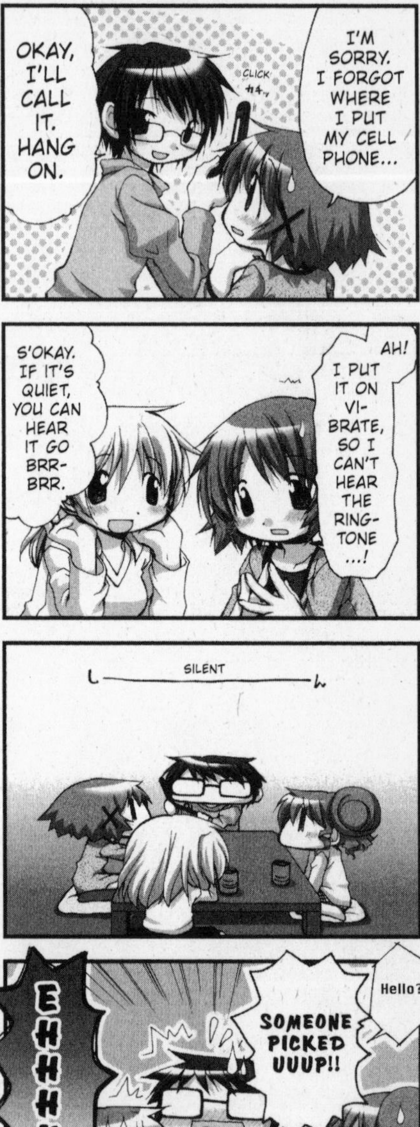

I'M SORRY. I FORGOT WHERE I PUT MY CELL PHONE...
CLICK
OKAY, I'LL CALL IT. HANG ON.
AH! I PUT IT ON VI-BRATE, SO I CAN'T HEAR THE RING-TONE ...!
S'OKAY. IF IT'S QUIET, YOU CAN HEAR IT GO BRR-BRR.
SILENT
Hello?
SOMEONE PICKED UUUP!!
EHHHHHH!!?

BRRR-BRRR

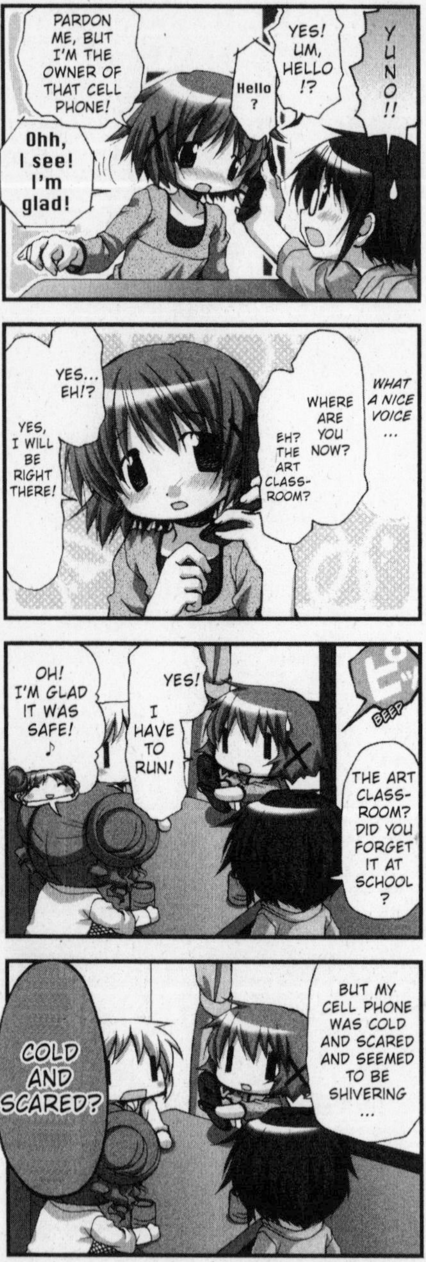

YUNO!!
YES! UM, HELLO!?
Hello?
PARDON ME, BUT I'M THE OWNER OF THAT CELL PHONE!
Ohh, I see! I'm glad!
WHAT A NICE VOICE ...
WHERE ARE YOU NOW?
EH? THE ART CLASS-ROOM?
YES... EH!?
YES, I WILL BE RIGHT THERE!
BEEP
THE ART CLASS-ROOM? DID YOU FORGET IT AT SCHOOL?
YES! I HAVE TO RUN!
OH! I'M GLAD IT WAS SAFE! ♪
BUT MY CELL PHONE WAS COLD AND SCARED AND SEEMED TO BE SHIVERING ...
COLD AND SCARED?

GIRL IN THE LIGHT

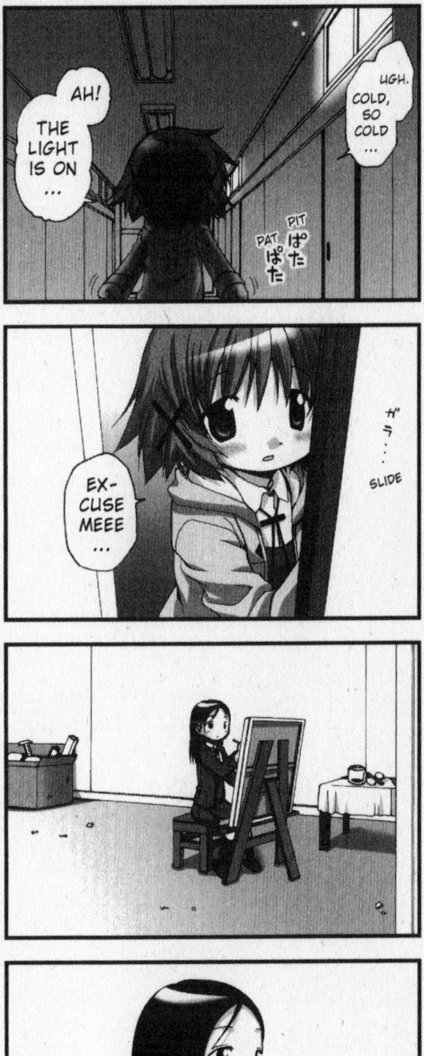
UGH. COLD, SO COLD...
AH! THE LIGHT IS ON...
PIT PAT
ぱたぱた
ガラ...
SLIDE
EX-CUSE MEEE...

FIRST CONTACT

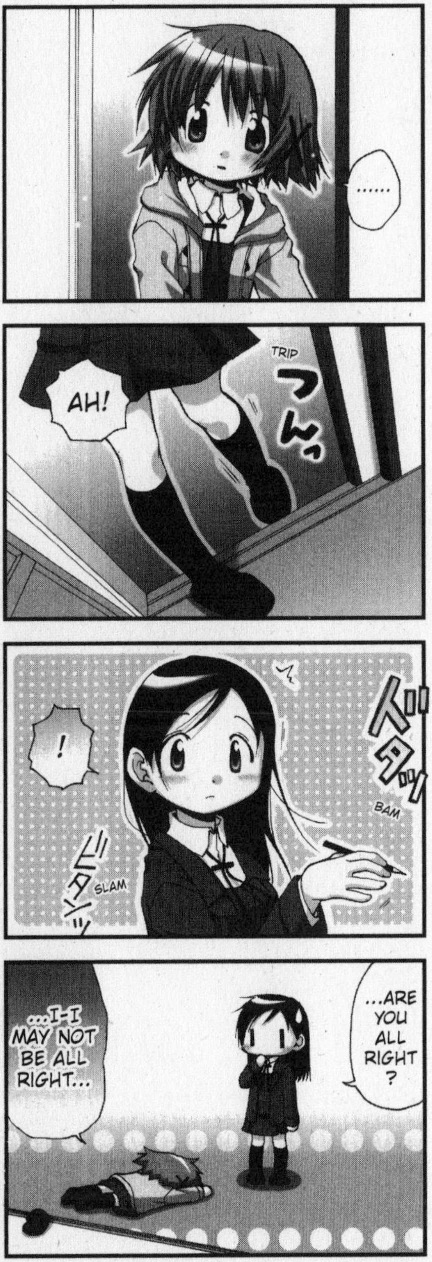
......
TRIP
つんっ
AH!
ドタッ
BAM
!
ビタンッ
SLAM
...ARE YOU ALL RIGHT?
...I-I MAY NOT BE ALL RIGHT...

REPORT WITH A SMILE

SO YOU'RE YUNO-SAN?
I'M ARISAWA, A THIRD-YEAR. PLEASED TO MEET YOU.
A THIRD-YEAR ...
AH.
HERE YOU GO, YOUR PHONE.
IT SURPRISED ME WHEN IT SUDDENLY STARTED GOING BRRR-BRRR~!
HEE-HEE! ふふ♥
I— I'M SORRY!!
I THOUGHT I WAS GOING TO HAVE A HEART ATTACK. ♡
I'M SO SORRY...

EXPERIMENTAL BODY

...HUH? BUT AREN'T THIRD-YEARS ON OPTIONAL ATTENDANCE RIGHT NOW ...?
?
YES.
I REALLY SHOULD BE AT THE LAB, BUT...
...I DIDN'T LIKE THE TENSION, SO I SKIPPED OUT! ♪
LAB?
TENSION?
IS IT... ELECTRIC SHOCK? OR MAYBE HYDROCHLORIC ACID...?
NN?

YOSHINOYA DISEASE

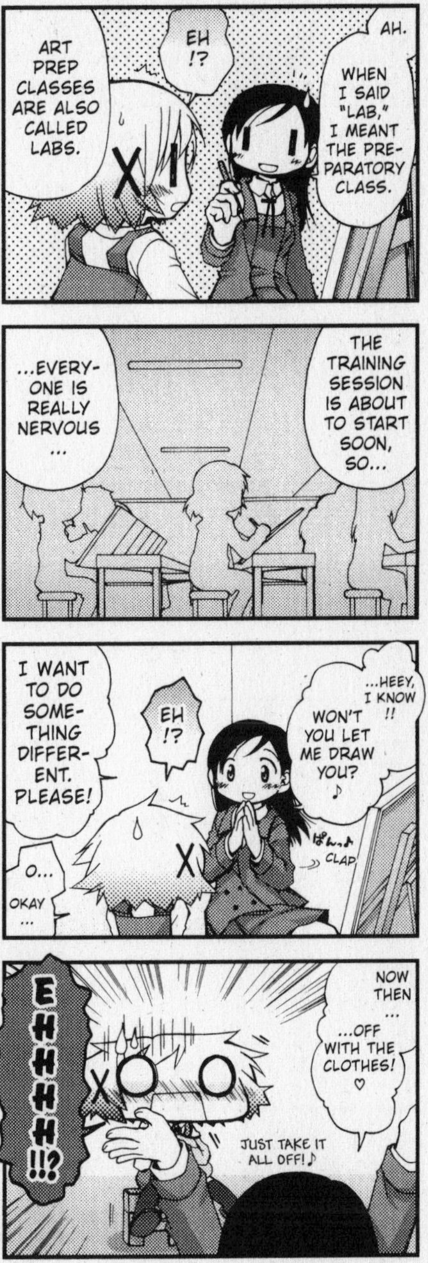
AH.
WHEN I SAID "LAB," I MEANT THE PREPARATORY CLASS.
EH !?
ART PREP CLASSES ARE ALSO CALLED LABS.
THE TRAINING SESSION IS ABOUT TO START SOON, SO...
...EVERYONE IS REALLY NERVOUS...
...HEEY, I KNOW !!
WON'T YOU LET ME DRAW YOU? ♪
EH !?
I WANT TO DO SOMETHING DIFFERENT. PLEASE!
CLAP
O... OKAY...
NOW THEN... ...OFF WITH THE CLOTHES! ♡
EHHHHH!!?
JUST TAKE IT ALL OFF!♪

A NEW ALIAS

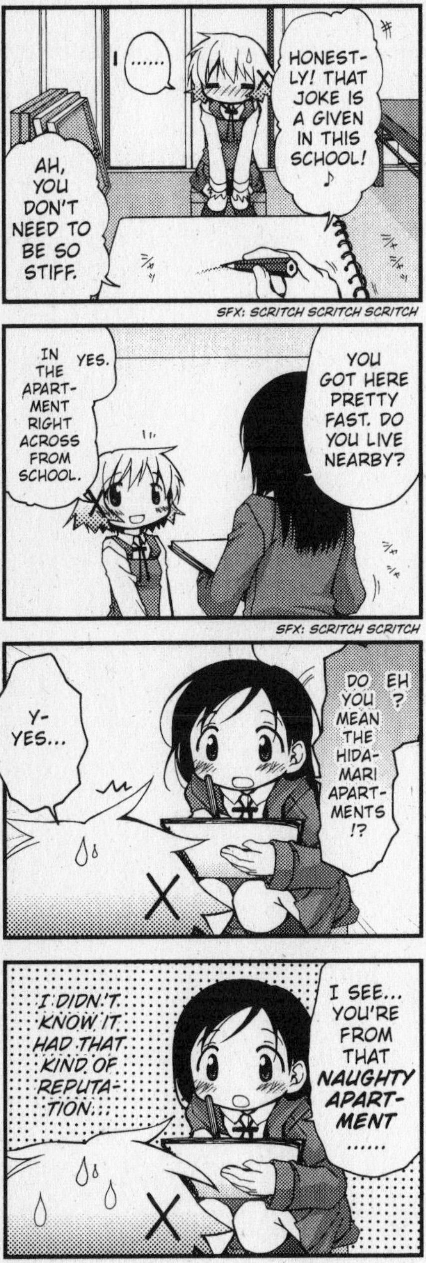
HONESTLY! THAT JOKE IS A GIVEN IN THIS SCHOOL! ♪
I ......
AH, YOU DON'T NEED TO BE SO STIFF.
SFX: SCRITCH SCRITCH SCRITCH
YOU GOT HERE PRETTY FAST. DO YOU LIVE NEARBY?
YES.
IN THE APARTMENT RIGHT ACROSS FROM SCHOOL.
SFX: SCRITCH SCRITCH
EH ?
DO YOU MEAN THE HIDAMARI APARTMENTS !?
Y-YES...
I SEE... YOU'RE FROM THAT NAUGHTY APARTMENT......
I DIDN'T KNOW IT HAD THAT KIND OF REPUTATION.

OBJECTIVE

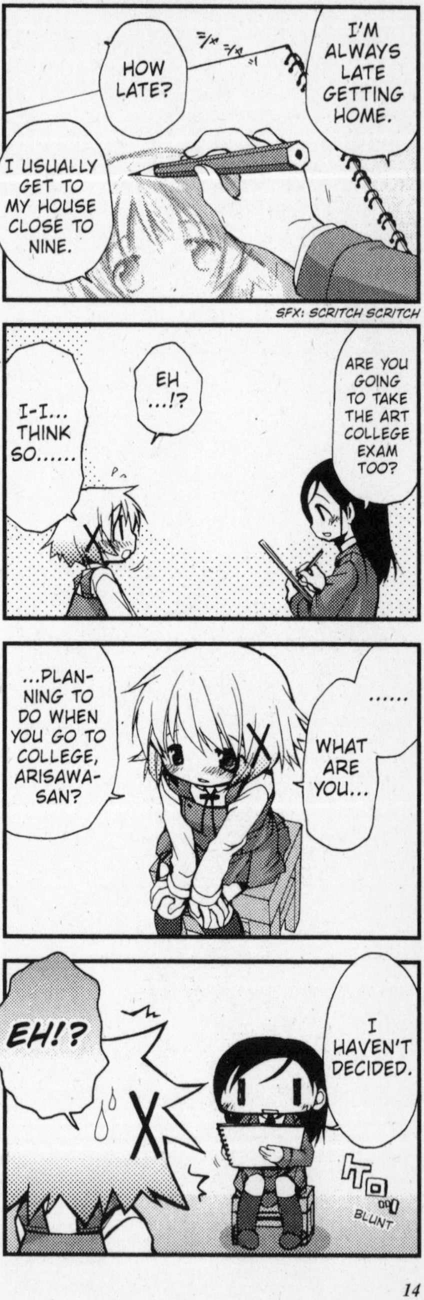
I'M ALWAYS LATE GETTING HOME.
HOW LATE?
I USUALLY GET TO MY HOUSE CLOSE TO NINE.
SFX: SCRITCH SCRITCH
ARE YOU GOING TO TAKE THE ART COLLEGE EXAM TOO?
EH ...!?
I-I... THINK SO......
...... WHAT ARE YOU...
...PLANNING TO DO WHEN YOU GO TO COLLEGE, ARISAWA-SAN?
I HAVEN'T DECIDED.
BLUNT
EH!?

DETERMINATION

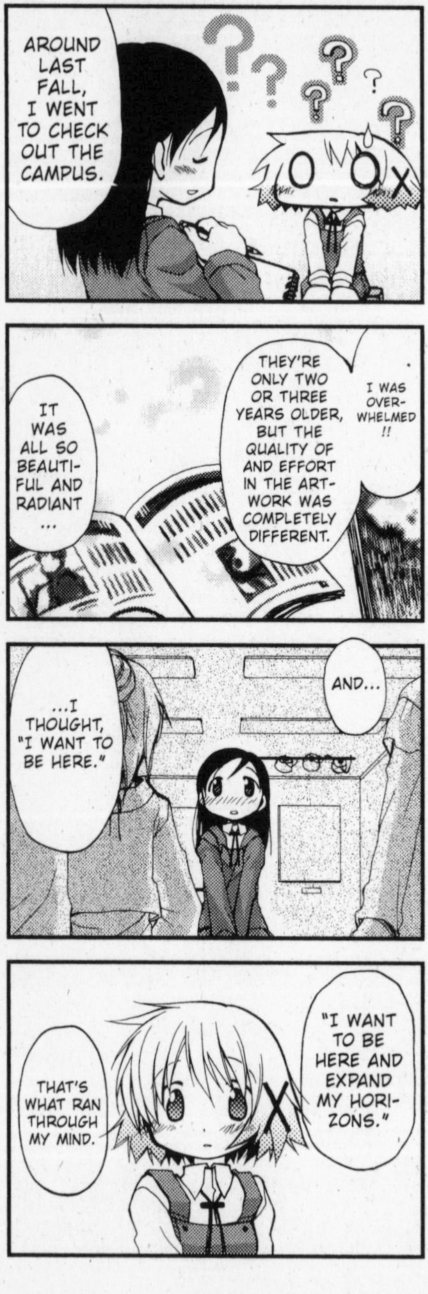
AROUND LAST FALL, I WENT TO CHECK OUT THE CAMPUS.
I WAS OVERWHELMED !!
THEY'RE ONLY TWO OR THREE YEARS OLDER, BUT THE QUALITY OF AND EFFORT IN THE ARTWORK WAS COMPLETELY DIFFERENT.
IT WAS ALL SO BEAUTIFUL AND RADIANT ...
AND...
...I THOUGHT, "I WANT TO BE HERE."
"I WANT TO BE HERE AND EXPAND MY HORIZONS."
THAT'S WHAT RAN THROUGH MY MIND.

STRAIGHTFORWARD WORDS

FIN-ISHED! ♪
IT'S A BIT ROUGH, BUT...WILL YOU TAKE A LOOK?
EH !?
YES!
WOW ...!
IT'S VERY GOOD... ...BUT IT'S NOT JUST THAT.
IT HAS THIS SENSE OF EXISTENCE WHICH MAKES IT A WARM AND RE-MARKABLE WORK...
AH!
I'M SORRY FOR SOUNDING SO ARROGANT!!
BUH!
NO, NO! I'M NOT UPSET...!
FIZZLE

SEE OFF

SORRY FOR KEEPING YOU SO LATE.
NOT AT ALL! I HAD FUN! ♪
ME TOO ......
IT'S BEEN A WHILE SINCE I ENJOYED DRAWING THAT MUCH.
THANK YOU.
WELL, SEE YOU LATER!
AH!
UM!
GOOD LUCK... ...ON YOUR EXAM!
...I'LL DO MY BEST!
HERE I GO!

SECRET

!
A CALL?
...OH, IT'S SAE-SAN!
ブブブブブブーッ
HELLO?
Hello, Yuno? Thank goodness!
It was late, so I was getting worried. Where are you now?
IN FRONT OF THE NAUGHTY APARTMENT. ♪
Eh?
Where's that?
ひだま

SFX: BRR BRR BRR BRR BRR BRR BRR BRR BRR

SIGN: HIDAMARI

THE ORIGINAL IS A CHARM

I'M HOME! I'M SORRY FOR WORRYING EVERYONE.
WEL-COME BAAACK, YUNO-CCHI AND MR. PHONE! ♪
AH. PLEASE WAIT ONE MO-MENT!
DIG DIG
UMM...
EH-HEH HEH! ♪
TA-DAAH! ☆
...HUH? WHAT ABOUT THE DOG?
WHAT ARE YOU TALKING ABOUT?
EAGER
EAGER
EAGER

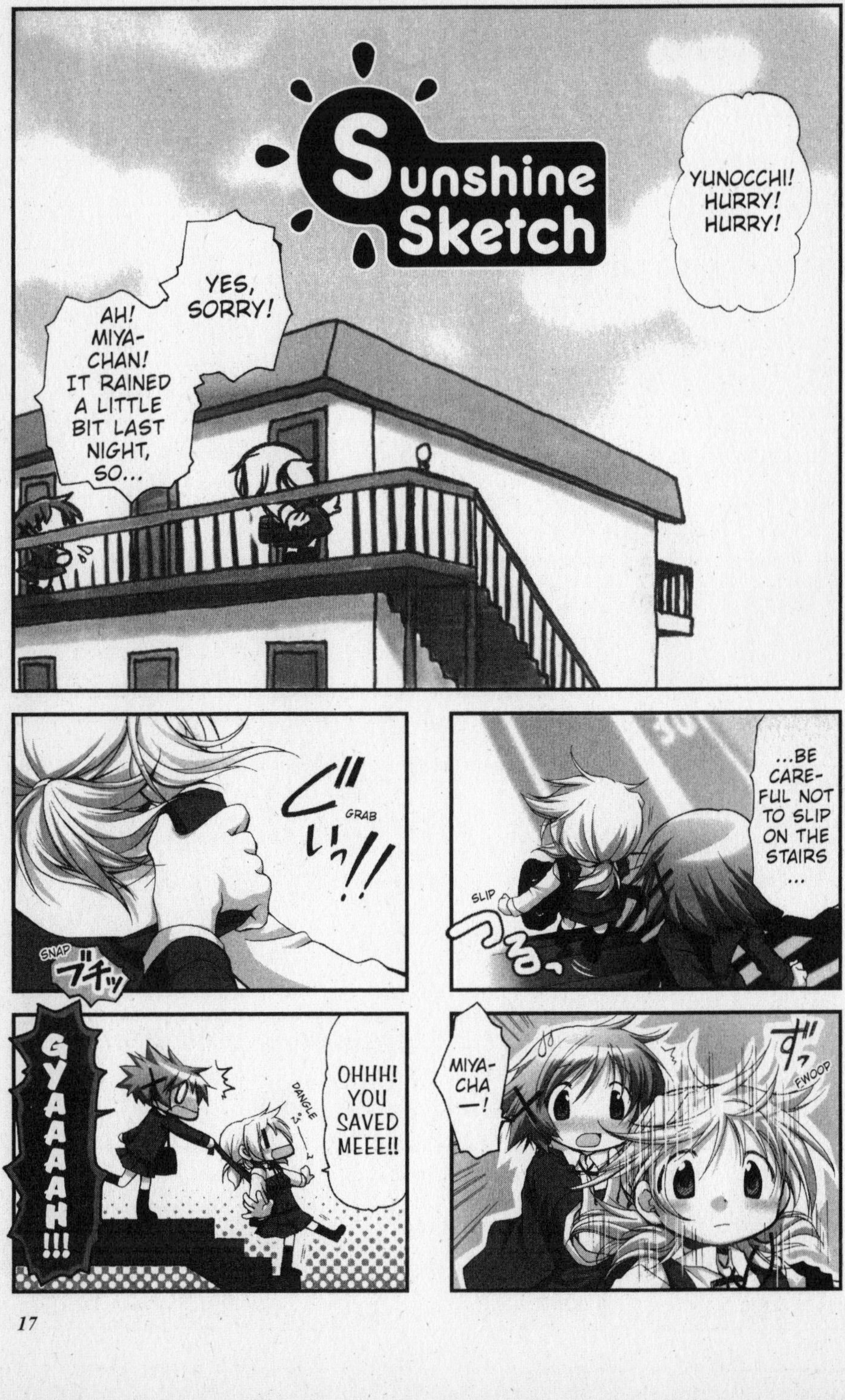
Sunshine Sketch
YUNOCCHI! HURRY! HURRY!
YES, SORRY!
AH! MIYA-CHAN! IT RAINED A LITTLE BIT LAST NIGHT, SO...
...BE CARE-FUL NOT TO SLIP ON THE STAIRS ...
SLIP
つる
ぐいっ!!
GRAB
SNAP
ブチッ
MIYA-CHA—!
ずっ
FWOOP
OHHH! YOU SAVED MEEE!!
DANGLE
GYAAAAAH!!!

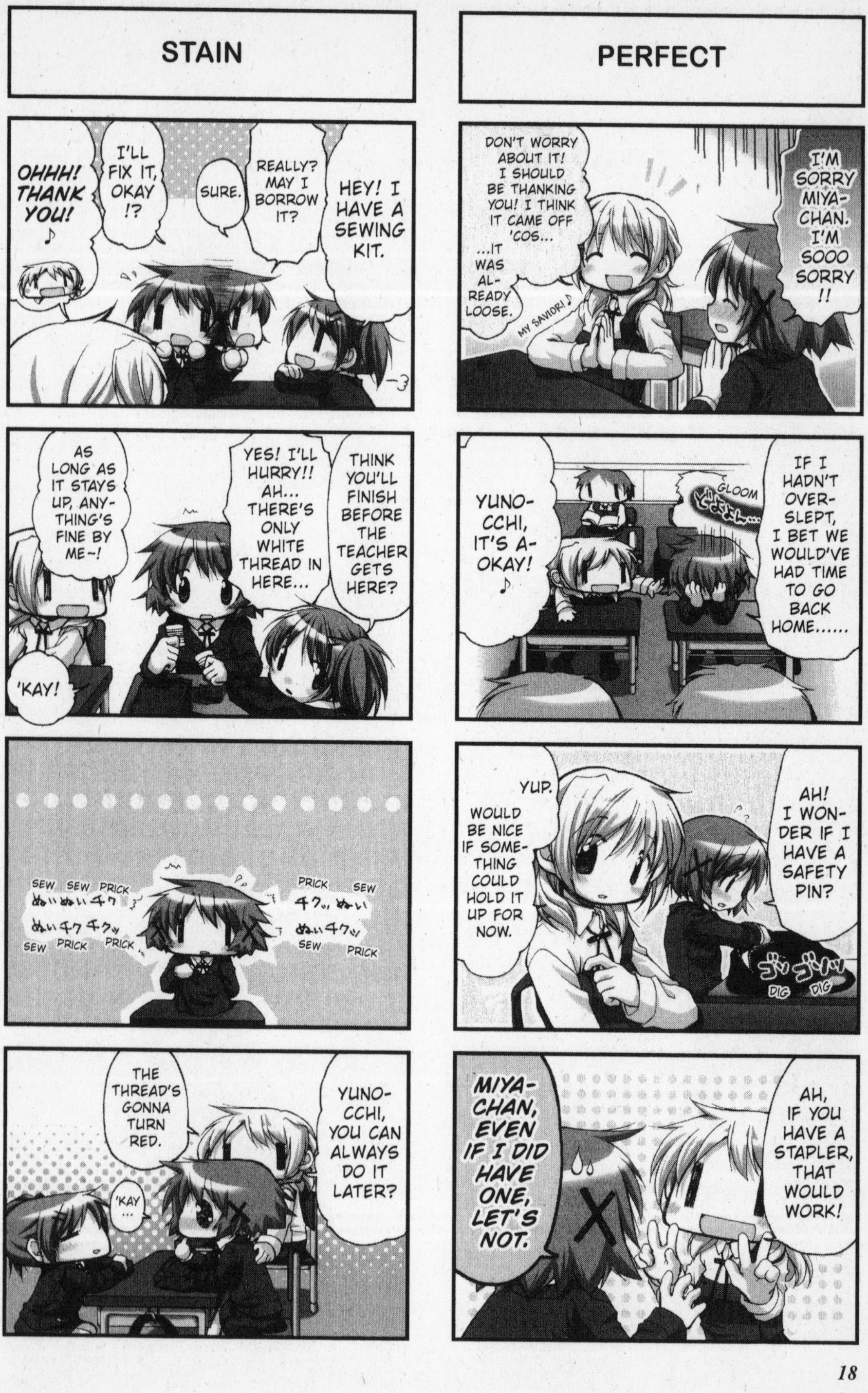
PERFECT
I'M SORRY MIYA-CHAN. I'M SOOO SORRY!!
DON'T WORRY ABOUT IT! I SHOULD BE THANKING YOU! I THINK IT CAME OFF 'COS...
...IT WAS AL-READY LOOSE.
MY SAVIOR! ♪
IF I HADN'T OVER-SLEPT, I BET WE WOULD'VE HAD TIME TO GO BACK HOME......
GLOOM
どよよん...
YUNO-CCHI, IT'S A-OKAY! ♪
AH! I WON-DER IF I HAVE A SAFETY PIN?
YUP.
WOULD BE NICE IF SOME-THING COULD HOLD IT UP FOR NOW.
ゴソゴソッ
DIG DIG
AH, IF YOU HAVE A STAPLER, THAT WOULD WORK!
MIYA-CHAN, EVEN IF I DID HAVE ONE, LET'S NOT.
STAIN
HEY! I HAVE A SEWING KIT.
REALLY? MAY I BORROW IT?
SURE.
I'LL FIX IT, OKAY!?
OHHH! THANK YOU! ♪
THINK YOU'LL FINISH BEFORE THE TEACHER GETS HERE?
YES! I'LL HURRY!! AH... THERE'S ONLY WHITE THREAD IN HERE...
AS LONG AS IT STAYS UP, ANY-THING'S FINE BY ME~!
'KAY!
PRICK SEW
チクッ ぬい
ぬい チクッ
SEW PRICK
SEW SEW PRICK
ぬいぬいチク
ぬいチクチクッ
SEW PRICK PRICK
YUNO-CCHI, YOU CAN ALWAYS DO IT LATER?
THE THREAD'S GONNA TURN RED.
'KAY...

HIGH SCHOOL BOYS

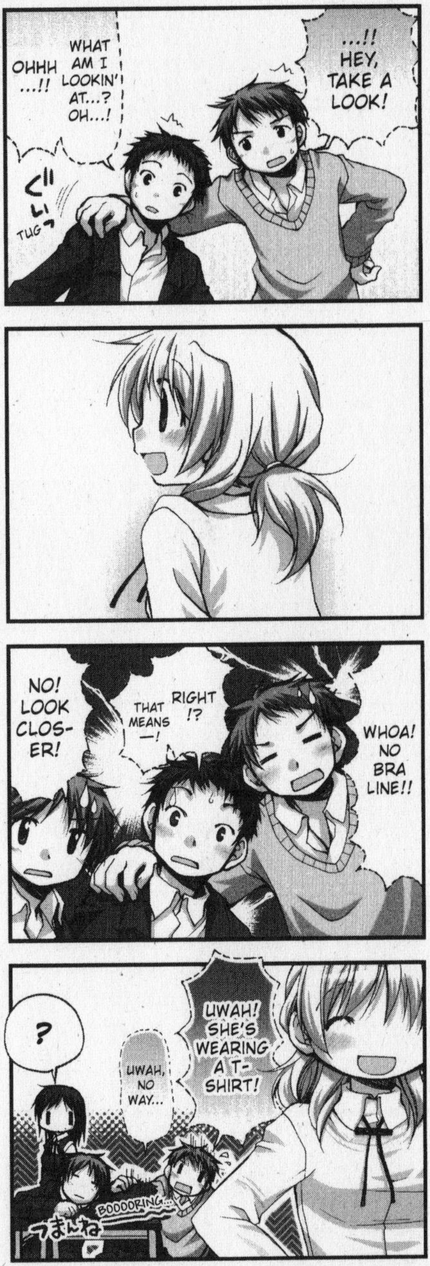
...!! HEY, TAKE A LOOK!
WHAT AM I LOOKIN' AT...? OH...!
OHHH ...!!
TUG
WHOA! NO BRA LINE!!
RIGHT !?
THAT MEANS —!
NO! LOOK CLOSER!
UWAH! SHE'S WEARING A T-SHIRT!
UWAH, NO WAY...
?
BOOOORING...

LOVE CALL

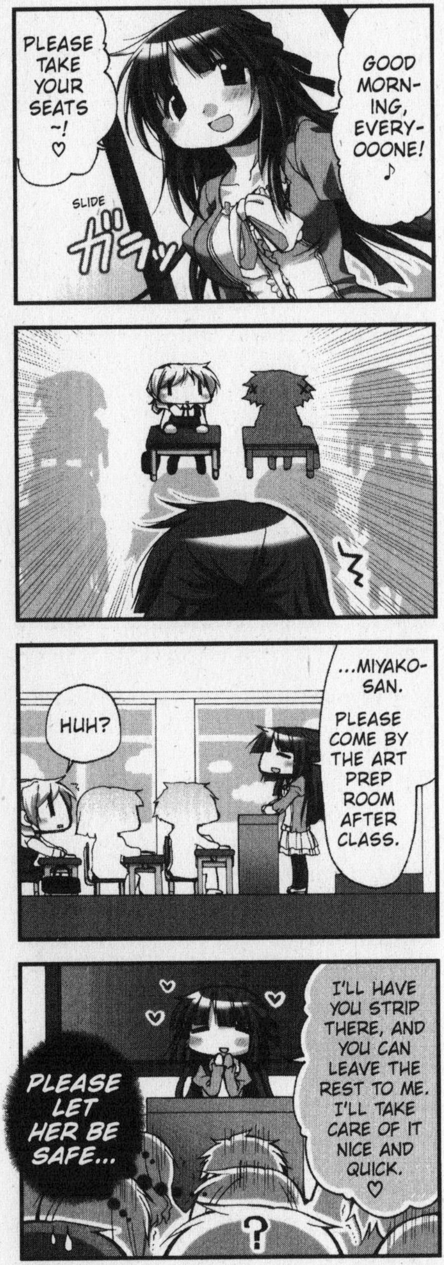
GOOD MORNING, EVERYOOONE! ♪
PLEASE TAKE YOUR SEATS ~! ♡
SLIDE
ガラッ
...MIYAKO-SAN. PLEASE COME BY THE ART PREP ROOM AFTER CLASS.
HUH?
I'LL HAVE YOU STRIP THERE, AND YOU CAN LEAVE THE REST TO ME. I'LL TAKE CARE OF IT NICE AND QUICK. ♡
PLEASE LET HER BE SAFE...
?

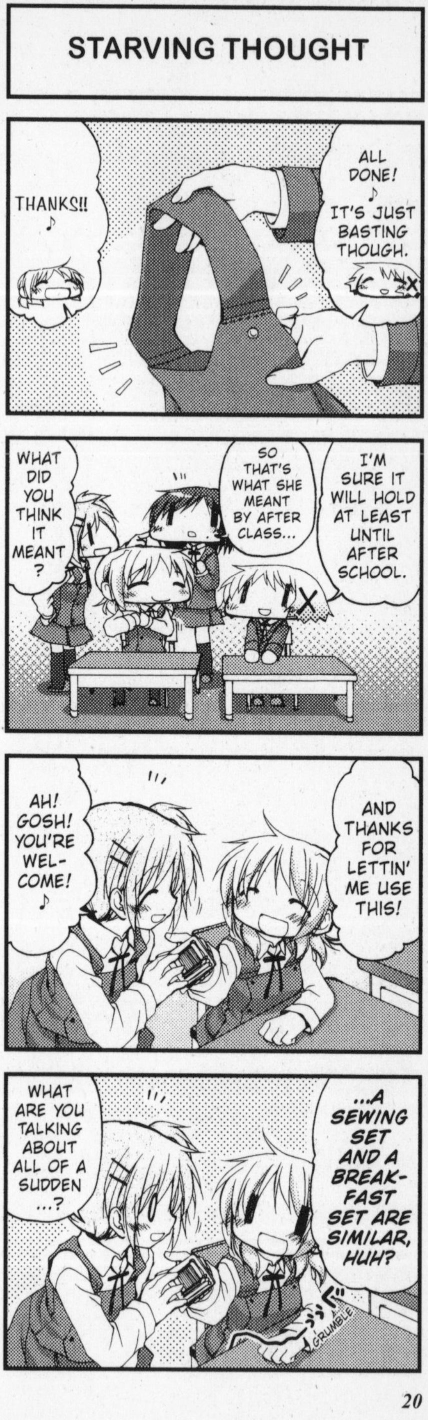
STARVING THOUGHT
ALL DONE! ♪ IT'S JUST BASTING THOUGH.
THANKS!! ♪
I'M SURE IT WILL HOLD AT LEAST UNTIL AFTER SCHOOL.
SO THAT'S WHAT SHE MEANT BY AFTER CLASS...
WHAT DID YOU THINK IT MEANT?
AND THANKS FOR LETTIN' ME USE THIS!
AH! GOSH! YOU'RE WELCOME! ♪
...A SEWING SET AND A BREAKFAST SET ARE SIMILAR, HUH?
WHAT ARE YOU TALKING ABOUT ALL OF A SUDDEN...?
GRUMBLE

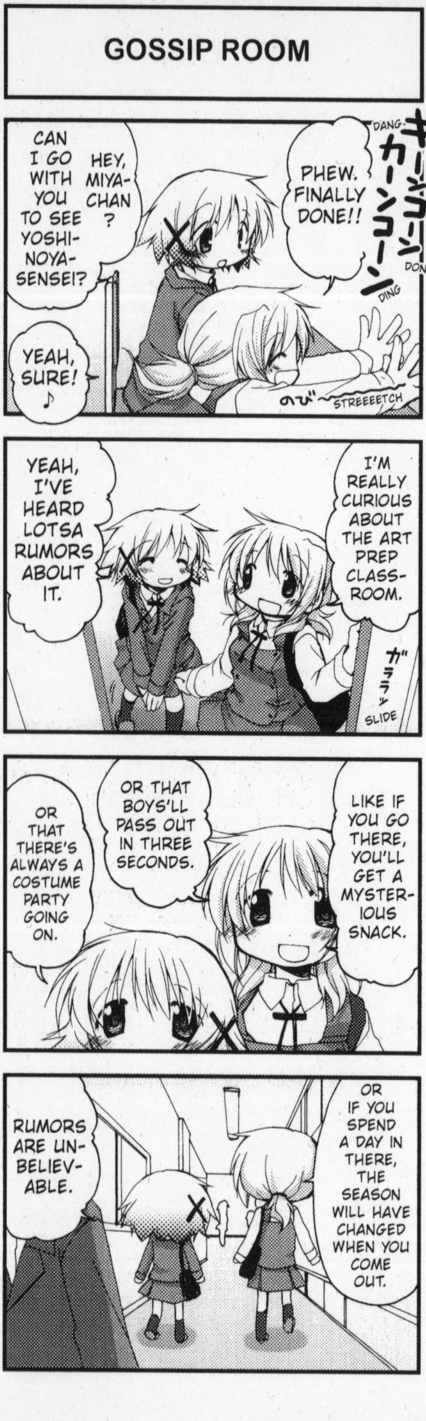
GOSSIP ROOM
キーンコーンカーンコーン
DING DANG DONG DING
PHEW. FINALLY DONE!!
HEY, MIYA-CHAN?
CAN I GO WITH YOU TO SEE YOSHINOYA-SENSEI?
YEAH, SURE! ♪
のび～ STREEEETCH
I'M REALLY CURIOUS ABOUT THE ART PREP CLASSROOM.
YEAH, I'VE HEARD LOTSA RUMORS ABOUT IT.
ガラッ SLIDE
LIKE IF YOU GO THERE, YOU'LL GET A MYSTERIOUS SNACK.
OR THAT BOYS'LL PASS OUT IN THREE SECONDS.
OR THAT THERE'S ALWAYS A COSTUME PARTY GOING ON.
OR IF YOU SPEND A DAY IN THERE, THE SEASON WILL HAVE CHANGED WHEN YOU COME OUT.
RUMORS ARE UNBELIEVABLE.

DRESSING ROOM

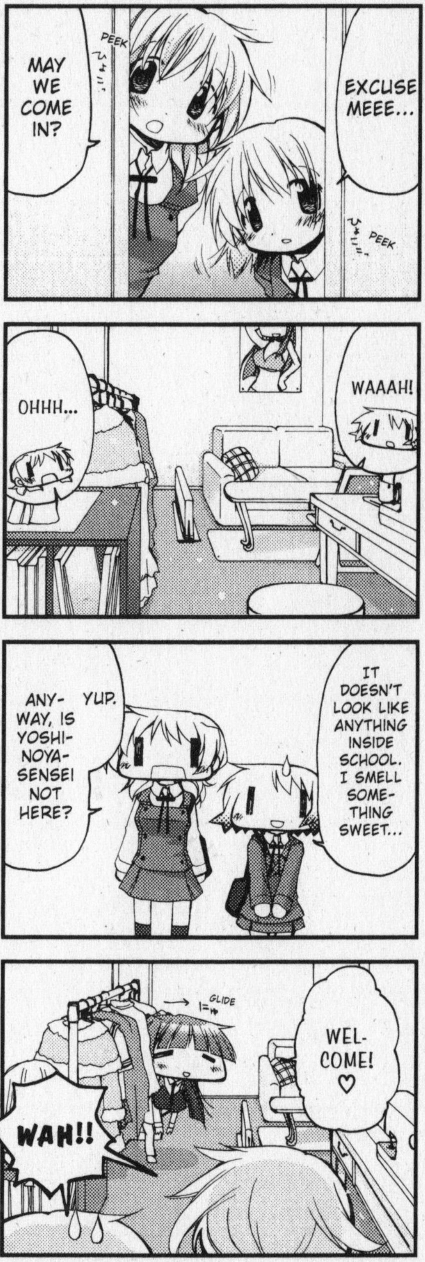
EXCUSE MEEE...
MAY WE COME IN?
PEEK
PEEK
WAAAH!
OHHH...
IT DOESN'T LOOK LIKE ANYTHING INSIDE SCHOOL. I SMELL SOMETHING SWEET...
YUP.
ANY-WAY, IS YOSHI-NOYA-SENSEI NOT HERE?
WEL-COME! ♡
GLIDE
WAH!!

NICE AND PROPER

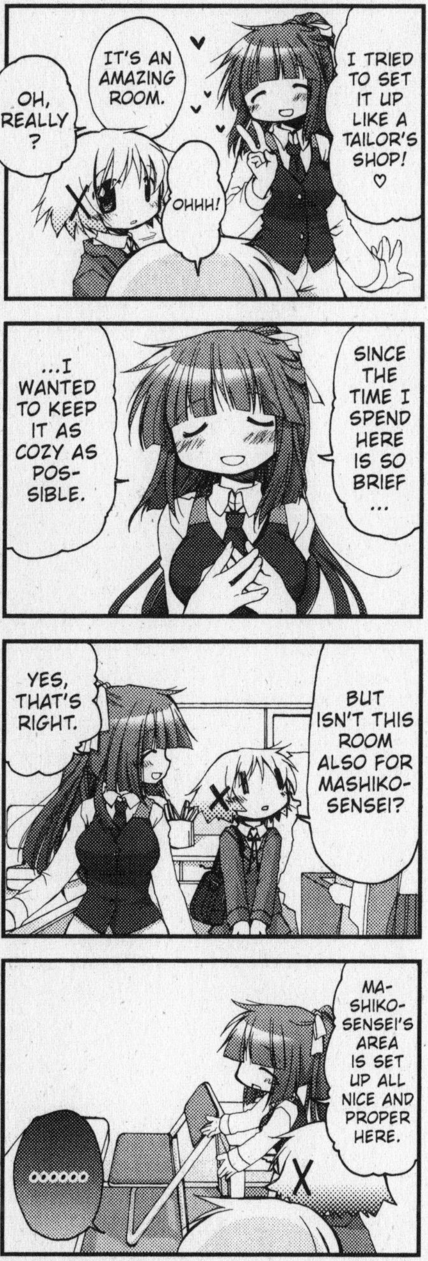
I TRIED TO SET IT UP LIKE A TAILOR'S SHOP! ♡
IT'S AN AMAZING ROOM.
OH, REALLY?
OHHH!
SINCE THE TIME I SPEND HERE IS SO BRIEF...
...I WANTED TO KEEP IT AS COZY AS POS-SIBLE.
BUT ISN'T THIS ROOM ALSO FOR MASHIKO-SENSEI?
YES, THAT'S RIGHT.
MA-SHIKO-SENSEI'S AREA IS SET UP ALL NICE AND PROPER HERE.
oooooo

NO OPTIONS

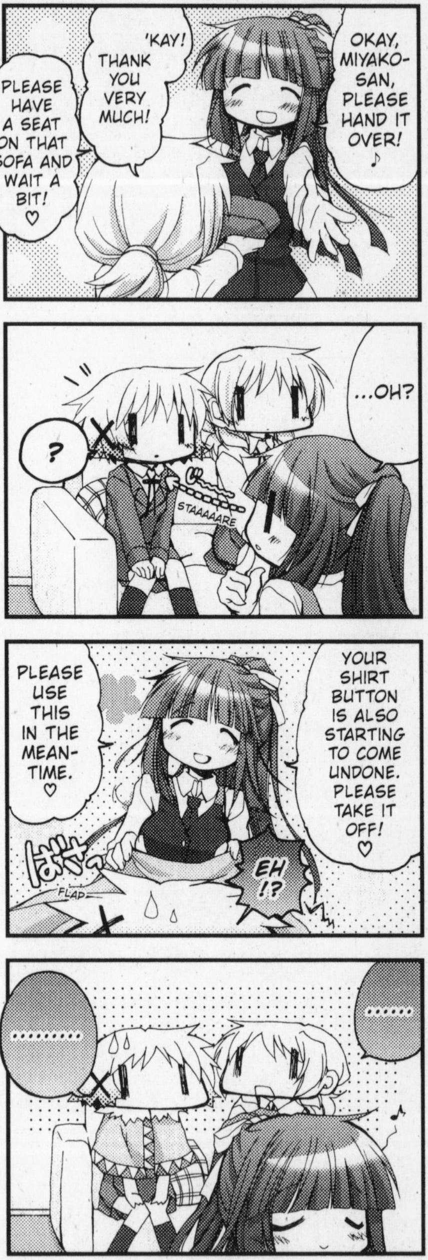
OKAY, MIYAKO-SAN, PLEASE HAND IT OVER! ♪
'KAY! THANK YOU VERY MUCH!
PLEASE HAVE A SEAT ON THAT SOFA AND WAIT A BIT! ♡
...OH?
STAAAAARE
?
YOUR SHIRT BUTTON IS ALSO STARTING TO COME UNDONE. PLEASE TAKE IT OFF! ♡
PLEASE USE THIS IN THE MEAN-TIME. ♡
EH !?
ばさっ
FLAP
......
....

HAPPINESS OF CREATION

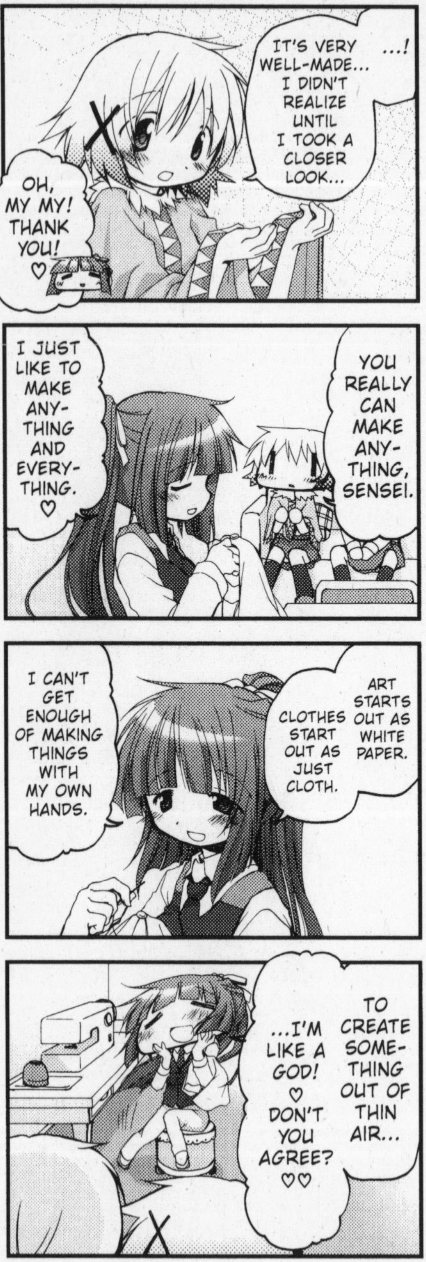
...!
IT'S VERY WELL-MADE... I DIDN'T REALIZE UNTIL I TOOK A CLOSER LOOK...
OH, MY MY! THANK YOU! ♡
YOU REALLY CAN MAKE ANY-THING, SENSEI.
I JUST LIKE TO MAKE ANY-THING AND EVERY-THING. ♡
ART STARTS OUT AS WHITE PAPER.
CLOTHES START OUT AS JUST CLOTH.
I CAN'T GET ENOUGH OF MAKING THINGS WITH MY OWN HANDS.
TO CREATE SOME-THING OUT OF THIN AIR...
...I'M LIKE A GOD! ♡ DON'T YOU AGREE? ♡♡

1 : 1 : 8

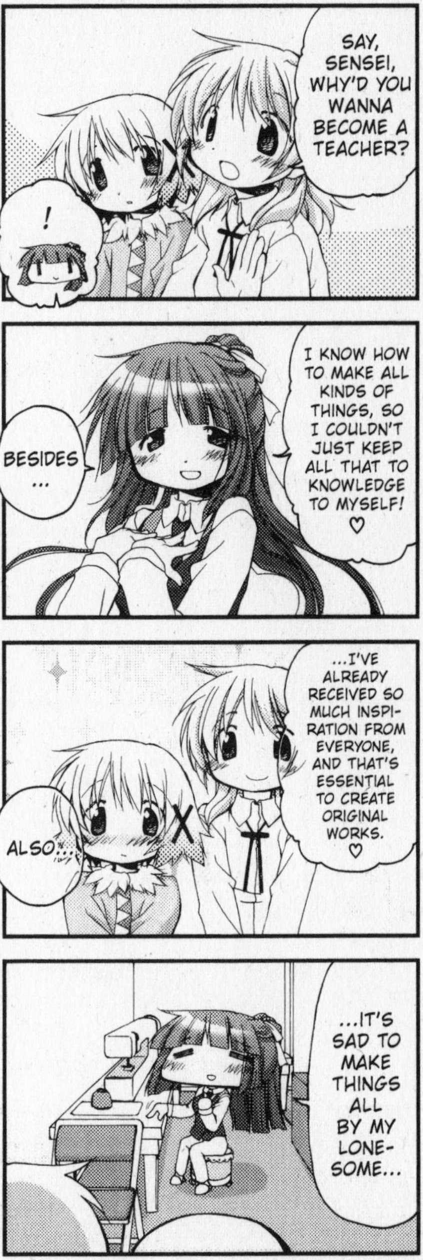

SAY, SENSEI, WHY'D YOU WANNA BECOME A TEACHER?
!
I KNOW HOW TO MAKE ALL KINDS OF THINGS, SO I COULDN'T JUST KEEP ALL THAT TO KNOWLEDGE TO MYSELF! ♡
BESIDES ...
...I'VE ALREADY RECEIVED SO MUCH INSPIRATION FROM EVERYONE, AND THAT'S ESSENTIAL TO CREATE ORIGINAL WORKS. ♡
ALSO...
...IT'S SAD TO MAKE THINGS ALL BY MY LONESOME...

ADOLESCENT GIRL

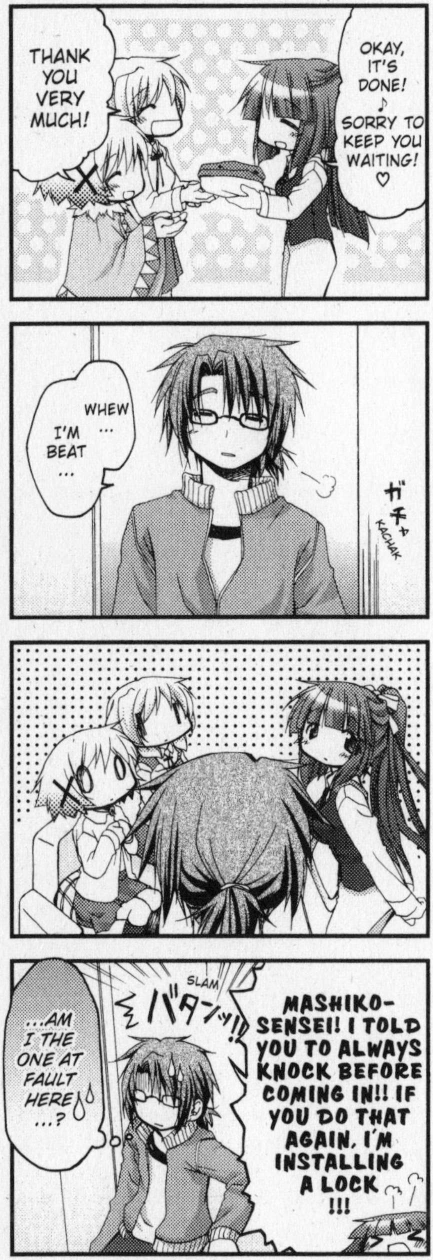

OKAY, IT'S DONE! ♪ SORRY TO KEEP YOU WAITING! ♡
THANK YOU VERY MUCH!
ガチャ
KACHAK
WHEW ... I'M BEAT ...
バタンッ!!
SLAM
MASHIKO-SENSEI! I TOLD YOU TO ALWAYS KNOCK BEFORE COMING IN!! IF YOU DO THAT AGAIN, I'M INSTALLING A LOCK !!!
...AM I THE ONE AT FAULT HERE ...?

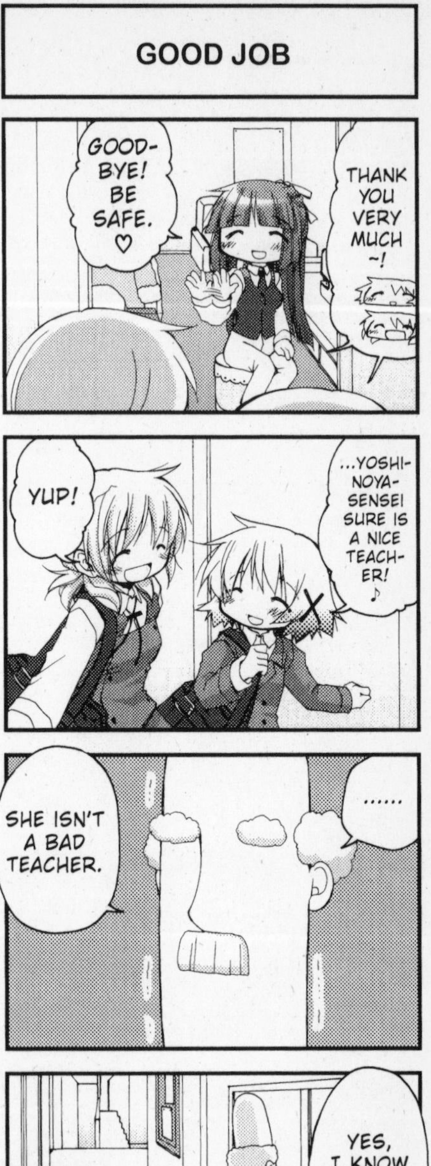
GOOD JOB
THANK YOU VERY MUCH ~!
GOOD-BYE! BE SAFE. ♡
...YOSHI-NOYA-SENSEI SURE IS A NICE TEACH-ER! ♪
YUP!
......
SHE ISN'T A BAD TEACHER.
YES, I KNOW SHE ISN'T A BAD TEACHER AT ALL...
....

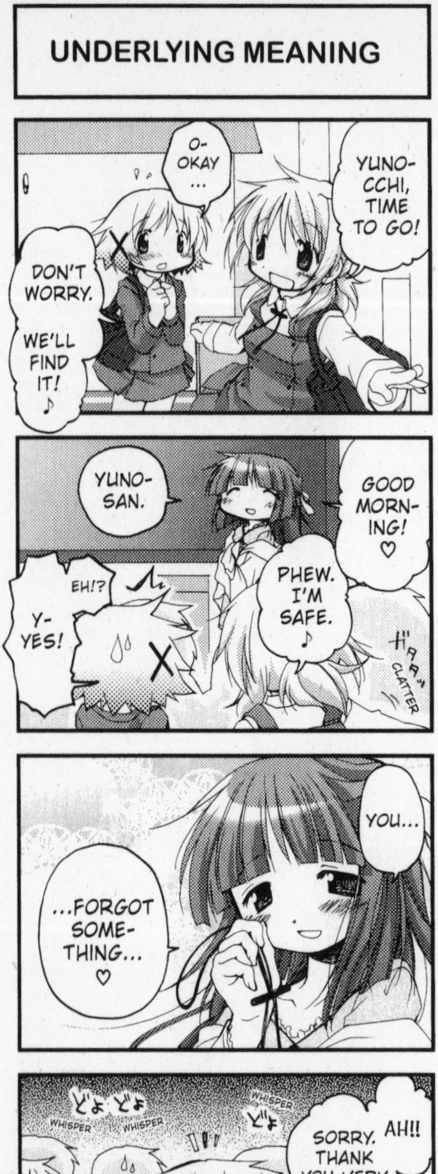
UNDERLYING MEANING
YUNO-CCHI, TIME TO GO!
O-OKAY ...
DON'T WORRY.
WE'LL FIND IT! ♪
GOOD MORN-ING! ♡
YUNO-SAN.
PHEW. I'M SAFE. ♪
CLATTER
EH!?
Y-YES!
YOU...
...FORGOT SOME-THING... ♡
AH!!
SORRY. THANK YOU VERY MUCH!
どよ WHISPER
どよ WHISPER
どよ WHISPER
どよ WHISPER
DASH
どよ WHISPER
YUNO-SAN ...!!?

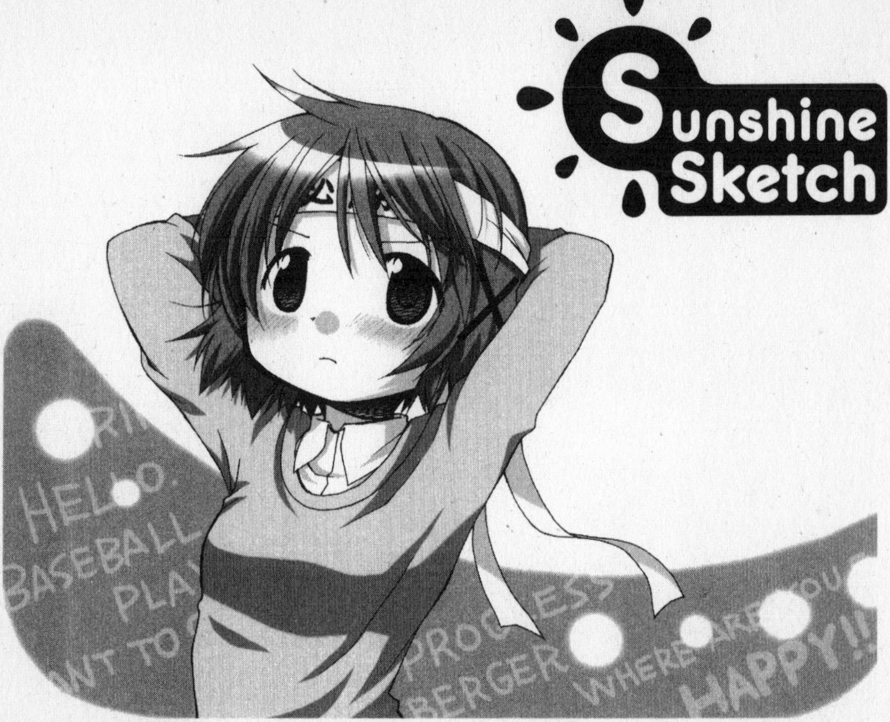
Sunshine Sketch
HELLO.
BASEBALL
PROGRESS
HAPPY!!

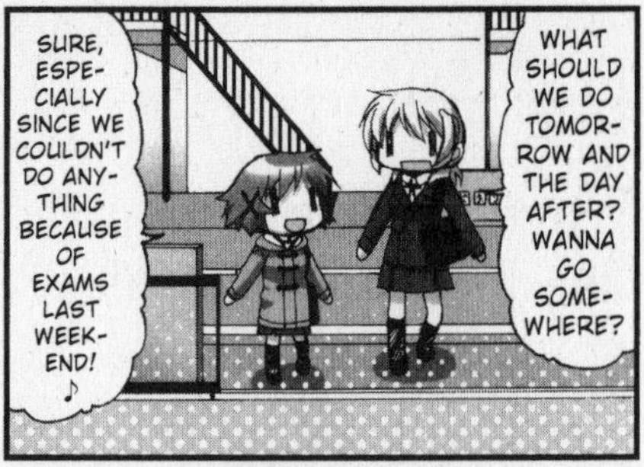
WHAT SHOULD WE DO TOMORROW AND THE DAY AFTER? WANNA GO SOMEWHERE?
SURE, ESPECIALLY SINCE WE COULDN'T DO ANYTHING BECAUSE OF EXAMS LAST WEEKEND! ♪

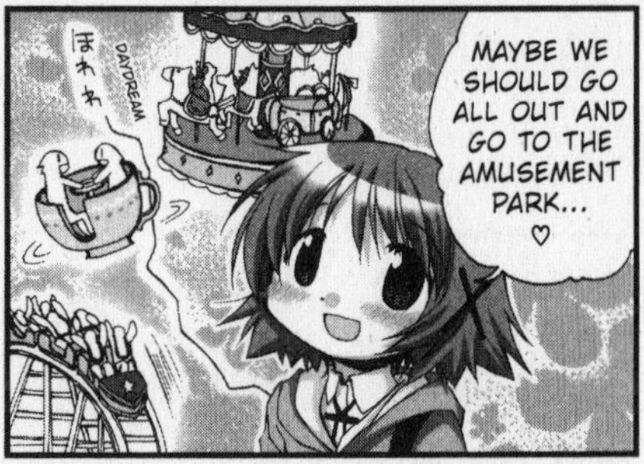
ほわわ
DAYDREAM
MAYBE WE SHOULD GO ALL OUT AND GO TO THE AMUSEMENT PARK... ♡

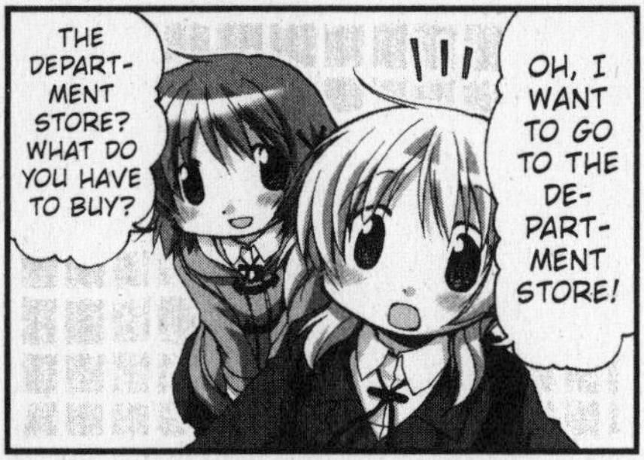
OH, I WANT TO GO TO THE DEPARTMENT STORE!
THE DEPARTMENT STORE? WHAT DO YOU HAVE TO BUY?

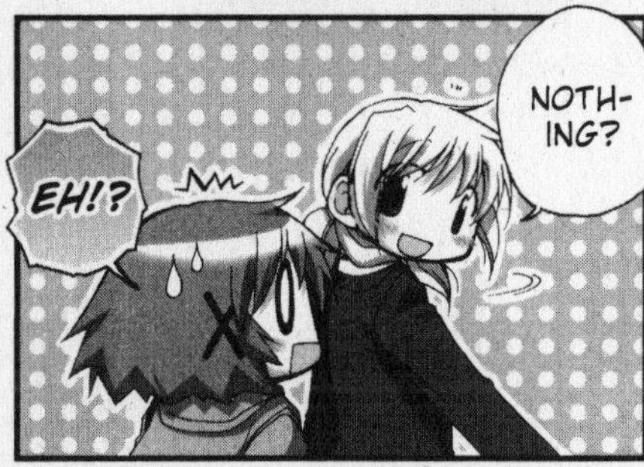
NOTHING?
EH!?

BLONDE BABE GRAMMAR

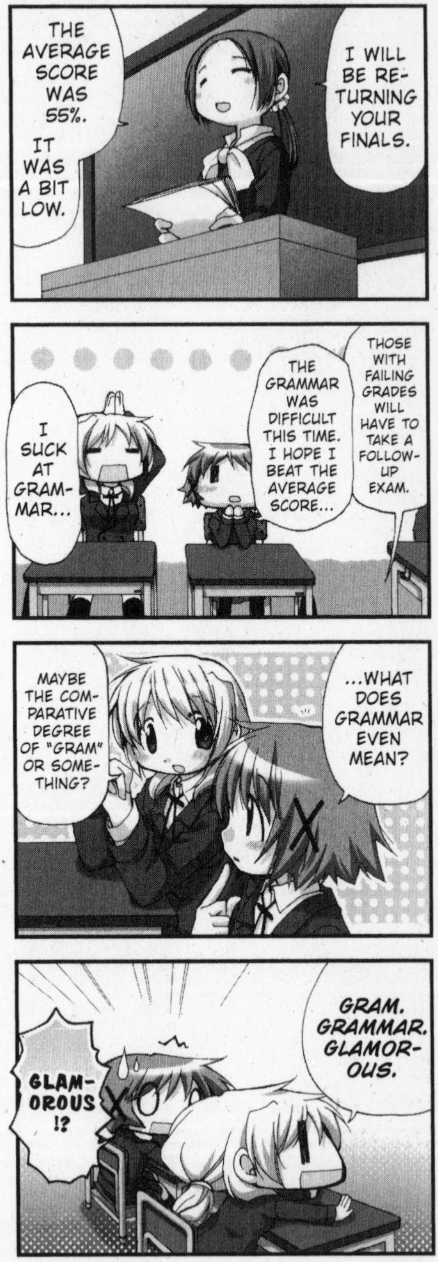
I WILL BE RE-TURNING YOUR FINALS.
THE AVERAGE SCORE WAS 55%.
IT WAS A BIT LOW.
THOSE WITH FAILING GRADES WILL HAVE TO TAKE A FOLLOW-UP EXAM.
THE GRAMMAR WAS DIFFICULT THIS TIME. I HOPE I BEAT THE AVERAGE SCORE...
I SUCK AT GRAM-MAR...
...WHAT DOES GRAMMAR EVEN MEAN?
MAYBE THE COM-PARATIVE DEGREE OF "GRAM" OR SOME-THING?
GRAM. GRAMMAR. GLAMOR-OUS.
GLAM-OROUS !?

SPEECHLESS

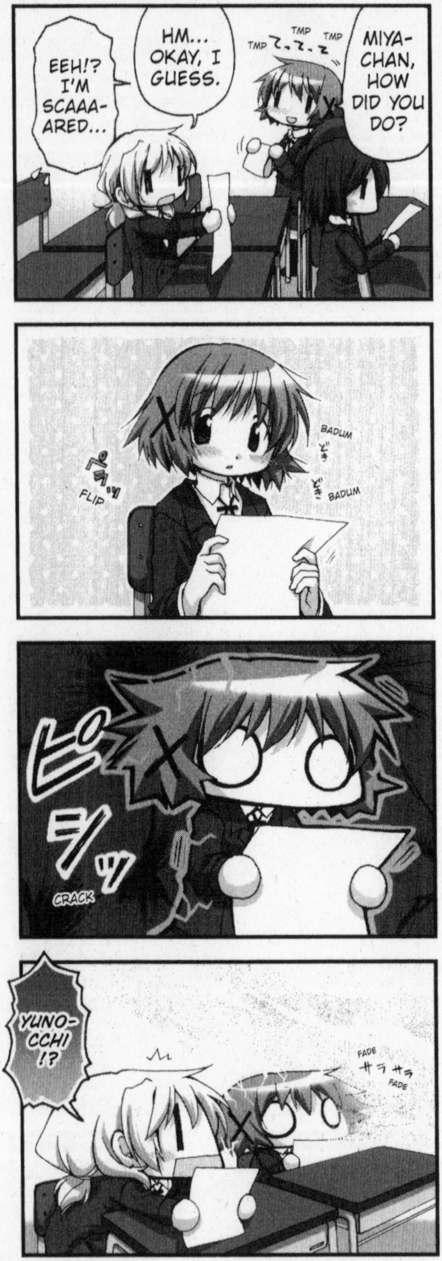
MIYA-CHAN, HOW DID YOU DO?
TMP TMP TMP
HM... OKAY, I GUESS.
EEH!? I'M SCAAAA-ARED...
BADUM
BADUM
FLIP
CRACK
FADE
FADE
YUNO-CCHI !?

SYMPATHETIC STORY

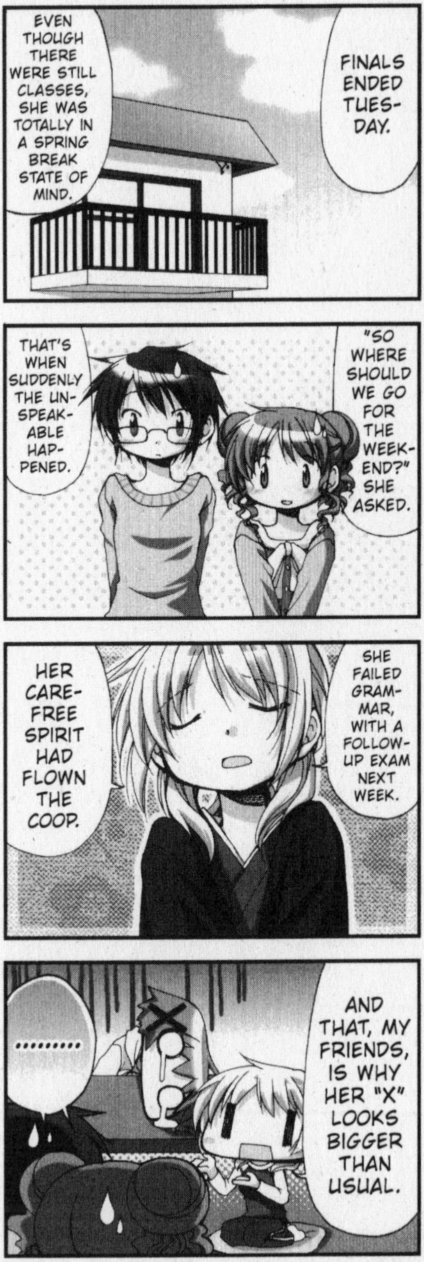
FINALS ENDED TUESDAY.
EVEN THOUGH THERE WERE STILL CLASSES, SHE WAS TOTALLY IN A SPRING BREAK STATE OF MIND.
"SO WHERE SHOULD WE GO FOR THE WEEKEND?" SHE ASKED.
THAT'S WHEN SUDDENLY THE UNSPEAKABLE HAPPENED.
SHE FAILED GRAMMAR, WITH A FOLLOW-UP EXAM NEXT WEEK.
HER CAREFREE SPIRIT HAD FLOWN THE COOP.
AND THAT, MY FRIENDS, IS WHY HER "X" LOOKS BIGGER THAN USUAL.
....

DEEPLY MOVED BY KINDNESS

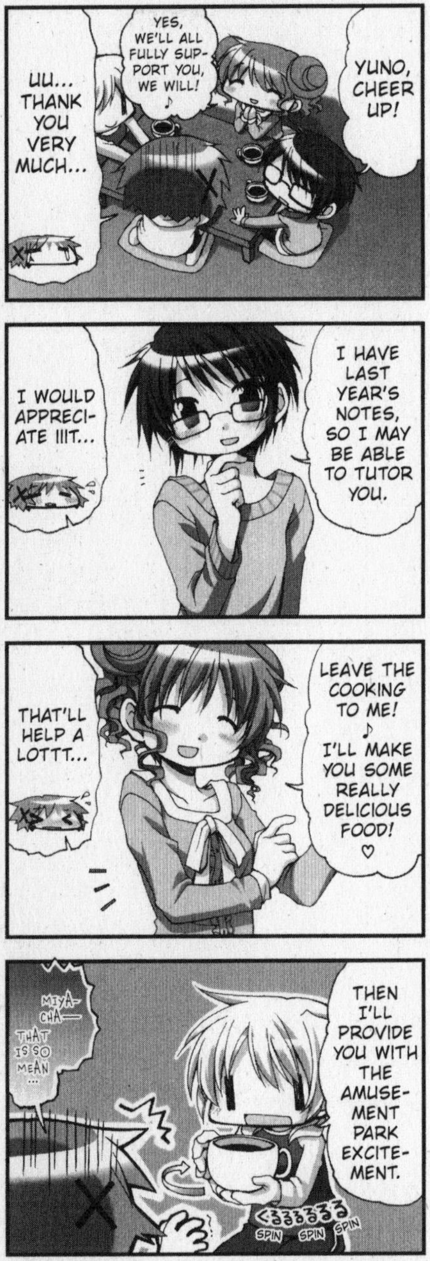
YUNO, CHEER UP!
YES, WE'LL ALL FULLY SUPPORT YOU, WE WILL! ♪
UU... THANK YOU VERY MUCH...
I HAVE LAST YEAR'S NOTES, SO I MAY BE ABLE TO TUTOR YOU.
I WOULD APPRECIATE IIIT...
LEAVE THE COOKING TO ME! ♪ I'LL MAKE YOU SOME REALLY DELICIOUS FOOD! ♡
THAT'LL HELP A LOTTT...
THEN I'LL PROVIDE YOU WITH THE AMUSEMENT PARK EXCITEMENT.
くるるるるるる
SPIN SPIN SPIN
MIYA-CHA— THAT IS SO MEAN ...

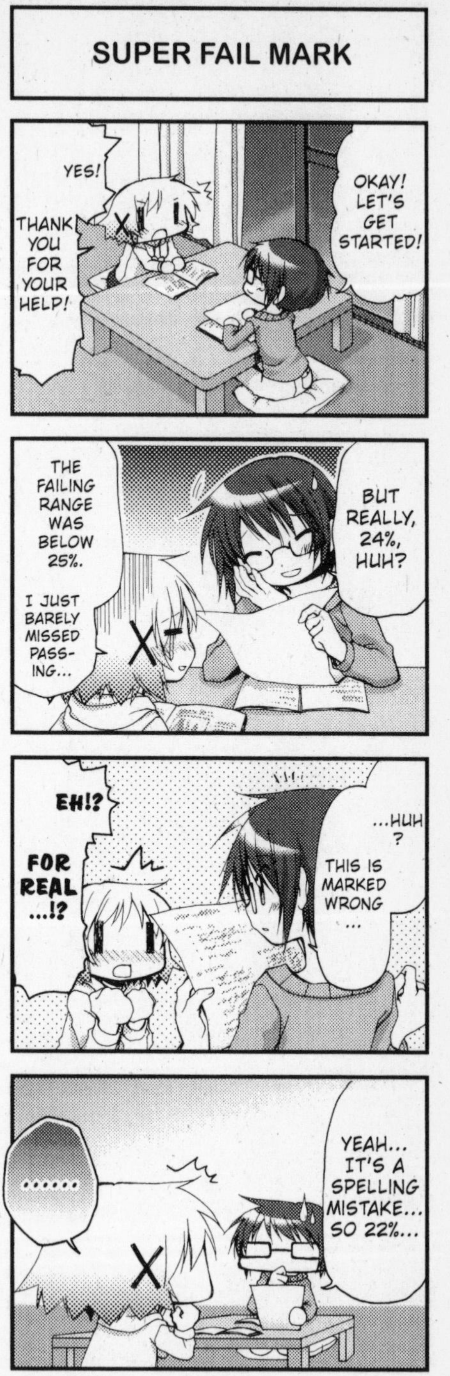
SUPER FAIL MARK
OKAY! LET'S GET STARTED!
YES!
THANK YOU FOR YOUR HELP!
BUT REALLY, 24%, HUH?
THE FAILING RANGE WAS BELOW 25%.
I JUST BARELY MISSED PASSING...
...HUH? THIS IS MARKED WRONG...
EH!?
FOR REAL...!?
YEAH... IT'S A SPELLING MISTAKE... SO 22%...
......

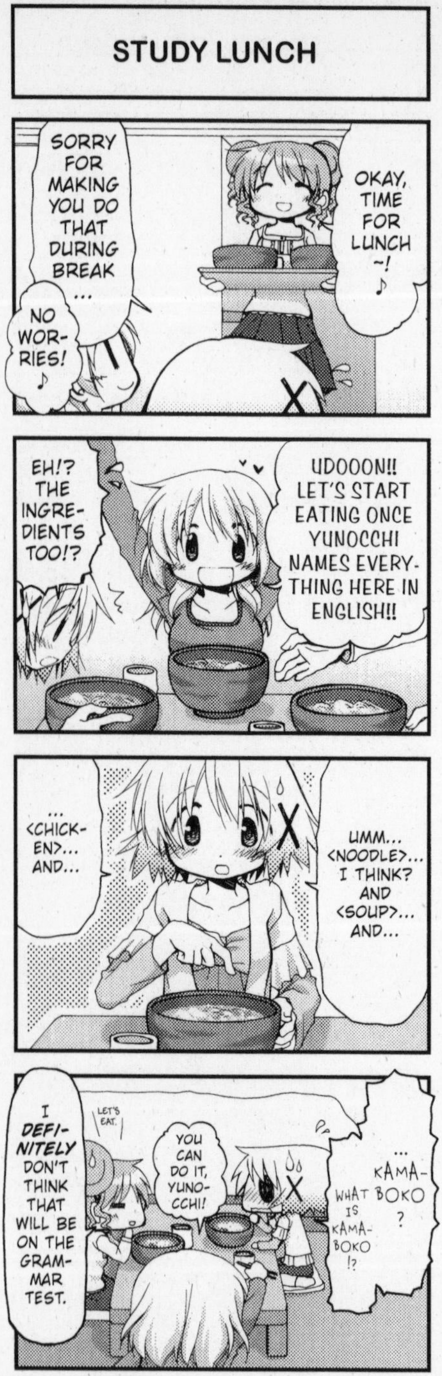
STUDY LUNCH
OKAY, TIME FOR LUNCH~! ♪
SORRY FOR MAKING YOU DO THAT DURING BREAK...
NO WORRIES! ♪
UDOOON!! LET'S START EATING ONCE YUNOCCHI NAMES EVERYTHING HERE IN ENGLISH!!
EH!? THE INGREDIENTS TOO!?
UMM... <NOODLE>... I THINK? AND <SOUP>... AND...
...<CHICKEN>... AND...
...KAMABOKO?
WHAT IS KAMABOKO!?
YOU CAN DO IT, YUNOCCHI!
LET'S EAT.
I *DEFINITELY* DON'T THINK THAT WILL BE ON THE GRAMMAR TEST.

FLY AWAY

GRADE-SCHOOL LEVEL

<THIS DRINK WILL MAKE YOU FEEL SICK>

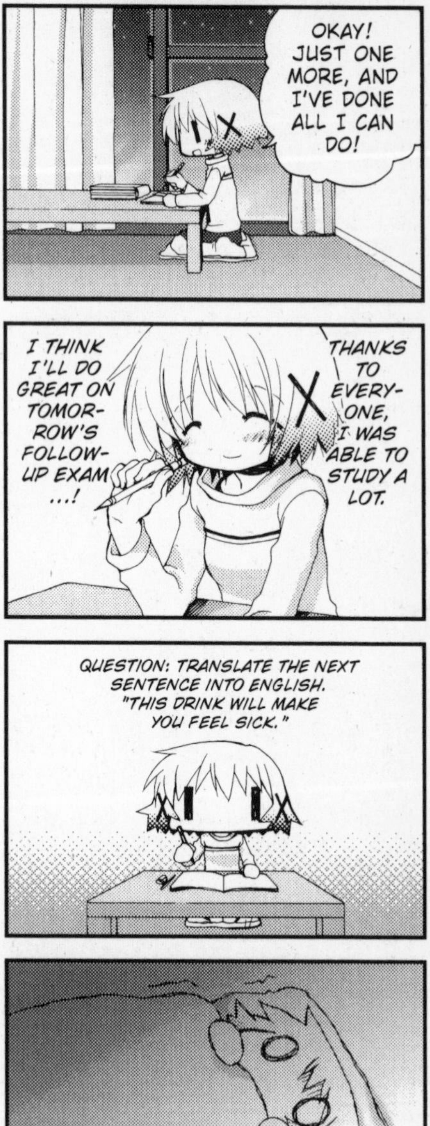
OKAY! JUST ONE MORE, AND I'VE DONE ALL I CAN DO!
THANKS TO EVERYONE, I WAS ABLE TO STUDY A LOT.
I THINK I'LL DO GREAT ON TOMORROW'S FOLLOW-UP EXAM ...!
QUESTION: TRANSLATE THE NEXT SENTENCE INTO ENGLISH. "THIS DRINK WILL MAKE YOU FEEL SICK."

RANDOM BLURB

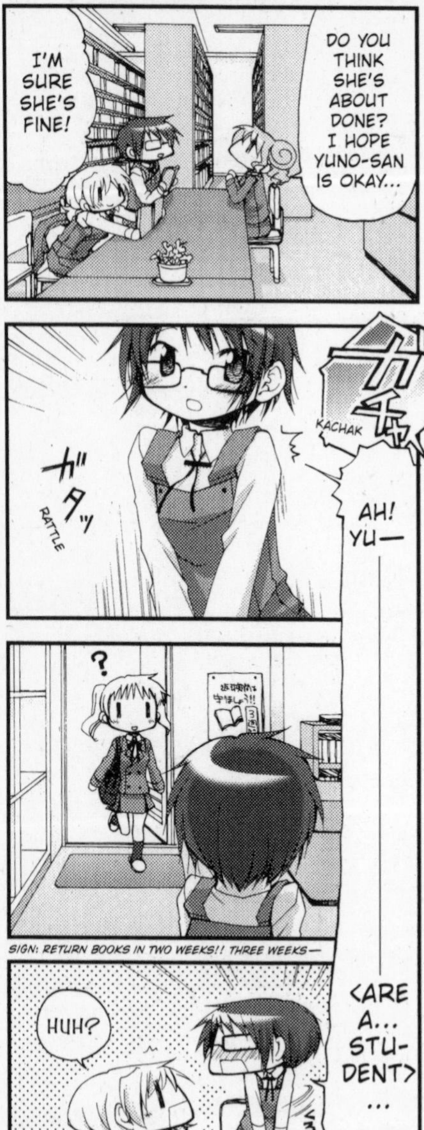
DO YOU THINK SHE'S ABOUT DONE? I HOPE YUNO-SAN IS OKAY...
I'M SURE SHE'S FINE!
KACHAK
RATTLE
AH! YU—
SIGN: RETURN BOOKS IN TWO WEEKS!! THREE WEEKS—
<ARE A... STU-DENT> ...
FWIP
HUH?

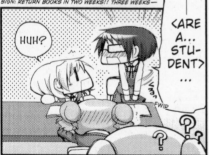

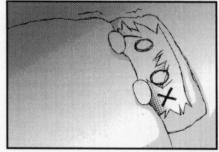

<FULL SUPPORT>

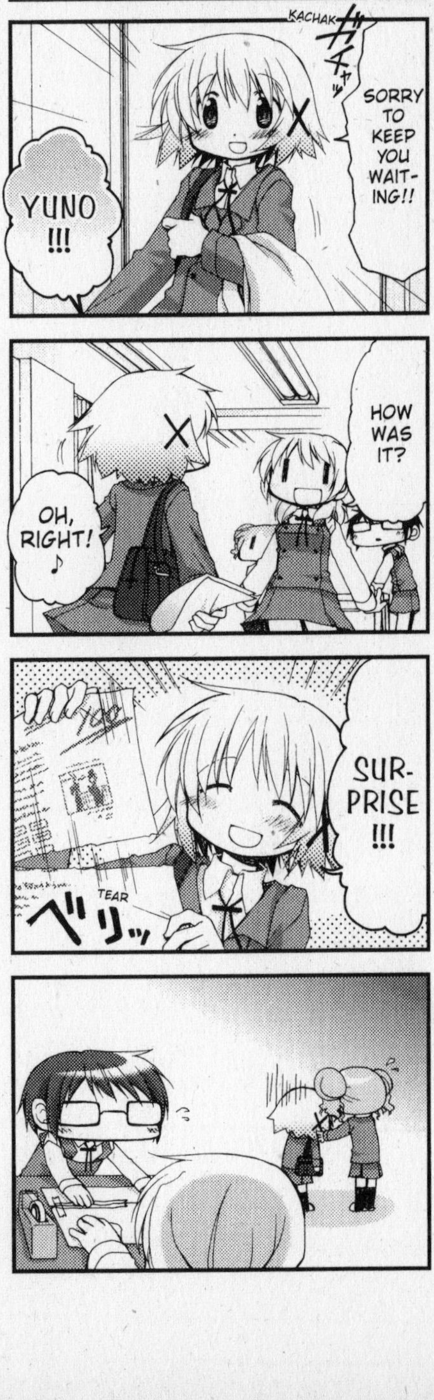
KACHAK
SORRY TO KEEP YOU WAITING!!
YUNO !!!
HOW WAS IT?
OH, RIGHT! ♪
SURPRISE !!!
TEAR

WITH ENGLISH

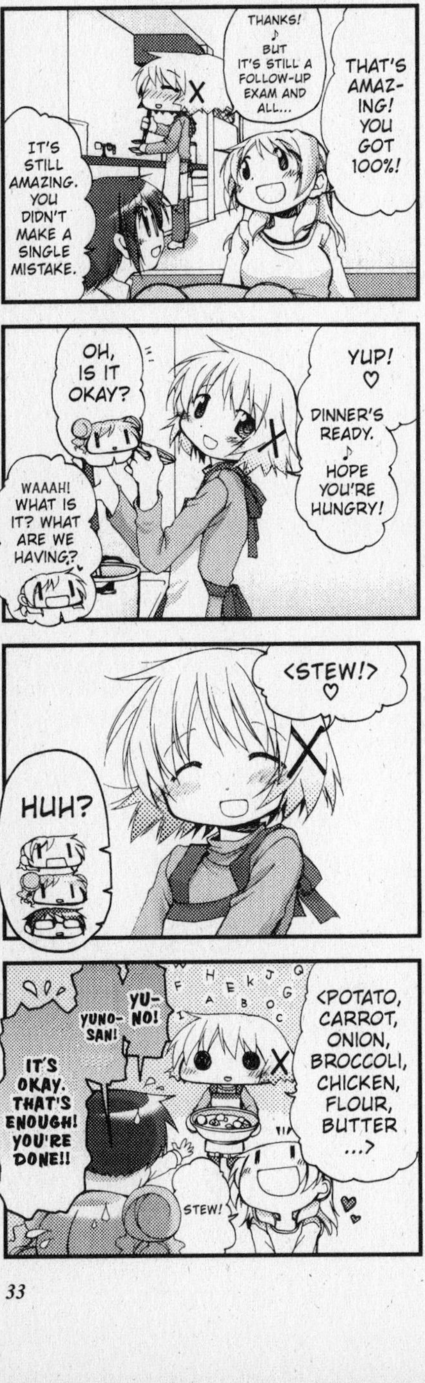
THAT'S AMAZING! YOU GOT 100%!
THANKS! ♪ BUT IT'S STILL A FOLLOW-UP EXAM AND ALL...
IT'S STILL AMAZING. YOU DIDN'T MAKE A SINGLE MISTAKE.
YUP! ♡ DINNER'S READY. ♪ HOPE YOU'RE HUNGRY!
OH, IS IT OKAY?
WAAAH! WHAT IS IT? WHAT ARE WE HAVING?
<STEW!> ♡
HUH?
<POTATO, CARROT, ONION, BROCCOLI, CHICKEN, FLOUR, BUTTER ...>
YU-NO!
YUNO-SAN!
IT'S OKAY. THAT'S ENOUGH! YOU'RE DONE!!
STEW!

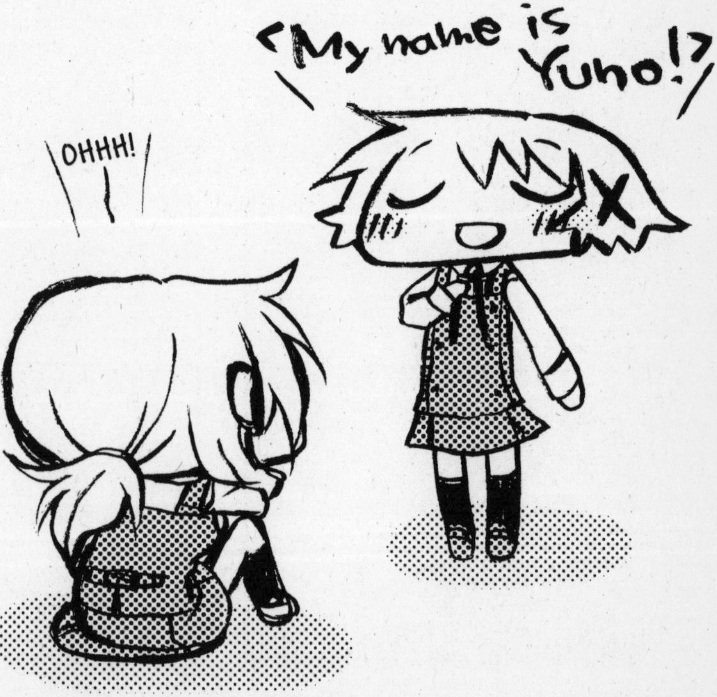
<My name is Yuno!>
OHHH!

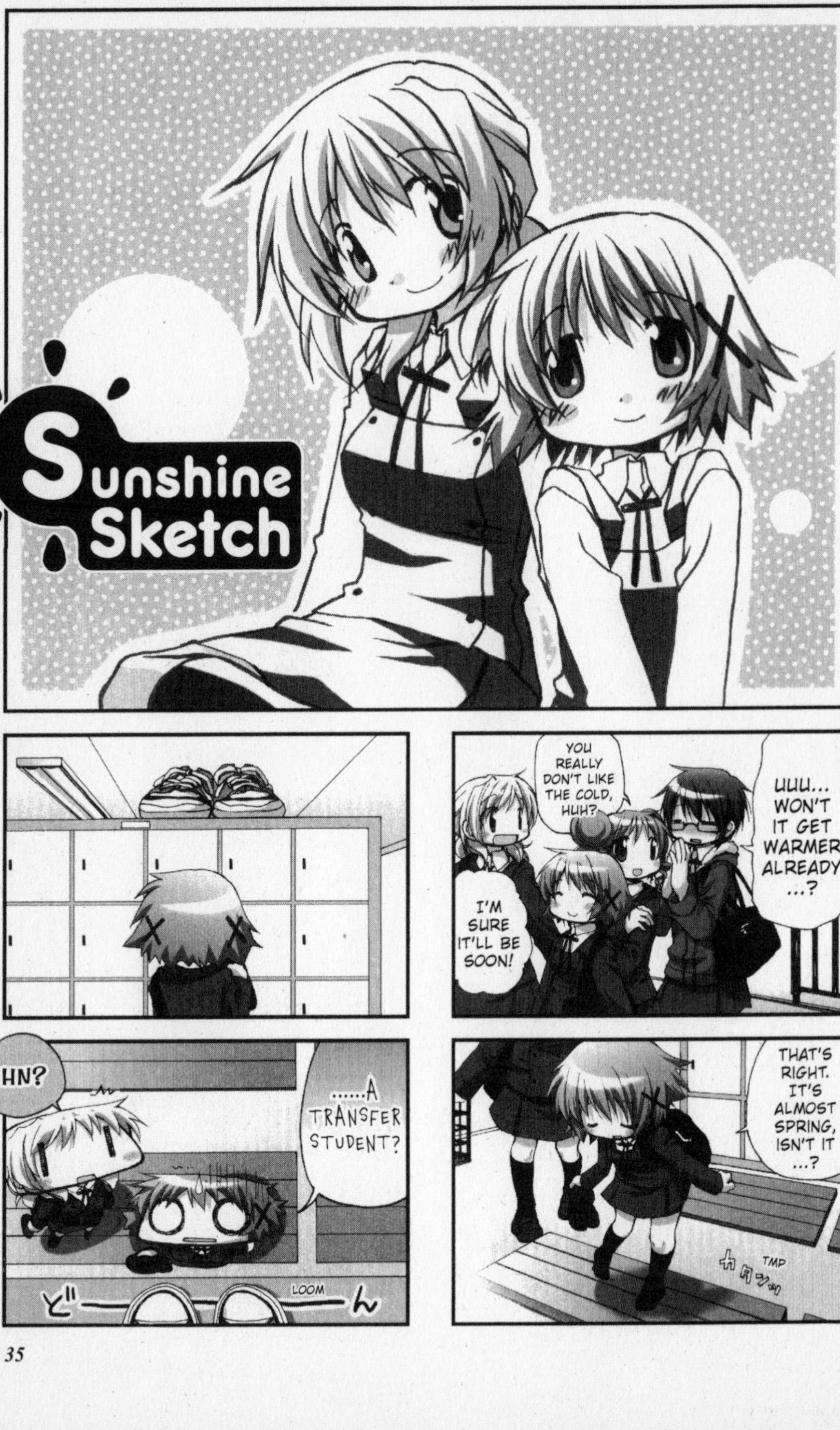
Sunshine Sketch
UUU... WON'T IT GET WARMER ALREADY ...?
YOU REALLY DON'T LIKE THE COLD, HUH?
I'M SURE IT'LL BE SOON!
THAT'S RIGHT. IT'S ALMOST SPRING, ISN'T IT ...?
TMP
......A TRANSFER STUDENT?
HN?
LOOM

48.5 CM

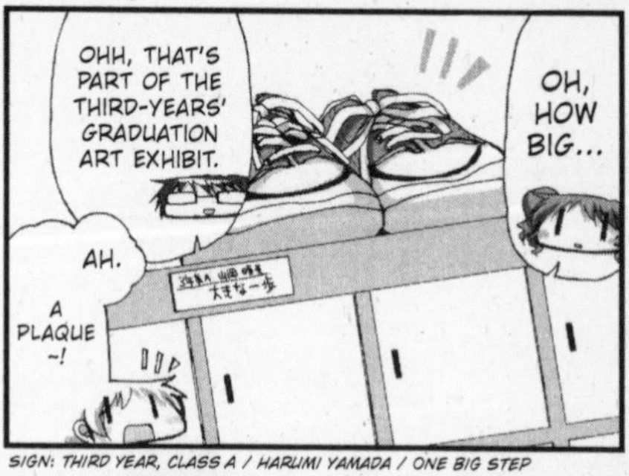
OH, HOW BIG...
OHH, THAT'S PART OF THE THIRD-YEARS' GRADUATION ART EXHIBIT.
AH.
A PLAQUE ~!

SIGN: THIRD YEAR, CLASS A / HARUMI YAMADA / ONE BIG STEP

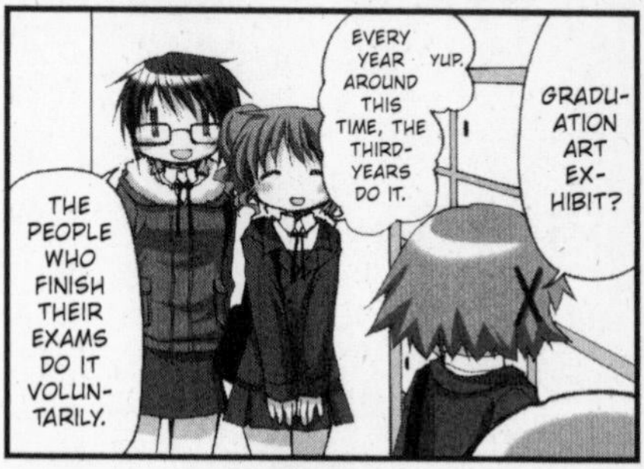
GRADU-ATION ART EX-HIBIT?
YUP.
EVERY YEAR AROUND THIS TIME, THE THIRD-YEARS DO IT.
THE PEOPLE WHO FINISH THEIR EXAMS DO IT VOLUN-TARILY.

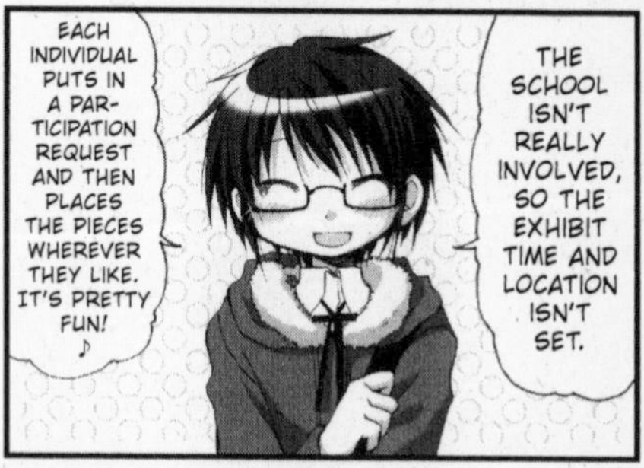
THE SCHOOL ISN'T REALLY INVOLVED, SO THE EXHIBIT TIME AND LOCATION ISN'T SET.
EACH INDIVIDUAL PUTS IN A PAR-TICIPATION REQUEST AND THEN PLACES THE PIECES WHEREVER THEY LIKE. IT'S PRETTY FUN! ♪

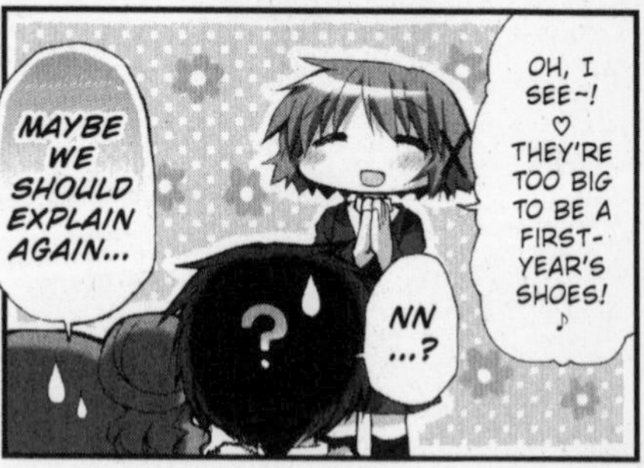
OH, I SEE~! ♡ THEY'RE TOO BIG TO BE A FIRST-YEAR'S SHOES! ♪
NN ...?
MAYBE WE SHOULD EXPLAIN AGAIN...

YAMABUKI ART MUSEUM

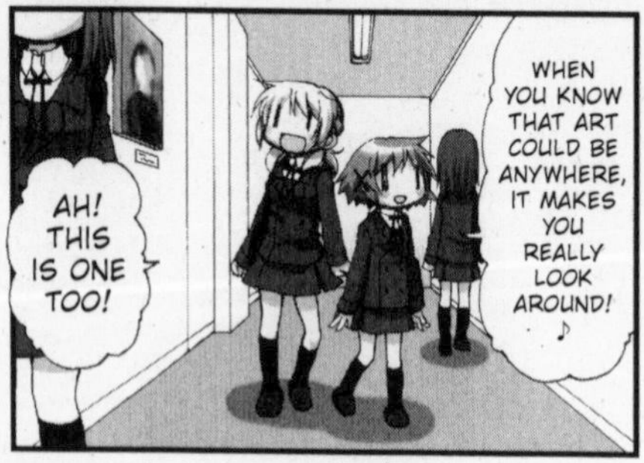
WHEN YOU KNOW THAT ART COULD BE ANYWHERE, IT MAKES YOU REALLY LOOK AROUND! ♪
AH! THIS IS ONE TOO!

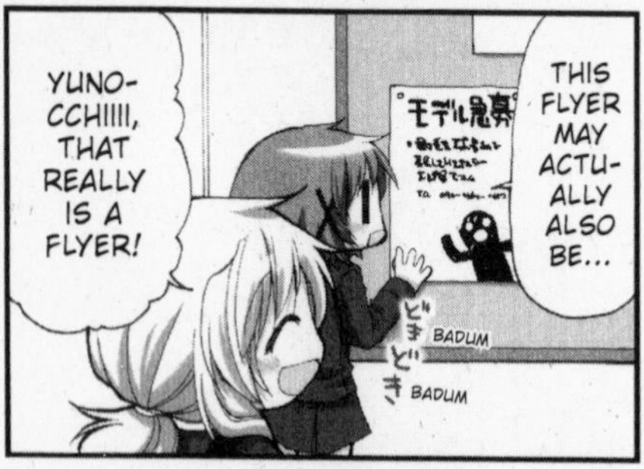
THIS FLYER MAY ACTU-ALLY ALSO BE...
YUNO-CCHIIII, THAT REALLY IS A FLYER!
どき BADUM
どき BADUM

SIGN: SEARCHING FOR MODELS

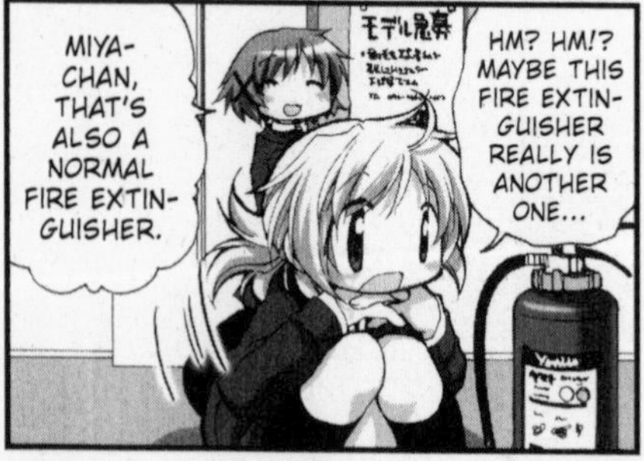
HM? HM!? MAYBE THIS FIRE EXTIN-GUISHER REALLY IS ANOTHER ONE...
MIYA-CHAN, THAT'S ALSO A NORMAL FIRE EXTIN-GUISHER.

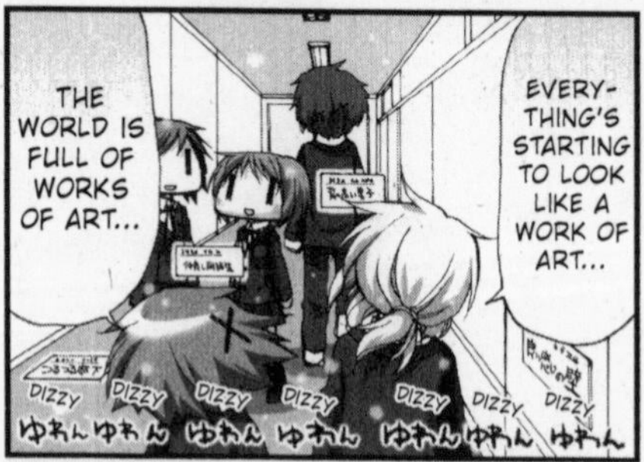
EVERY-THING'S STARTING TO LOOK LIKE A WORK OF ART...
THE WORLD IS FULL OF WORKS OF ART...
DIZZY DIZZY DIZZY DIZZY DIZZY DIZZY DIZZY
ゆわん ゆわん ゆわん ゆわん ゆわん ゆわん ゆわん

SIGNS: VERY NICE WALL / TALL GUY / FRIENDLY COLLEAGUES / SHINY FLOOR

SANTA ANA WINDS

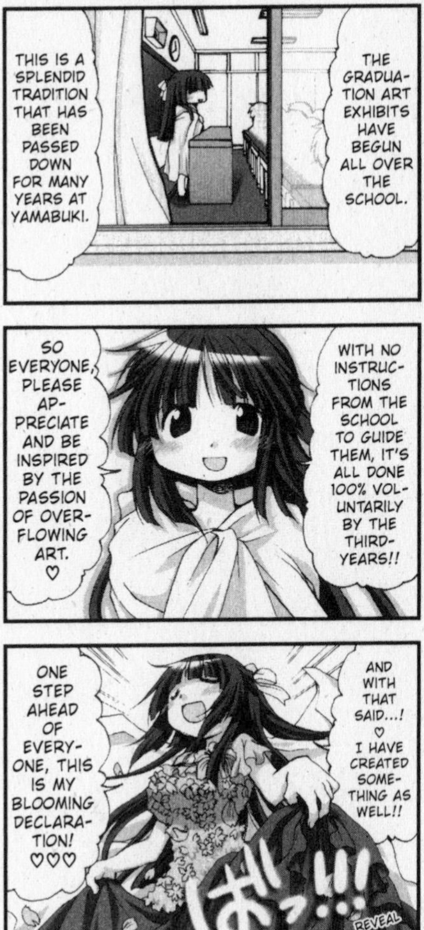
THE GRADUATION ART EXHIBITS HAVE BEGUN ALL OVER THE SCHOOL.
THIS IS A SPLENDID TRADITION THAT HAS BEEN PASSED DOWN FOR MANY YEARS AT YAMABUKI.
WITH NO INSTRUCTIONS FROM THE SCHOOL TO GUIDE THEM, IT'S ALL DONE 100% VOLUNTARILY BY THE THIRD-YEARS!!
SO EVERYONE, PLEASE APPRECIATE AND BE INSPIRED BY THE PASSION OF OVERFLOWING ART. ♡
AND WITH THAT SAID...! ♡ I HAVE CREATED SOMETHING AS WELL!!
ONE STEP AHEAD OF EVERYONE, THIS IS MY BLOOMING DECLARATION! ♡♡♡
ばっ!!
REVEAL
ひゅ
FWOOSH
OH, BUT THE LIVES OF FLOWERS ARE SOOOOO BRIEF!!
ばささささ
FLAP FLAP FLAP FLAP

CREATION, PART 2

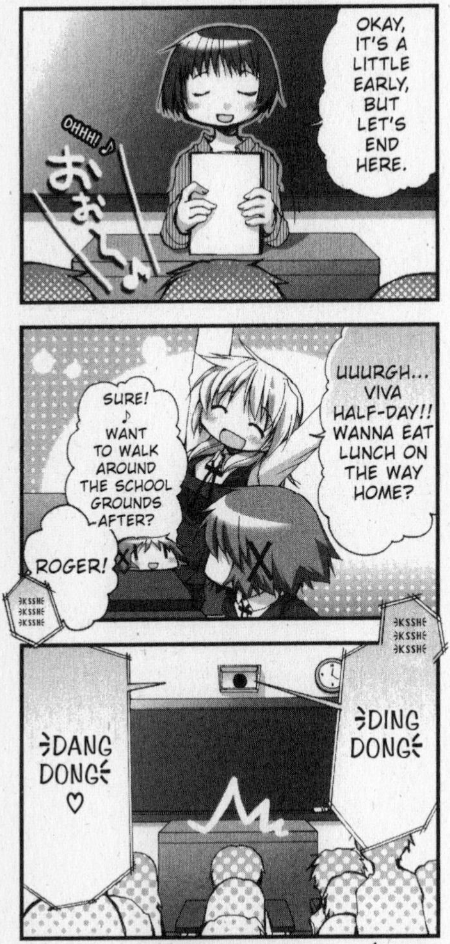
OKAY, IT'S A LITTLE EARLY, BUT LET'S END HERE.
おぉ〜♪
OHHH! ♪
UUURGH... VIVA HALF-DAY!! WANNA EAT LUNCH ON THE WAY HOME?
SURE! ♪ WANT TO WALK AROUND THE SCHOOL GROUNDS AFTER?
ROGER!
KSSH KSSH KSSH
KSSH KSSH KSSH
DING DONG
DANG DONG ♡
PING PONG PANG PO-POOON ♡♡
YOSHINOYA-SENSEI...
YOU'RE GOING TO BE FORCED TO GRADUATE...

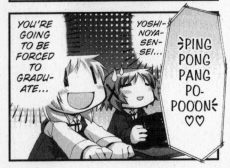

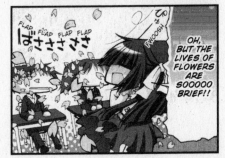

BIRD LEAVING FOOTPRINTS

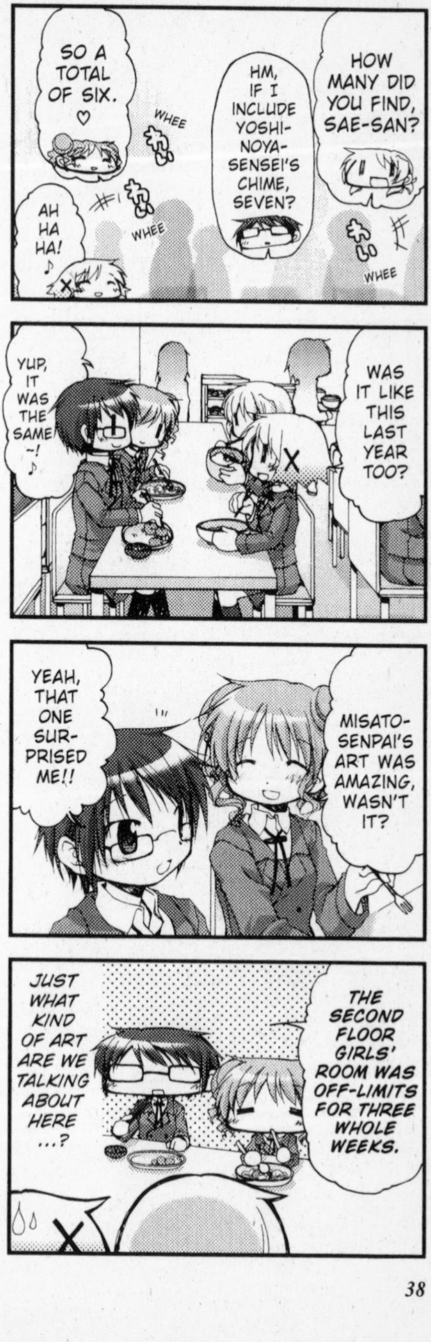
HOW MANY DID YOU FIND, SAE-SAN?
HM, IF I INCLUDE YOSHI-NOYA-SENSEI'S CHIME, SEVEN?
SO A TOTAL OF SIX. ♡
WHEE
WHEE
WHEE
AH HA HA! ♪
WAS IT LIKE THIS LAST YEAR TOO?
YUP, IT WAS THE SAME ~! ♪
MISATO-SENPAI'S ART WAS AMAZING, WASN'T IT?
YEAH, THAT ONE SUR-PRISED ME!!
THE SECOND FLOOR GIRLS' ROOM WAS OFF-LIMITS FOR THREE WHOLE WEEKS.
JUST WHAT KIND OF ART ARE WE TALKING ABOUT HERE ...?

LIMITS TO BEING UNIQUE

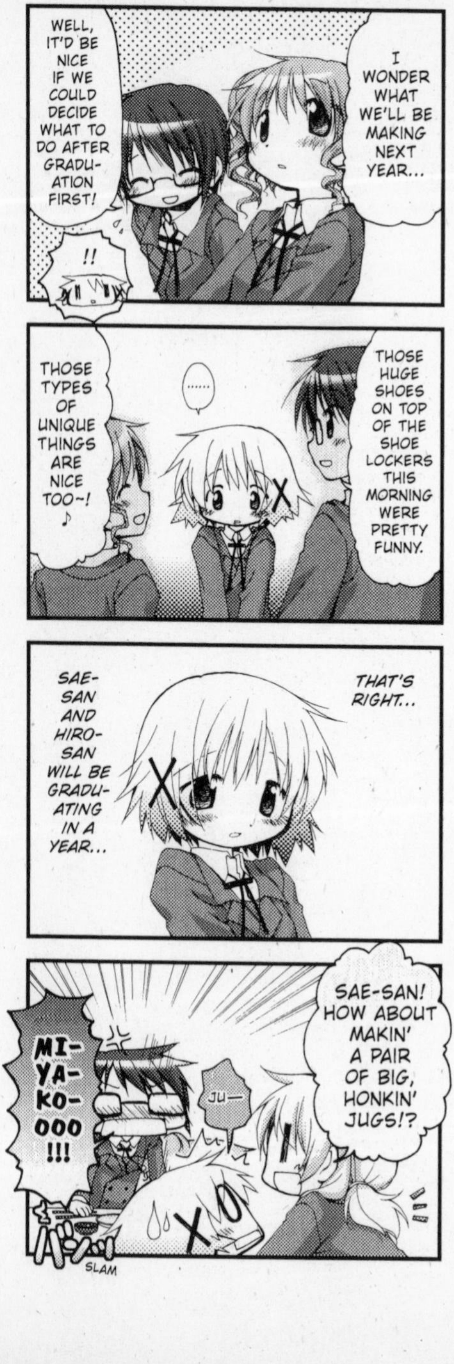
I WONDER WHAT WE'LL BE MAKING NEXT YEAR...
WELL, IT'D BE NICE IF WE COULD DECIDE WHAT TO DO AFTER GRADU-ATION FIRST!
!!
THOSE HUGE SHOES ON TOP OF THE SHOE LOCKERS THIS MORNING WERE PRETTY FUNNY.
......
THOSE TYPES OF UNIQUE THINGS ARE NICE TOO~! ♪
THAT'S RIGHT...
SAE-SAN AND HIRO-SAN WILL BE GRADU-ATING IN A YEAR...
SAE-SAN! HOW ABOUT MAKIN' A PAIR OF BIG, HONKIN' JUGS!?
JU—
MI-YA-KO-OOO !!!
SLAM

COLLAPSE

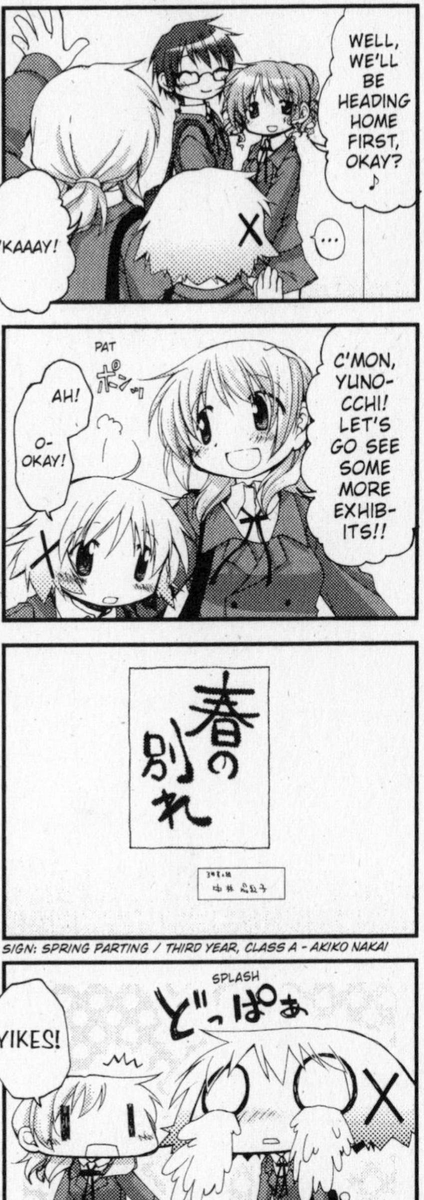

WELL, WE'LL BE HEADING HOME FIRST, OKAY? ♪
'KAAAY!
...
C'MON, YUNO-CCHI! LET'S GO SEE SOME MORE EXHIB-ITS!!
PAT
ポンッ
AH!
O-OKAY!
春の別れ
SIGN: SPRING PARTING / THIRD YEAR, CLASS A - AKIKO NAKAI
SPLASH
どっぱぁ
YIKES!

STILL HEALING WOUND

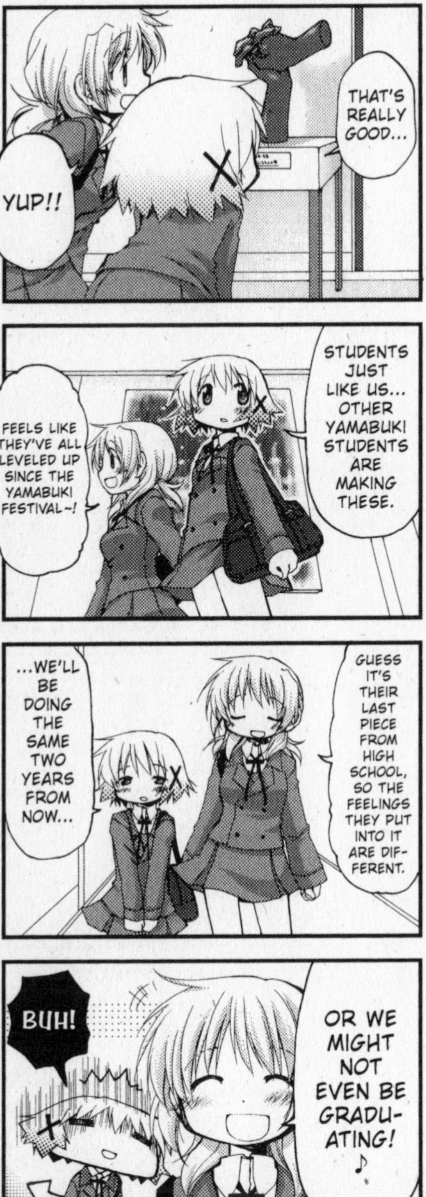

THAT'S REALLY GOOD...
YUP!!
STUDENTS JUST LIKE US... OTHER YAMABUKI STUDENTS ARE MAKING THESE.
FEELS LIKE THEY'VE ALL LEVELED UP SINCE THE YAMABUKI FESTIVAL~!
GUESS IT'S THEIR LAST PIECE FROM HIGH SCHOOL, SO THE FEELINGS THEY PUT INTO IT ARE DIFFERENT.
...WE'LL BE DOING THE SAME TWO YEARS FROM NOW...
OR WE MIGHT NOT EVEN BE GRADUATING! ♪
BUH!
STAB

FLYING BODY ATTACK

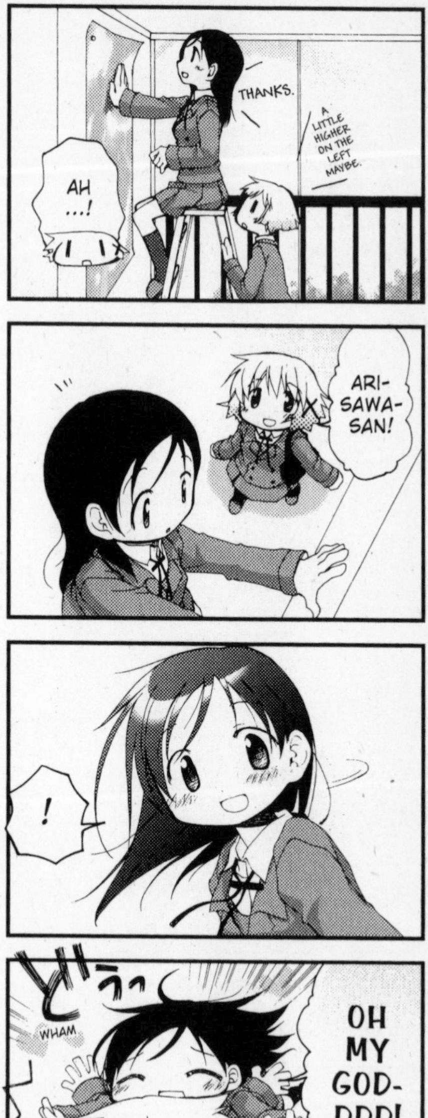
A LITTLE HIGHER ON THE LEFT MAYBE.
THANKS.
AH ...!
ARI-SAWA-SAN!
!
OH MY GOD-DDD! ♡
WHAM
GYAH!

FLIP SIDE TO AN EMOTIONAL REUNION

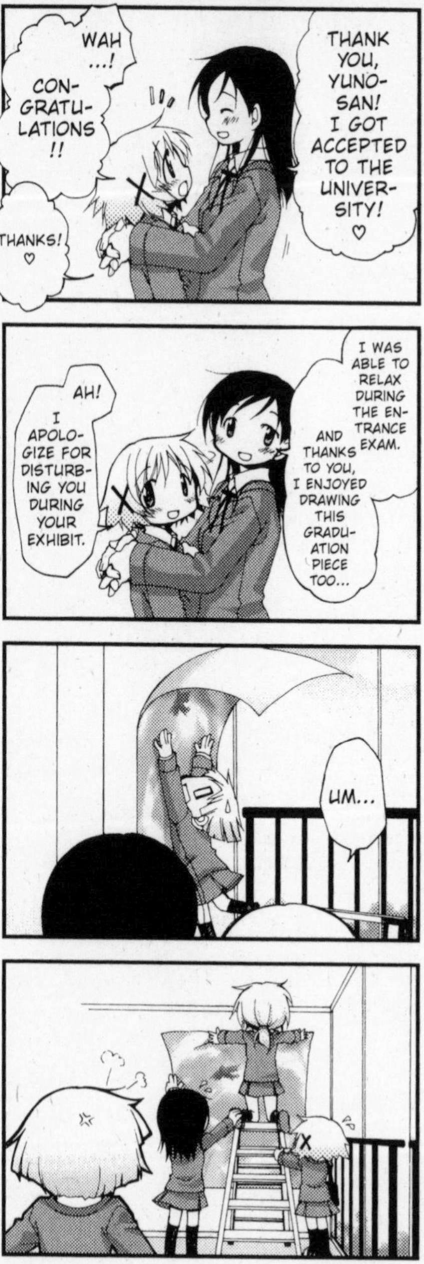
THANK YOU, YUNO-SAN! I GOT ACCEPTED TO THE UNIVERSITY! ♡
WAH ...!
CON-GRATU-LATIONS !!
THANKS! ♡
I WAS ABLE TO RELAX DURING THE EN-TRANCE EXAM.
AND THANKS TO YOU, I ENJOYED DRAWING THIS GRADU-ATION PIECE TOO...
AH! I APOLO-GIZE FOR DISTURB-ING YOU DURING YOUR EXHIBIT.
UM...

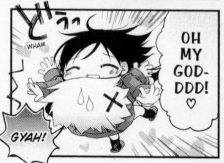

PASSING THE BATON

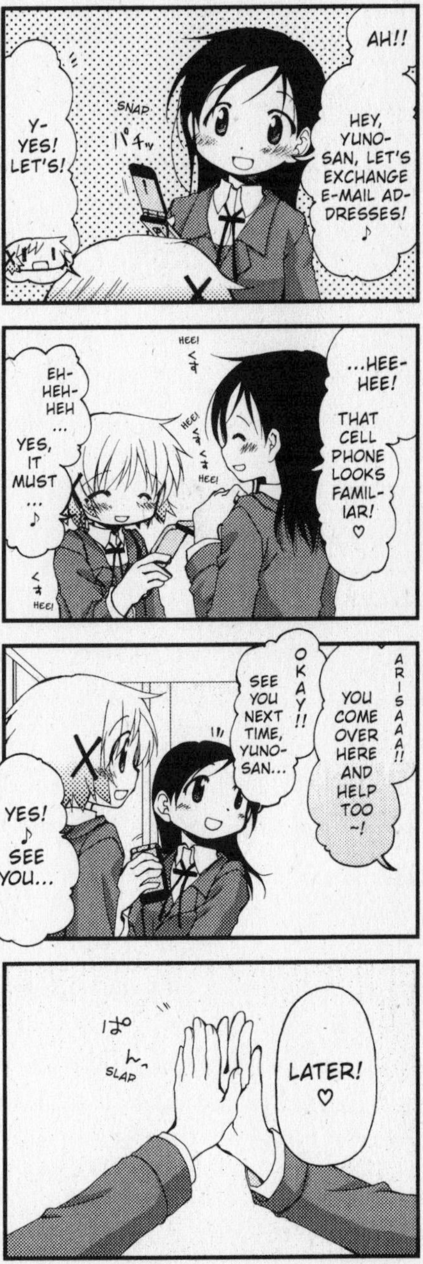
AH!!
HEY, YUNO-SAN, LET'S EXCHANGE E-MAIL ADDRESSES! ♪
SNAP パチッ
Y-YES! LET'S!
...HEE-HEE! THAT CELL PHONE LOOKS FAMILIAR! ♡
HEE! くす
HEE! くす くす HEE!
EH-HEH-HEH... YES, IT MUST... ♪
くす HEE!
ARISAAAA!!
YOU COME OVER HERE AND HELP TOO~!
OKAY!!
SEE YOU NEXT TIME, YUNO-SAN...
YES! ♪ SEE YOU...
LATER! ♡
ぱん SLAP

CALL ME

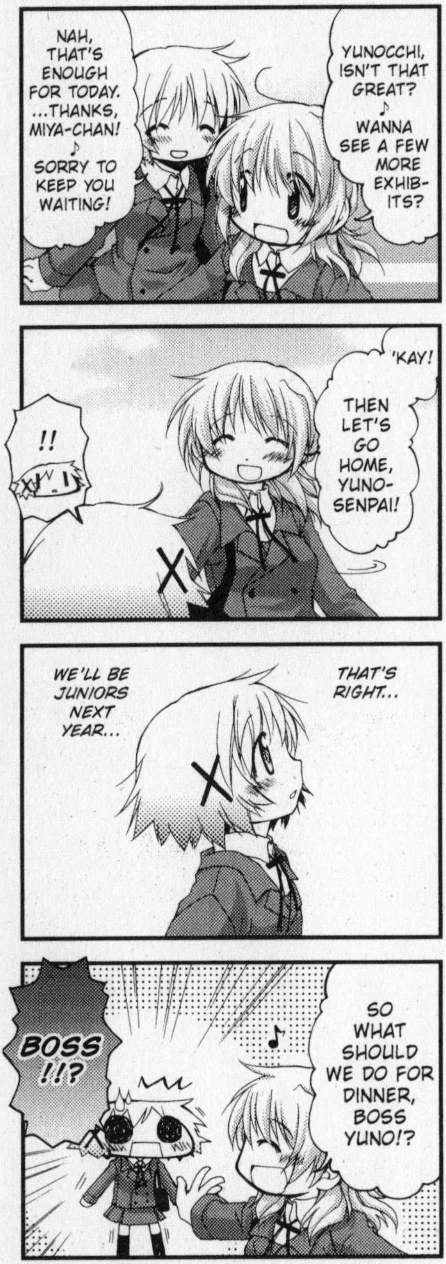
YUNOCCHI, ISN'T THAT GREAT? ♪ WANNA SEE A FEW MORE EXHIBITS?
NAH, THAT'S ENOUGH FOR TODAY. ...THANKS, MIYA-CHAN! ♪ SORRY TO KEEP YOU WAITING!
'KAY! THEN LET'S GO HOME, YUNO-SENPAI!
!!
THAT'S RIGHT...
WE'LL BE JUNIORS NEXT YEAR...
SO WHAT SHOULD WE DO FOR DINNER, BOSS YUNO!?
BOSS!!?

SPRING

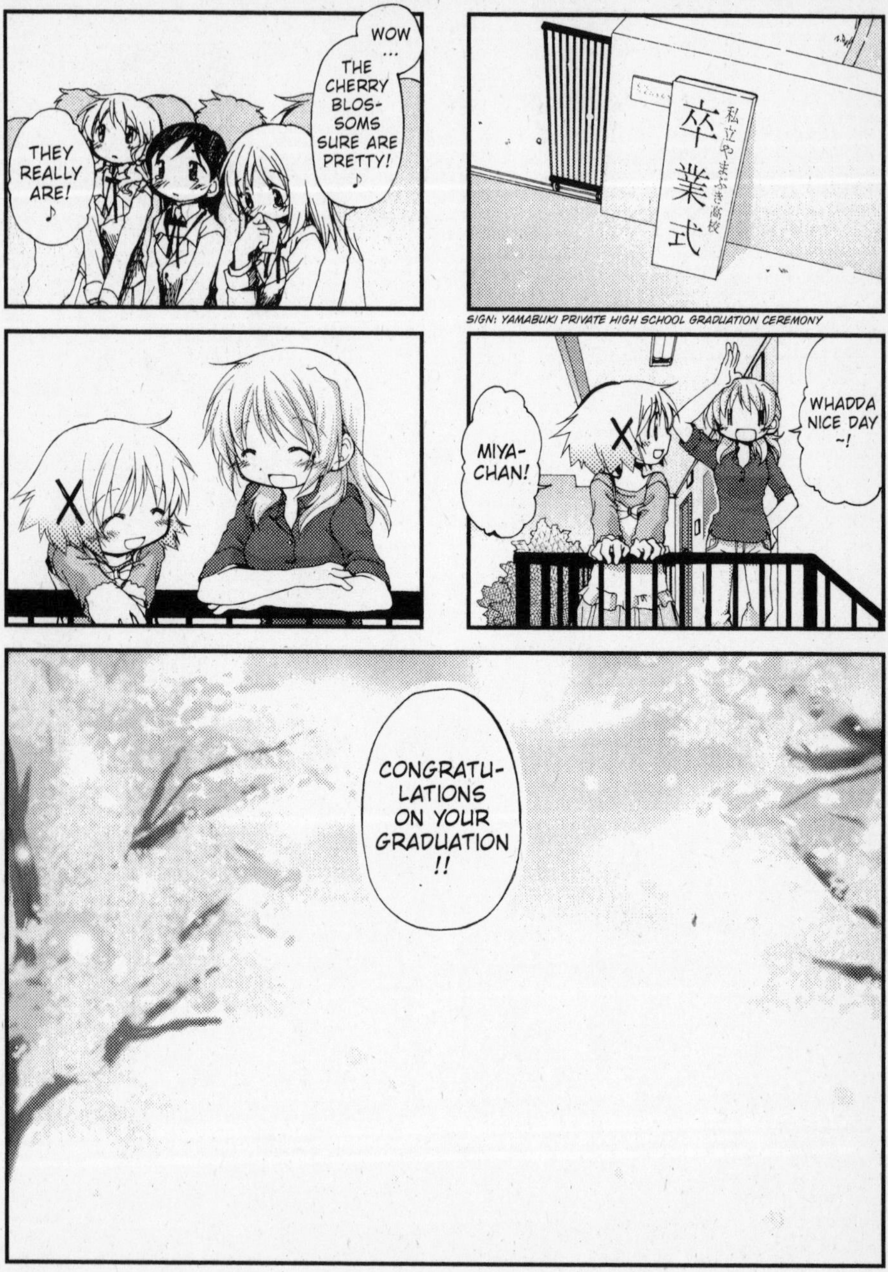
私立やまぶき高校
卒業式
WOW... THE CHERRY BLOSSOMS SURE ARE PRETTY! ♪
THEY REALLY ARE! ♪
WHADDA NICE DAY ~!
MIYA-CHAN!
CONGRATULATIONS ON YOUR GRADUATION!!

SIGN: YAMABUKI PRIVATE HIGH SCHOOL GRADUATION CEREMONY

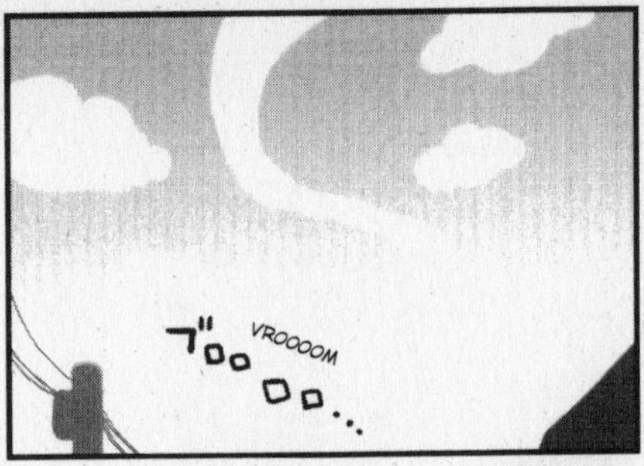
VROOOOM
ブロロ ロロ...
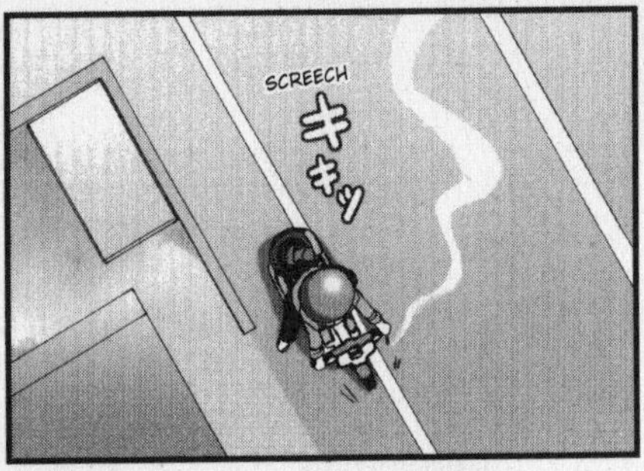
SCREECH
キキッ
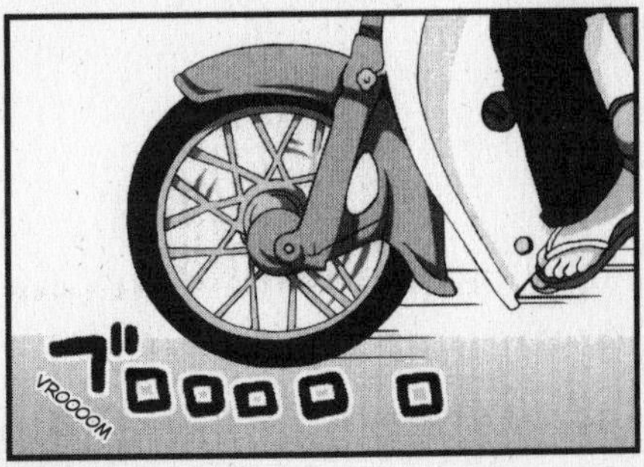
ブロロロロ ロ
VROOOOM
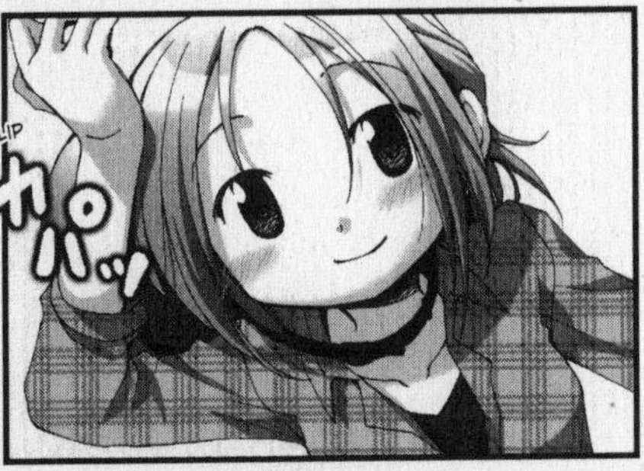
FLIP
カパッ
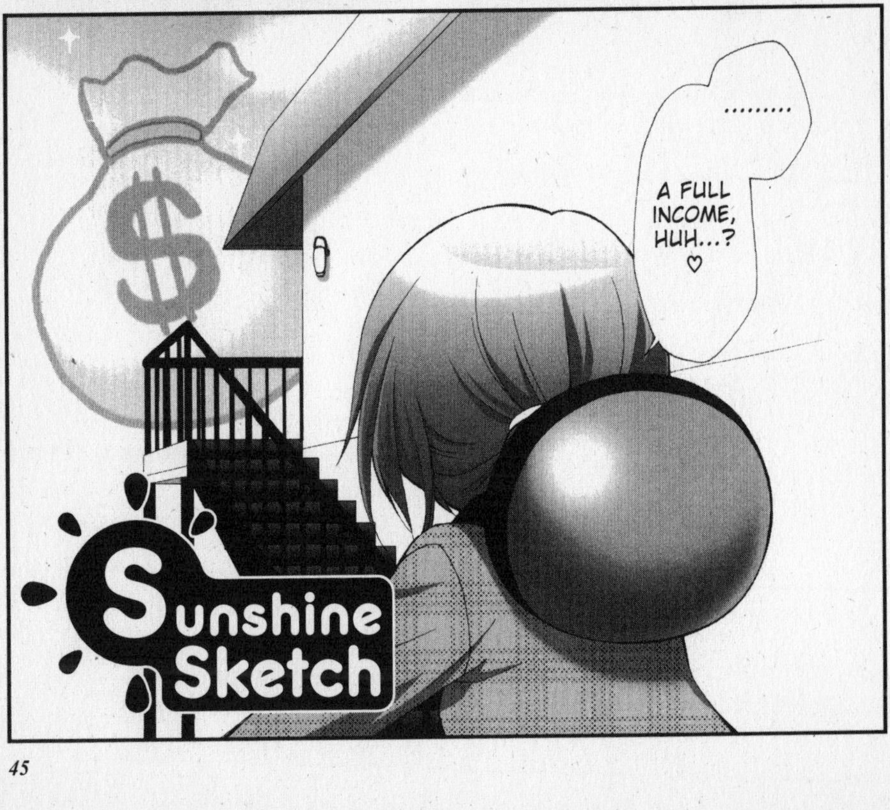
....
A FULL INCOME, HUH...? ♡
Sunshine Sketch

STILL UNAWARE

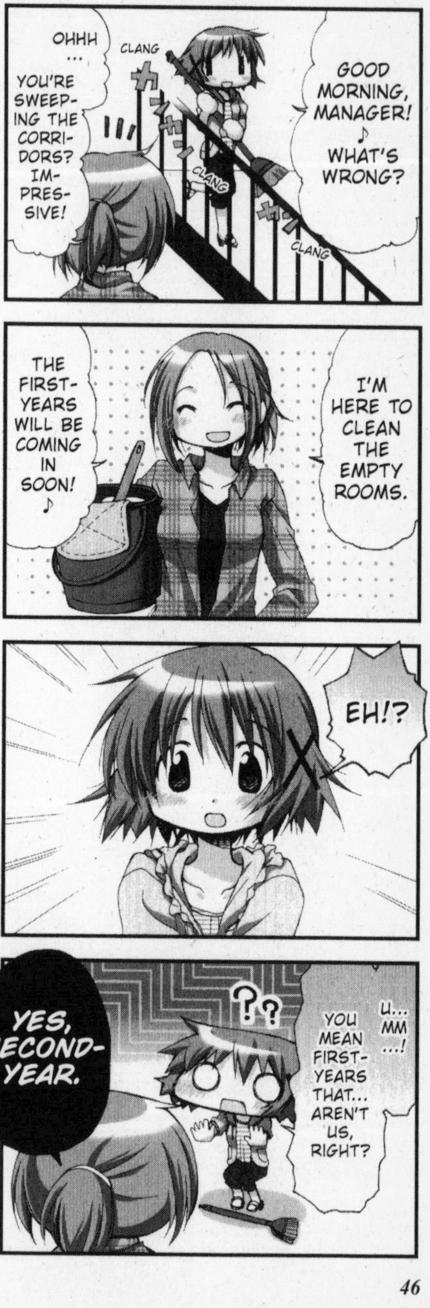
GOOD MORNING, MANAGER! ♪ WHAT'S WRONG?
CLANG
CLANG
CLANG
OHHH... YOU'RE SWEEPING THE CORRIDORS? IMPRESSIVE!
I'M HERE TO CLEAN THE EMPTY ROOMS.
THE FIRST-YEARS WILL BE COMING IN SOON! ♪
EH!?
U...MM...!
YOU MEAN FIRST-YEARS THAT... AREN'T US, RIGHT?
YES, SECOND-YEAR.

TELEPHONE GAME

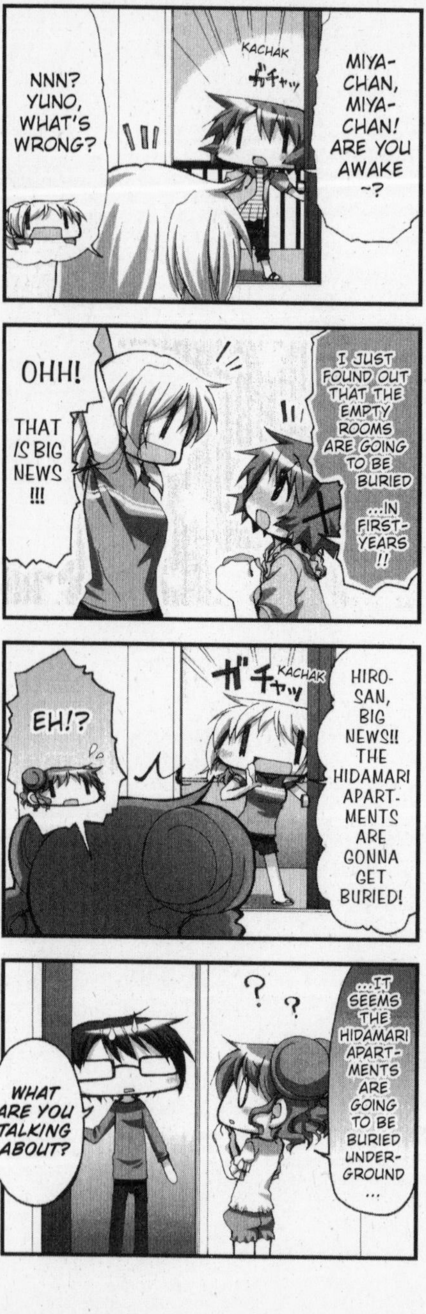
MIYA-CHAN, MIYA-CHAN! ARE YOU AWAKE ~?
KACHAK
ガチャッ
NNN? YUNO, WHAT'S WRONG?
I JUST FOUND OUT THAT THE EMPTY ROOMS ARE GOING TO BE BURIED ...IN FIRST-YEARS!!
OHH!
THAT IS BIG NEWS!!!
HIRO-SAN, BIG NEWS!! THE HIDAMARI APARTMENTS ARE GONNA GET BURIED!
KACHAK
ガチャッ
EH!?
...IT SEEMS THE HIDAMARI APARTMENTS ARE GOING TO BE BURIED UNDERGROUND...
WHAT ARE YOU TALKING ABOUT?

WHERE'S THE MONEY?

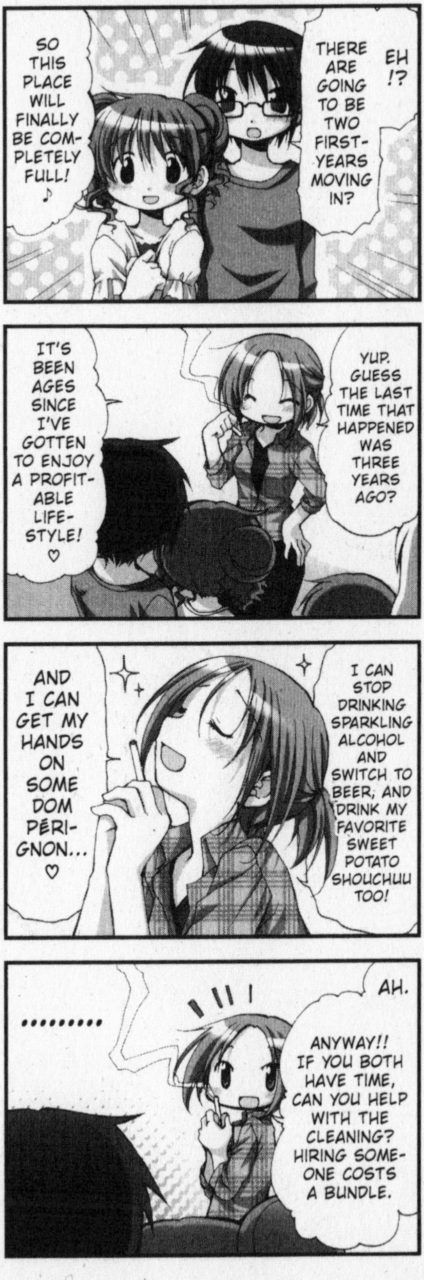

EH!?
THERE ARE GOING TO BE TWO FIRST-YEARS MOVING IN?
SO THIS PLACE WILL FINALLY BE COMPLETELY FULL! ♪
YUP. GUESS THE LAST TIME THAT HAPPENED WAS THREE YEARS AGO?
IT'S BEEN AGES SINCE I'VE GOTTEN TO ENJOY A PROFITABLE LIFESTYLE! ♡
I CAN STOP DRINKING SPARKLING ALCOHOL AND SWITCH TO BEER, AND DRINK MY FAVORITE SWEET POTATO SHOUCHUU TOO!
AND I CAN GET MY HANDS ON SOME DOM PÉRIGNON... ♡
AH.
ANYWAY!! IF YOU BOTH HAVE TIME, CAN YOU HELP WITH THE CLEANING? HIRING SOMEONE COSTS A BUNDLE.
....

TEN TO ONE

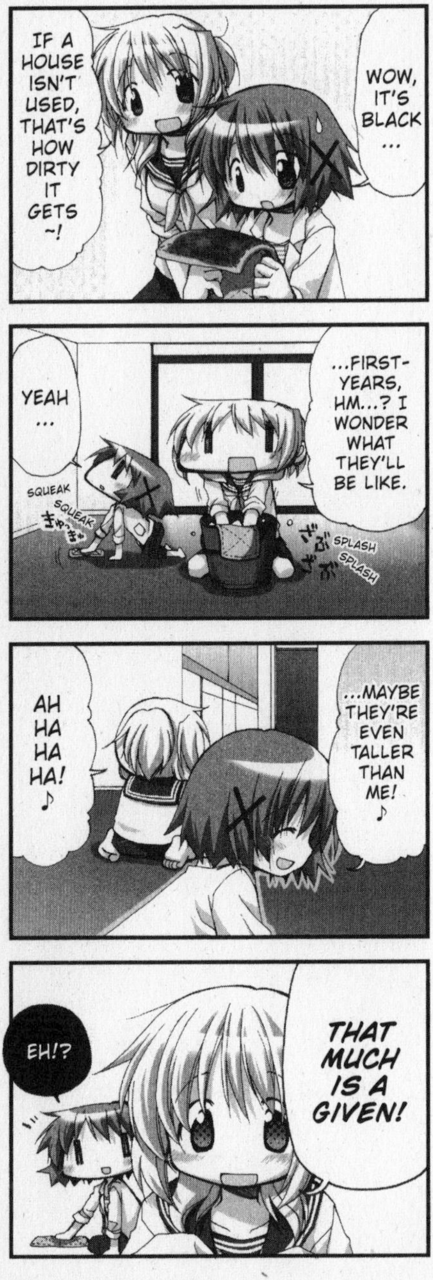

WOW, IT'S BLACK...
IF A HOUSE ISN'T USED, THAT'S HOW DIRTY IT GETS~!
...FIRST-YEARS, HM...? I WONDER WHAT THEY'LL BE LIKE.
ざぶざぶ
SPLASH SPLASH
YEAH...
SQUEAK SQUEAK
きゅっきゅ
...MAYBE THEY'RE EVEN TALLER THAN ME! ♪
AH HA HA HA! ♪
THAT MUCH IS A GIVEN!
EH!?

LOVE CLEANING

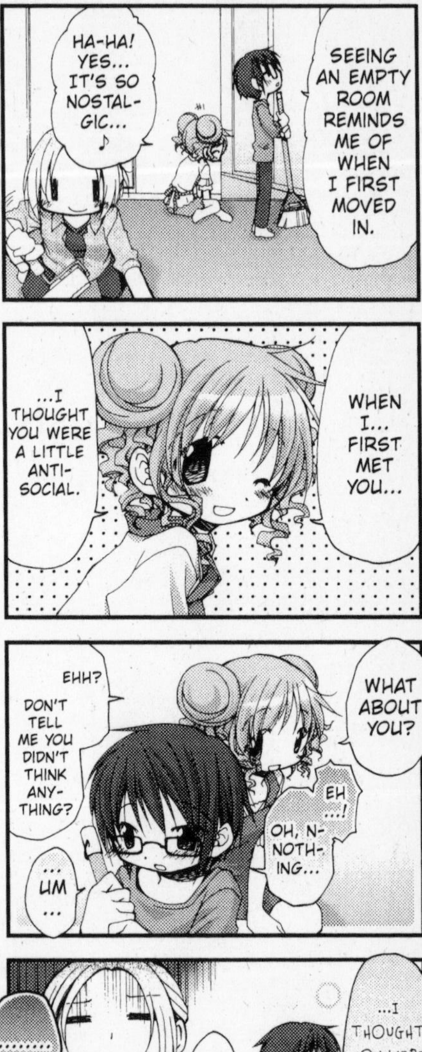
SEEING AN EMPTY ROOM REMINDS ME OF WHEN I FIRST MOVED IN.
HA-HA! YES... IT'S SO NOSTALGIC... ♪
WHEN I... FIRST MET YOU...
...I THOUGHT YOU WERE A LITTLE ANTI-SOCIAL.
WHAT ABOUT YOU?
EH ...!
OH, N-NOTHING...
EHH?
DON'T TELL ME YOU DIDN'T THINK ANYTHING?
...UM...
...I THOUGHT YOU WERE LIKE A SUGAR CANDY...
......
....

YOUNG STOMACHS

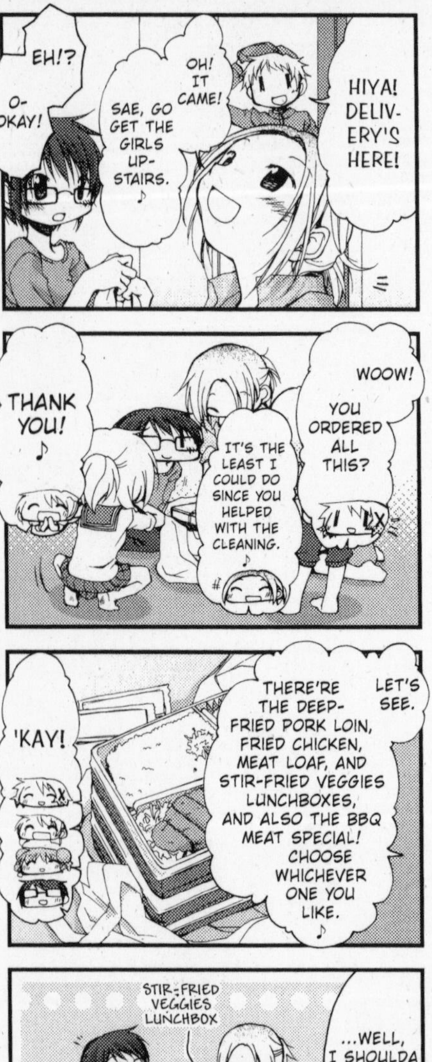
HIYA! DELIVERY'S HERE!
OH! IT CAME!
SAE, GO GET THE GIRLS UPSTAIRS. ♪
EH!?
O-OKAY!
WOOW!
YOU ORDERED ALL THIS?
IT'S THE LEAST I COULD DO SINCE YOU HELPED WITH THE CLEANING. ♪
THANK YOU! ♪
LET'S SEE.
THERE'RE THE DEEP-FRIED PORK LOIN, FRIED CHICKEN, MEAT LOAF, AND STIR-FRIED VEGGIES LUNCHBOXES, AND ALSO THE BBQ MEAT SPECIAL! CHOOSE WHICHEVER ONE YOU LIKE. ♪
'KAY!
...WELL, I SHOULDA KNOWN THIS WOULD BE THE ONE LEFT......
STIR-FRIED VEGGIES LUNCHBOX
EH!?

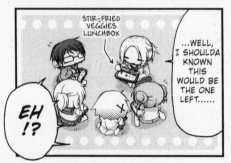

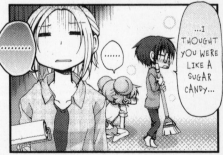

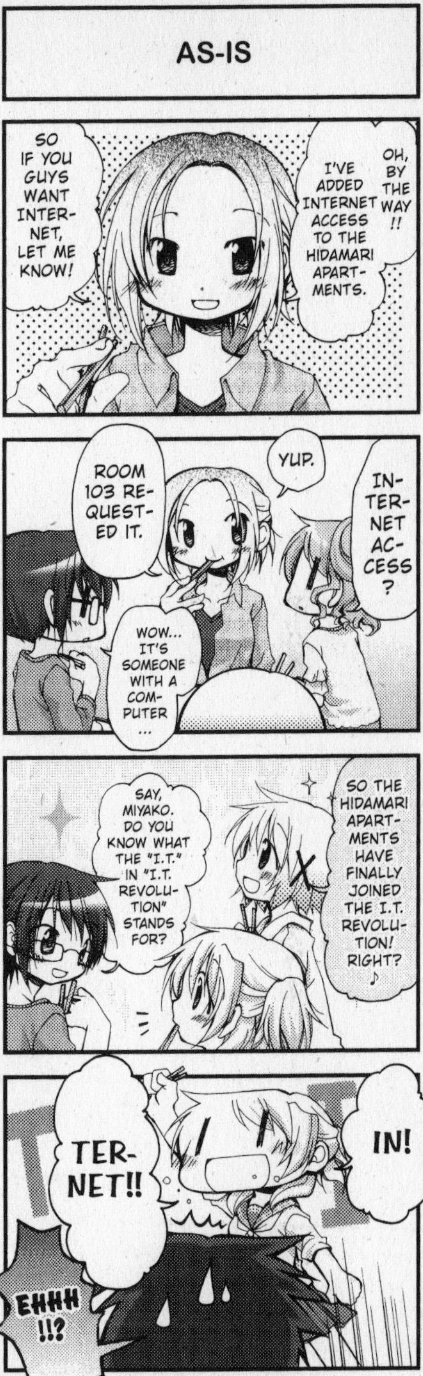
AS-IS
OH, BY THE WAY!!
I'VE ADDED INTERNET ACCESS TO THE HIDAMARI APARTMENTS.
SO IF YOU GUYS WANT INTERNET, LET ME KNOW!
INTERNET ACCESS?
YUP.
ROOM 103 REQUESTED IT.
WOW... IT'S SOMEONE WITH A COMPUTER...
SO THE HIDAMARI APARTMENTS HAVE FINALLY JOINED THE I.T. REVOLUTION! RIGHT? ♪
SAY, MIYAKO. DO YOU KNOW WHAT THE "I.T." IN "I.T. REVOLUTION" STANDS FOR?
IN!
TER-NET!!
EHHH!!?

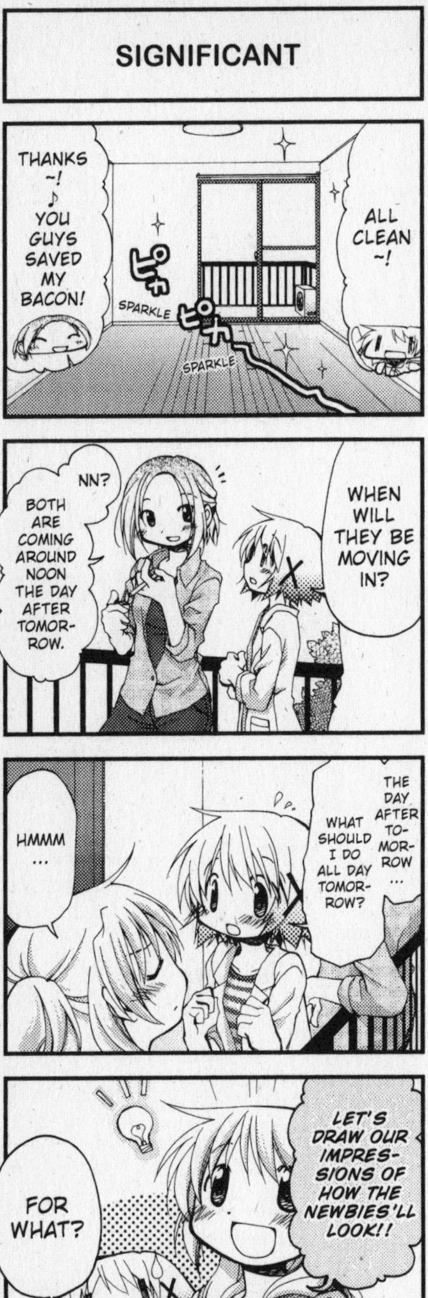
SIGNIFICANT
ALL CLEAN~!
ピカ SPARKLE
ピカ SPARKLE
THANKS~! ♪ YOU GUYS SAVED MY BACON!
WHEN WILL THEY BE MOVING IN?
NN?
BOTH ARE COMING AROUND NOON THE DAY AFTER TOMORROW.
THE DAY AFTER TOMORROW...
WHAT SHOULD I DO ALL DAY TOMORROW?
HMMM...
LET'S DRAW OUR IMPRESSIONS OF HOW THE NEWBIES'LL LOOK!!
FOR WHAT?

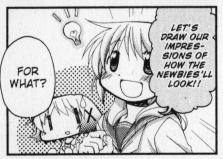

MOVING DAY

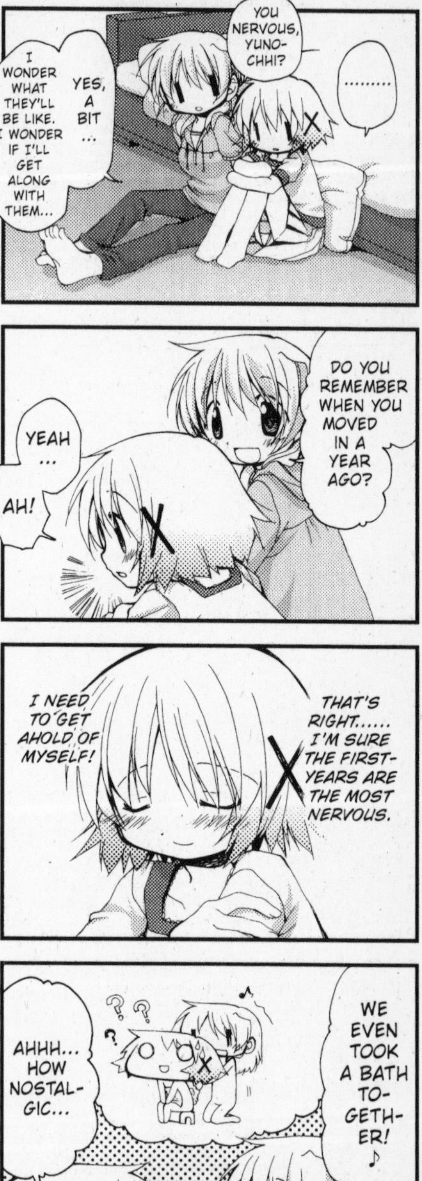
YOU NERVOUS, YUNO-CHHI?
....
YES, A BIT ...
I WONDER WHAT THEY'LL BE LIKE. I WONDER IF I'LL GET ALONG WITH THEM...
DO YOU REMEMBER WHEN YOU MOVED IN A YEAR AGO?
YEAH ...
AH!
THAT'S RIGHT...... I'M SURE THE FIRST-YEARS ARE THE MOST NERVOUS.
I NEED TO GET AHOLD OF MYSELF!
WE EVEN TOOK A BATH TO-GETH-ER! ♪
AHHH... HOW NOSTAL-GIC...

WELCOME MOOD

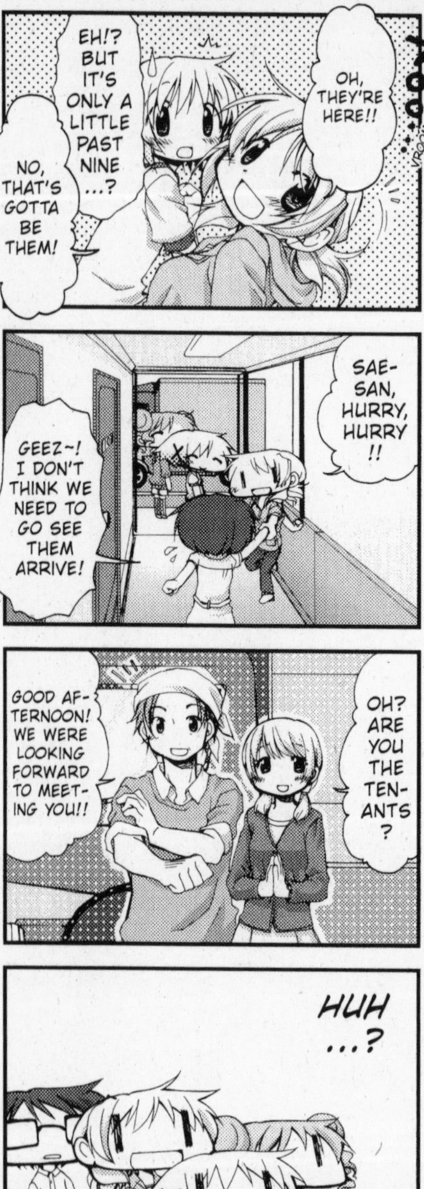
OH, THEY'RE HERE!!
VROOM
EH!? BUT IT'S ONLY A LITTLE PAST NINE ...?
NO, THAT'S GOTTA BE THEM!
SAE-SAN, HURRY, HURRY !!
GEEZ~! I DON'T THINK WE NEED TO GO SEE THEM ARRIVE!
OH? ARE YOU THE TEN-ANTS ?
GOOD AF-TERNOON! WE WERE LOOKING FORWARD TO MEET-ING YOU!!
HUH ...?

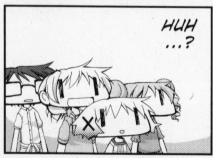

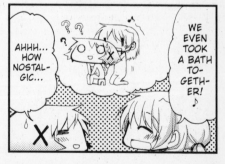

PICK UP GIRLS

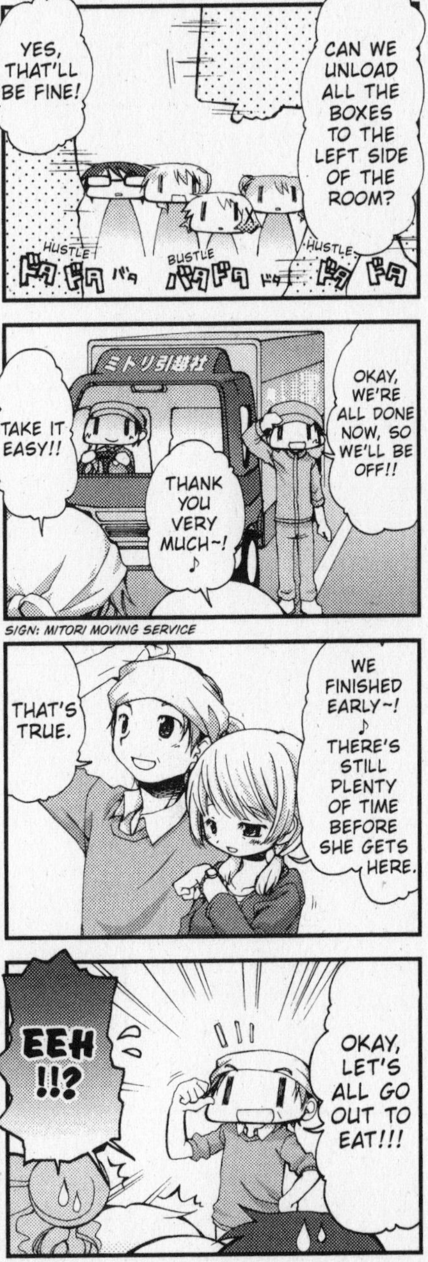
CAN WE UNLOAD ALL THE BOXES TO THE LEFT SIDE OF THE ROOM?
YES, THAT'LL BE FINE!
HUSTLE
BUSTLE
HUSTLE
ミトリ引越社
OKAY, WE'RE ALL DONE NOW, SO WE'LL BE OFF!!
THANK YOU VERY MUCH~! ♪
TAKE IT EASY!!
SIGN: MITORI MOVING SERVICE
WE FINISHED EARLY~! ♪ THERE'S STILL PLENTY OF TIME BEFORE SHE GETS HERE.
THAT'S TRUE.
OKAY, LET'S ALL GO OUT TO EAT!!!
EEH!!?

ALONE

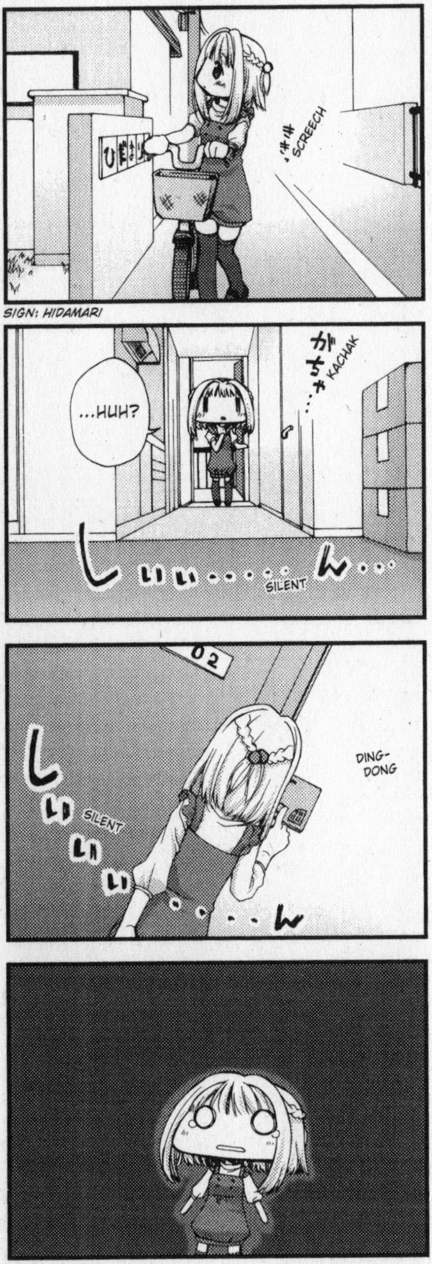
SCREECH
SIGN: HIDAMARI
KACHAK
...HUH?
SILENT
02
DING-DONG
SILENT

CONFUSED

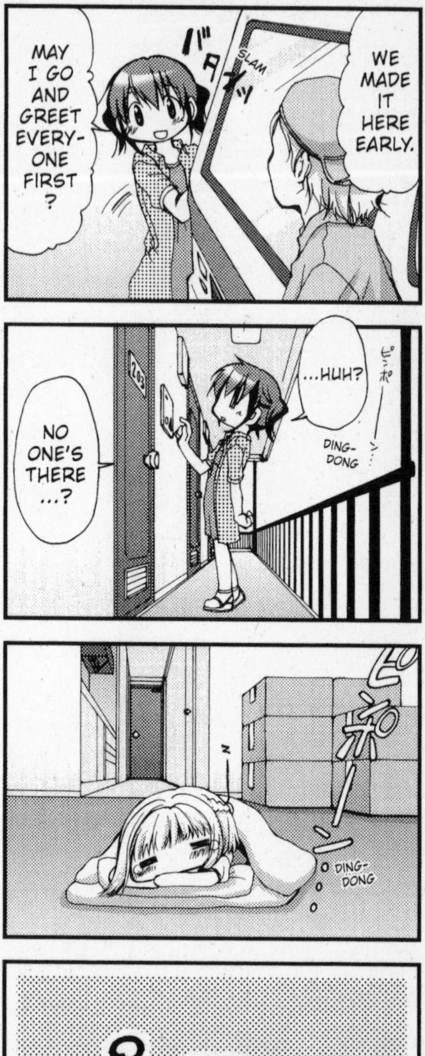
WE MADE IT HERE EARLY.
SLAM
MAY I GO AND GREET EVERY-ONE FIRST?
...HUH?
DING-DONG
NO ONE'S THERE ...?
z
DING-DONG
?

WELCOME TO THE HIDAMARI APARTMENTS

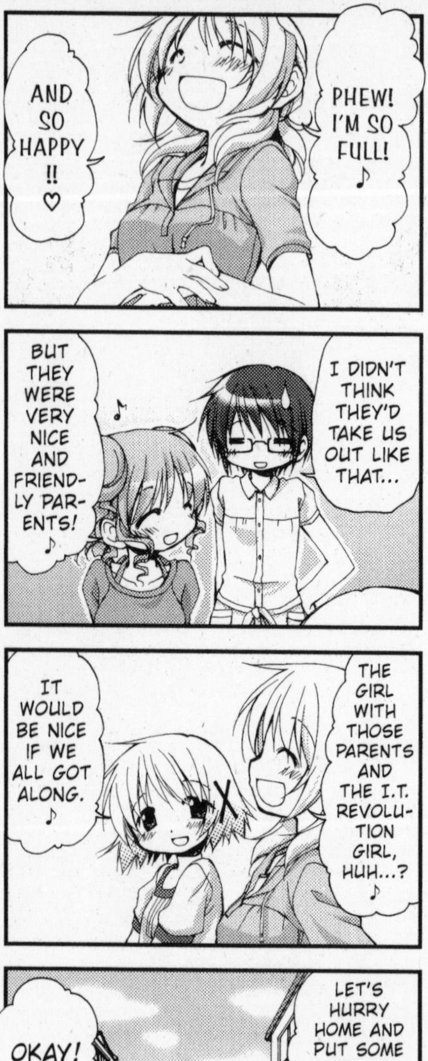
PHEW! I'M SO FULL! ♪
AND SO HAPPY!! ♡
I DIDN'T THINK THEY'D TAKE US OUT LIKE THAT...
BUT THEY WERE VERY NICE AND FRIEND-LY PAR-ENTS! ♪
THE GIRL WITH THOSE PARENTS AND THE I.T. REVOLU-TION GIRL, HUH...? ♪
IT WOULD BE NICE IF WE ALL GOT ALONG. ♪
LET'S HURRY HOME AND PUT SOME TEA ON WHILE WE WAIT FOR THEM! ♪
OKAY!

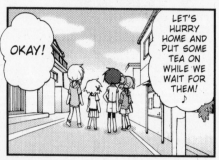

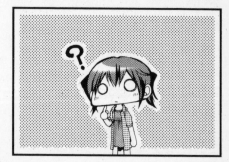

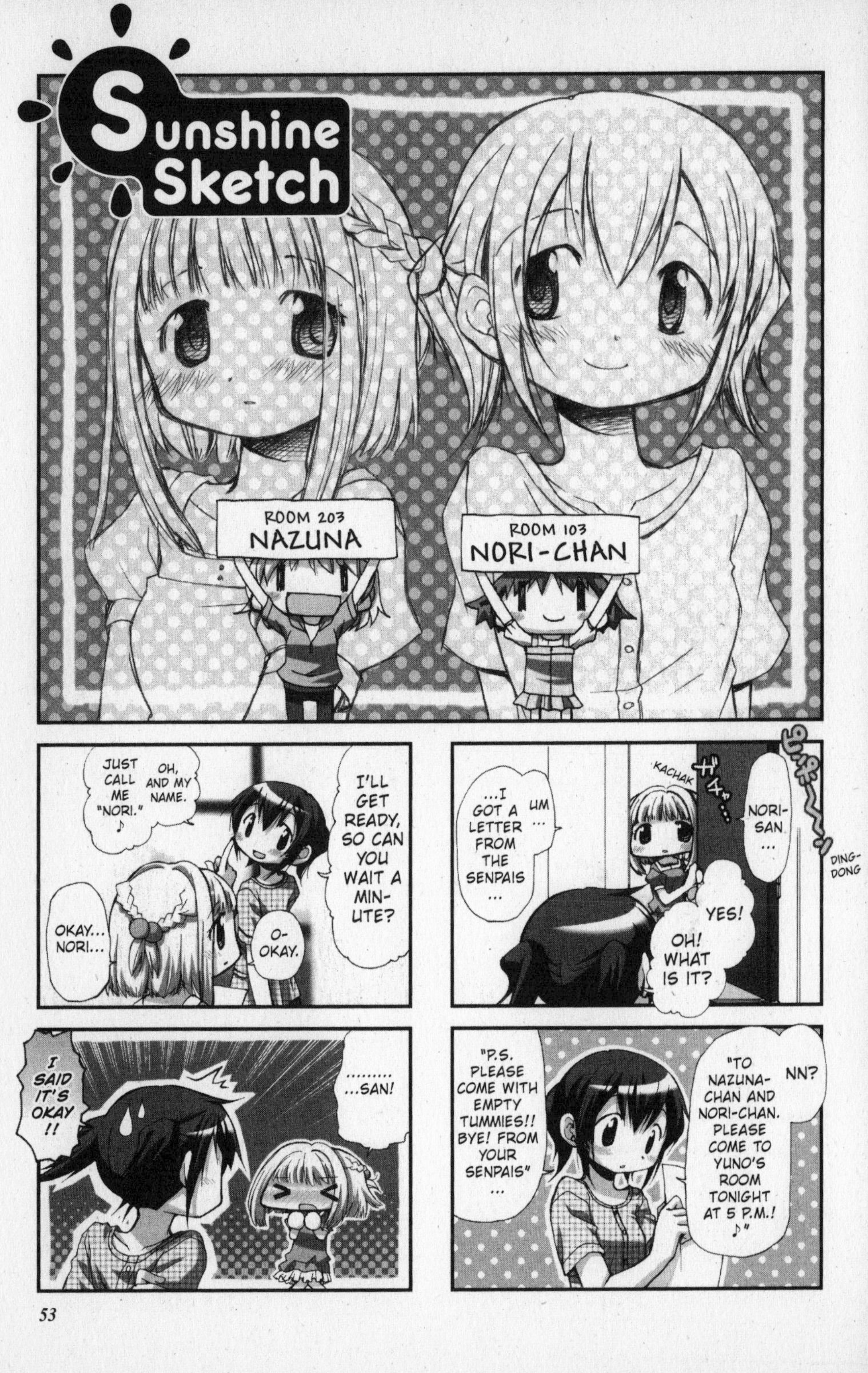
Sunshine Sketch
ROOM 103 NORI-CHAN
ROOM 203 NAZUNA
DING-DONG
NORI-SAN …
KACHAK
UM …
…I GOT A LETTER FROM THE SENPAIS …
YES!
OH! WHAT IS IT?
I'LL GET READY, SO CAN YOU WAIT A MIN-UTE?
OH, AND MY NAME.
JUST CALL ME "NORI." ♪
O-OKAY.
OKAY… NORI…
NN?
"TO NAZUNA-CHAN AND NORI-CHAN. PLEASE COME TO YUNO'S ROOM TONIGHT AT 5 P.M.! ♪"
"P.S. PLEASE COME WITH EMPTY TUMMIES!! BYE! FROM YOUR SENPAIS" …
……… …SAN!
I SAID IT'S OKAY!!

FRIENDLY SENIORS

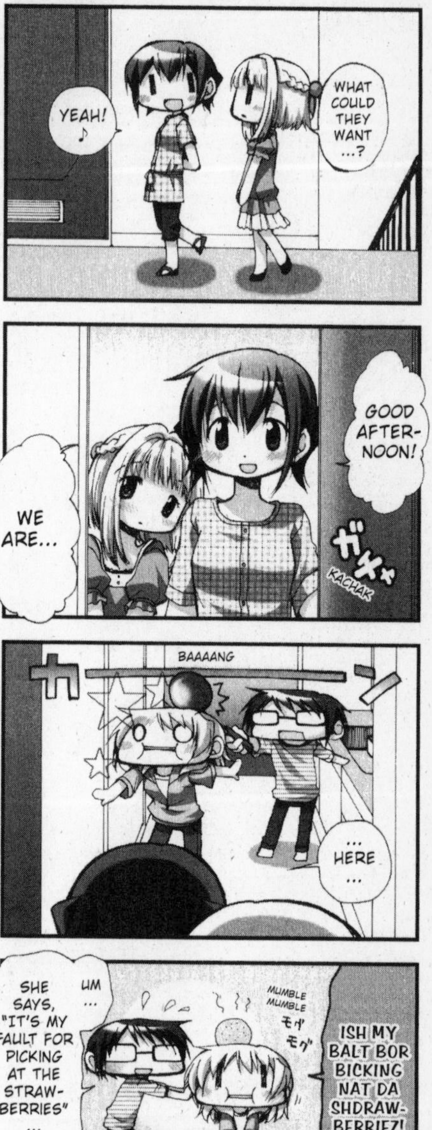
WHAT COULD THEY WANT ...?
YEAH! ♪
GOOD AFTER-NOON!
KACHAK
WE ARE...
BAAAANG
... HERE ...
ISH MY BALT BOR BICKING NAT DA SHDRAW-BERRIEZ!
MUMBLE MUMBLE
UM ...
SHE SAYS, "IT'S MY FAULT FOR PICKING AT THE STRAW-BERRIES" ...

BIG WELCOME

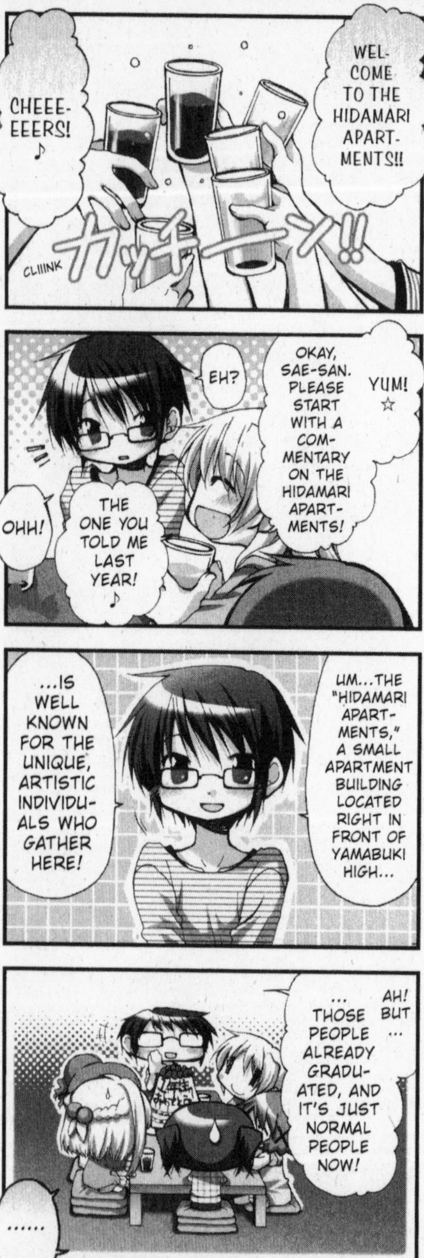
WEL-COME TO THE HIDAMARI APART-MENTS!!
CHEEEEERS! ♪
CLIIINK
YUM! ☆
OKAY, SAE-SAN. PLEASE START WITH A COM-MENTARY ON THE HIDAMARI APART-MENTS!
EH?
THE ONE YOU TOLD ME LAST YEAR! ♪
OHH!
UM...THE "HIDAMARI APART-MENTS," A SMALL APARTMENT BUILDING LOCATED RIGHT IN FRONT OF YAMABUKI HIGH...
...IS WELL KNOWN FOR THE UNIQUE, ARTISTIC INDIVIDU-ALS WHO GATHER HERE!
AH! BUT ...
... THOSE PEOPLE ALREADY GRADU-ATED, AND IT'S JUST NORMAL PEOPLE NOW!
......

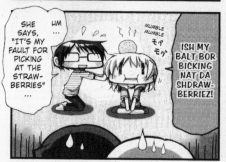

YES / NO

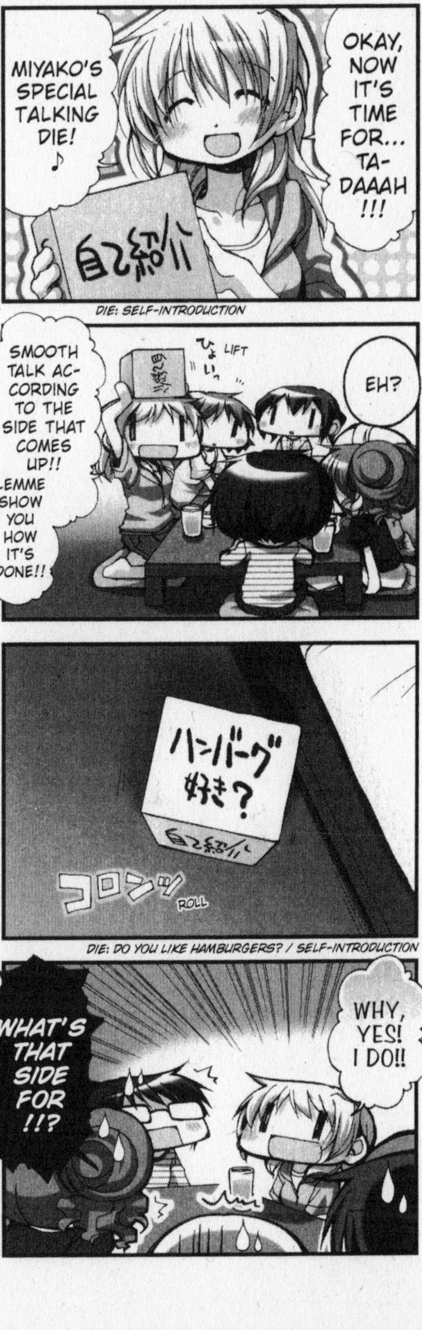
OKAY, NOW IT'S TIME FOR... TA-DAAAH!!!
MIYAKO'S SPECIAL TALKING DIE! ♪
自己紹介
EH?
ひょいっ LIFT
SMOOTH TALK ACCORDING TO THE SIDE THAT COMES UP!! LEMME SHOW YOU HOW IT'S DONE!!
ハンバーグ好き？
自己紹介
コロンッ ROLL
WHY, YES! I DO!!
WHAT'S THAT SIDE FOR!!?
DIE: SELF-INTRODUCTION
DIE: DO YOU LIKE HAMBURGERS? / SELF-INTRODUCTION

TALKLESS

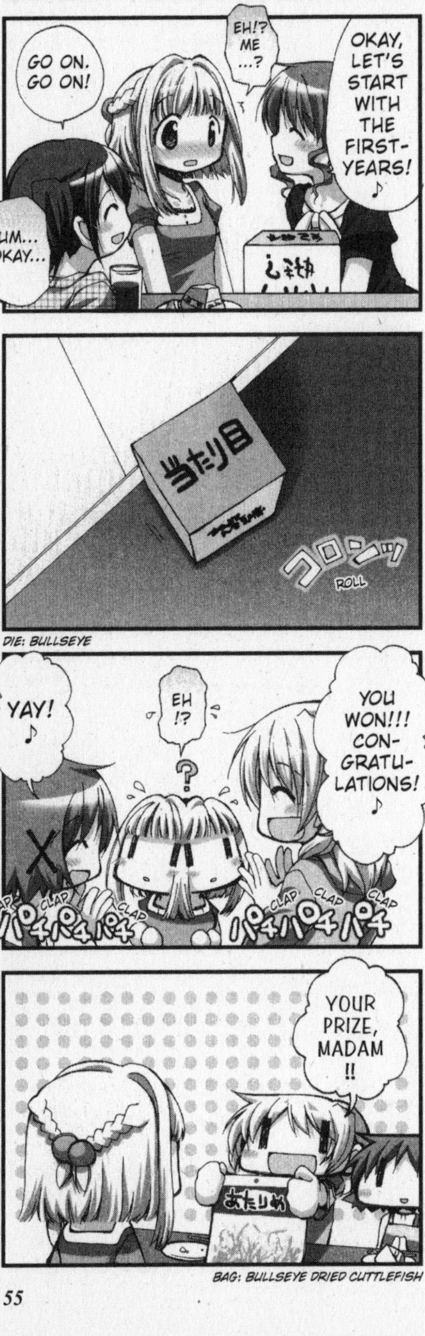
OKAY, LET'S START WITH THE FIRST-YEARS! ♪
EH!? ME ...?
GO ON. GO ON!
UM... OKAY...
当たり目
コロンッ ROLL
YOU WON!!! CONGRATULATIONS! ♪
EH!?
YAY! ♪
CLAP CLAP パチパチパチ
CLAP CLAP パチパチパチ
YOUR PRIZE, MADAM!!
あたりめ
DIE: BULLSEYE
BAG: BULLSEYE DRIED CUTTLEFISH

DOES NOT COMPUTE

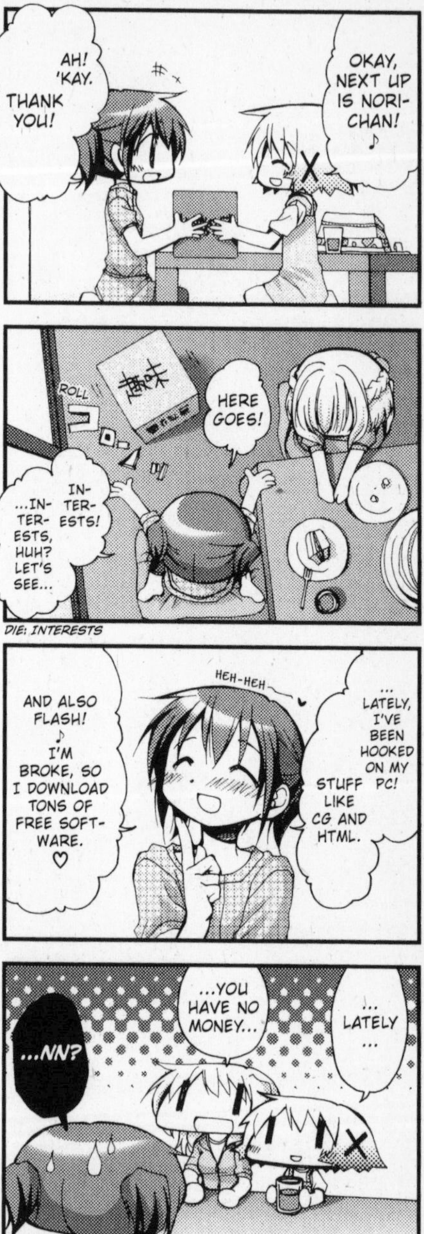
OKAY, NEXT UP IS NORI-CHAN! ♪
AH! 'KAY. THANK YOU!
HERE GOES!
ROLL
IN-TER-ESTS!
...IN-TER-ESTS, HUH? LET'S SEE...
DIE: INTERESTS
HEH-HEH
... LATELY, I'VE BEEN HOOKED ON MY PC!
STUFF LIKE CG AND HTML.
AND ALSO FLASH! ♪ I'M BROKE, SO I DOWNLOAD TONS OF FREE SOFTWARE. ♡
... LATELY ...
...YOU HAVE NO MONEY...
...NN?

CULTURE GAP

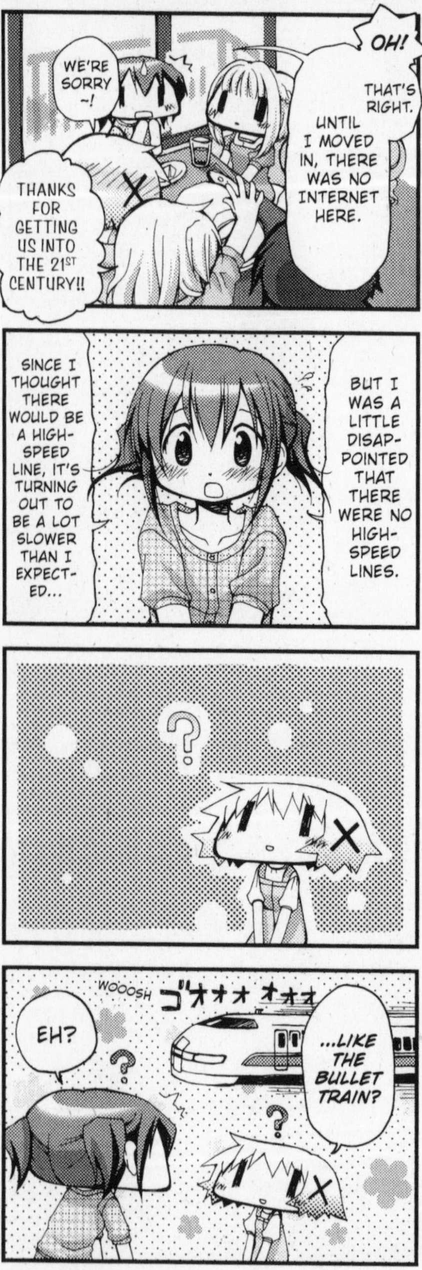
OH!
THAT'S RIGHT.
UNTIL I MOVED IN, THERE WAS NO INTERNET HERE.
WE'RE SORRY ~!
THANKS FOR GETTING US INTO THE 21ST CENTURY!!
BUT I WAS A LITTLE DISAPPOINTED THAT THERE WERE NO HIGH-SPEED LINES.
SINCE I THOUGHT THERE WOULD BE A HIGH-SPEED LINE, IT'S TURNING OUT TO BE A LOT SLOWER THAN I EXPECTED...
?
WOOOSH ゴオオオ オオオ
...LIKE THE BULLET TRAIN?
EH?
?
?

DEEP

THERE! ♪
なずなさんからセンパイたちへ質問!!
EH!? I HAVE TO ASK SOMETHING!?
コロンッ
ROLL
YUP, YUP.
OKAY THEN...
......
WHY ARE ALL OF YOU DRAWING ART...?
WHY... HUH?
THAT'S A DEEP QUESTION.
HOW ABOUT STARTING WITH THE ONE WHO ROLLED THE DIE—YUNO?
...... WHY...
...DO I DRAW ......
WHY ......
WHY ...
PERPLEXED
もんもんもん
もんもん
ACK... YUNO !!!

DIE: A QUESTION FOR THE SENPAIS FROM NAZUNA-SAN!!

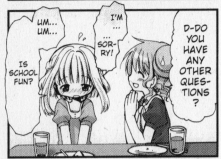

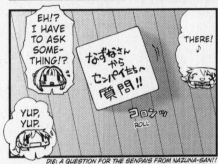

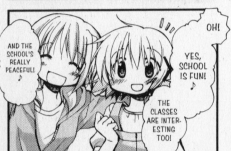

EXTREME REACTION

D-DO YOU HAVE ANY OTHER QUESTIONS?
I'M ... ...SORRY!
UM... UM...
IS SCHOOL FUN?
OH!
YES, SCHOOL IS FUN! ♪
THE CLASSES ARE INTERESTING TOO!
AND THE SCHOOL'S REALLY PEACEFUL! ♪
THERE ARE FUNNY TEACHERS. ♪
ONE ALWAYS WEARS WEIRD OUTFITS ~!
SHE'S REALLY SEXY AND HAS A HABIT OF TAKING IT OFF. ♪
...HUH?

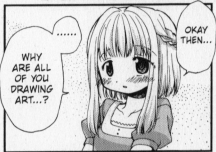

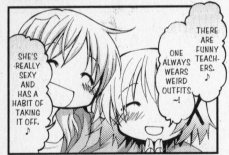

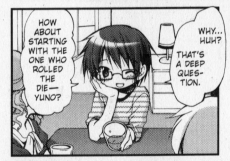

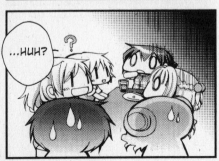

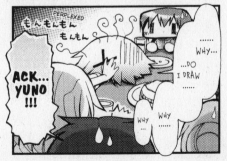

IT'LL BE OKAY

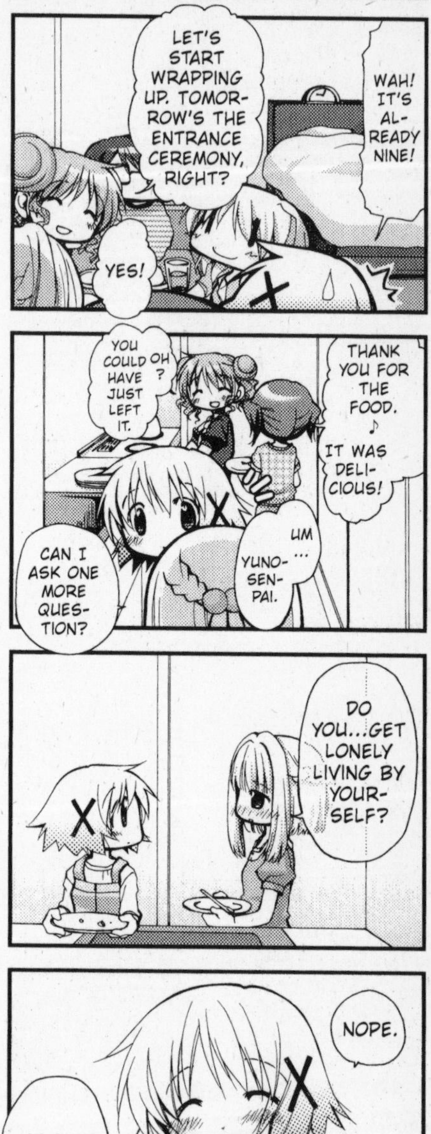

WAH! IT'S ALREADY NINE!
LET'S START WRAPPING UP. TOMORROW'S THE ENTRANCE CEREMONY, RIGHT?
YES!
THANK YOU FOR THE FOOD. ♪
IT WAS DELICIOUS!
OH?
YOU COULD HAVE JUST LEFT IT.
UM... YUNO-SENPAI.
CAN I ASK ONE MORE QUESTION?
DO YOU...GET LONELY LIVING BY YOURSELF?
NOPE.
NOT AT ALL!

IT JUST STARTED

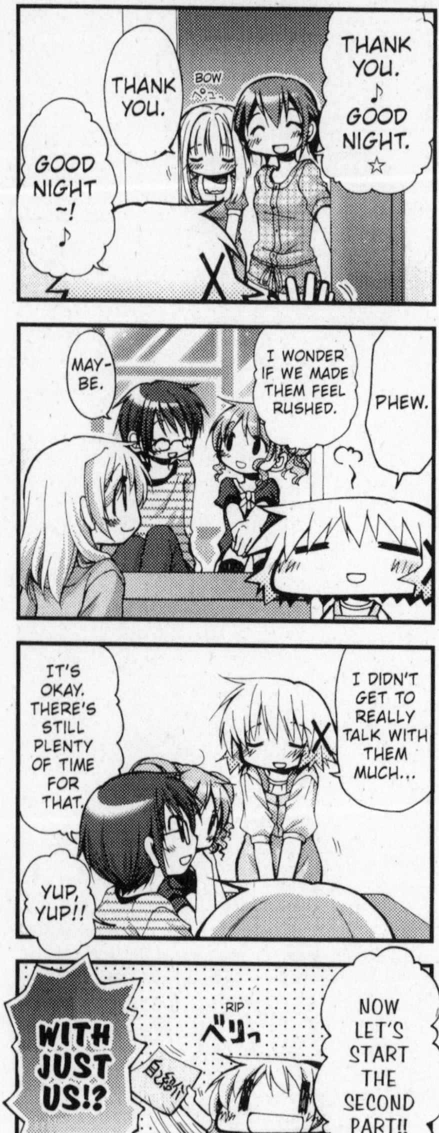

THANK YOU. ♪ GOOD NIGHT. ☆
BOW
THANK YOU.
GOOD NIGHT ~! ♪
PHEW.
I WONDER IF WE MADE THEM FEEL RUSHED.
MAYBE.
I DIDN'T GET TO REALLY TALK WITH THEM MUCH...
IT'S OKAY. THERE'S STILL PLENTY OF TIME FOR THAT.
YUP, YUP!!
NOW LET'S START THE SECOND PART!!
RIP
WITH JUST US!?

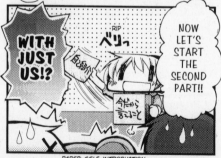

PAPER: SELF-INTRODUCTION
DIE: NOW WE CAN SAY IT

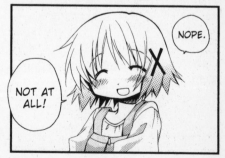

BAPTISM

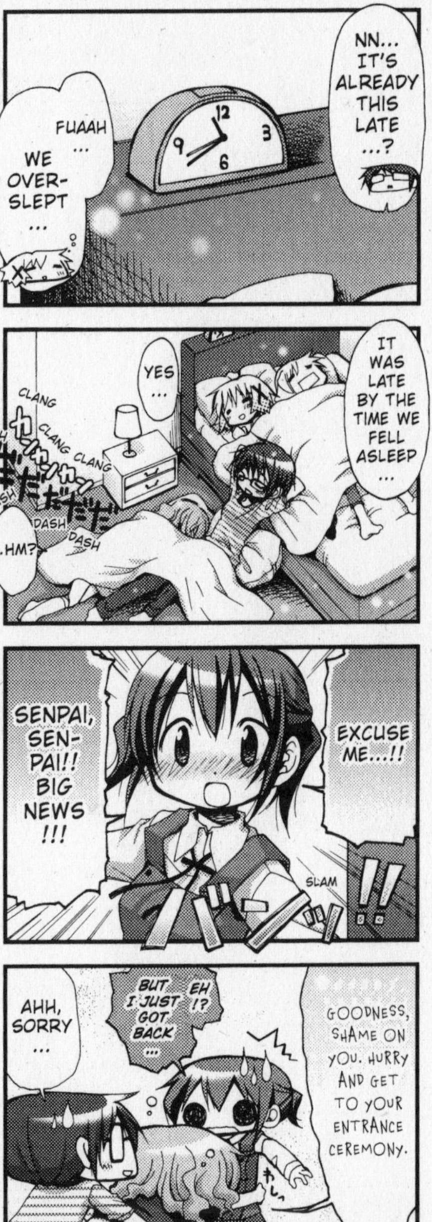
NN... IT'S ALREADY THIS LATE ...?
FUAAH ... WE OVERSLEPT ...
IT WAS LATE BY THE TIME WE FELL ASLEEP ...
YES ...
CLANG CLANG CLANG
DASH DASH DASH DASH
...HM?
EXCUSE ME...!!
SENPAI, SENPAI!! BIG NEWS !!!
SLAM
GOODNESS, SHAME ON YOU. HURRY AND GET TO YOUR ENTRANCE CEREMONY.
EH !?
BUT I JUST GOT BACK ...
AHH, SORRY ...
SFX: WASHI (GRAB)

HIDAMARI APARTMENT FIRST

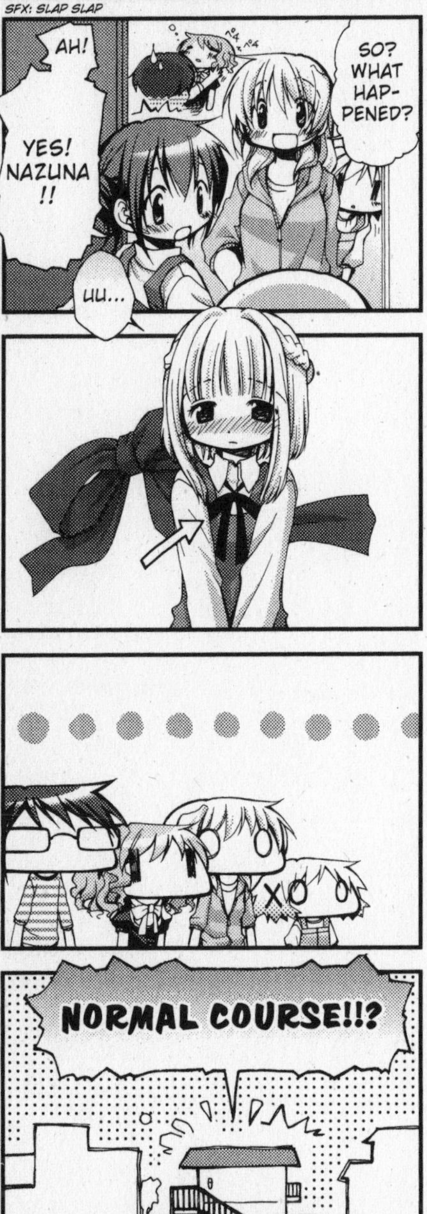
SFX: SLAP SLAP
SO? WHAT HAPPENED?
AH!
YES! NAZUNA !!
UU...
NORMAL COURSE!!?

NEGATIVE ↔ POSITIVE

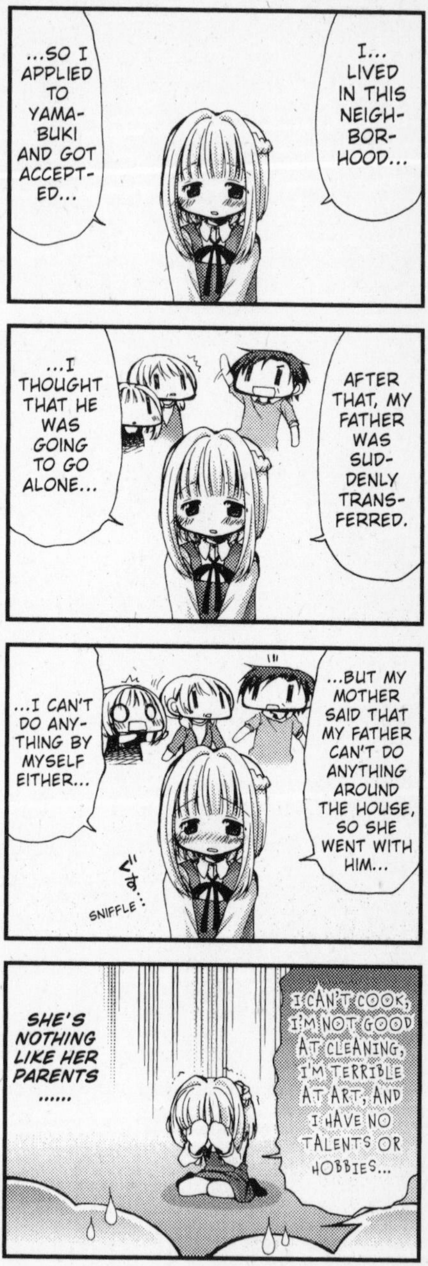
I... LIVED IN THIS NEIGHBORHOOD...
...SO I APPLIED TO YAMABUKI AND GOT ACCEPTED...
AFTER THAT, MY FATHER WAS SUDDENLY TRANSFERRED.
...I THOUGHT THAT HE WAS GOING TO GO ALONE...
...BUT MY MOTHER SAID THAT MY FATHER CAN'T DO ANYTHING AROUND THE HOUSE, SO SHE WENT WITH HIM...
...I CAN'T DO ANYTHING BY MYSELF EITHER...
SNIFFLE
I CAN'T COOK, I'M NOT GOOD AT CLEANING, I'M TERRIBLE AT ART, AND I HAVE NO TALENTS OR HOBBIES...
SHE'S NOTHING LIKE HER PARENTS ......

STRAIGHT PUNCH

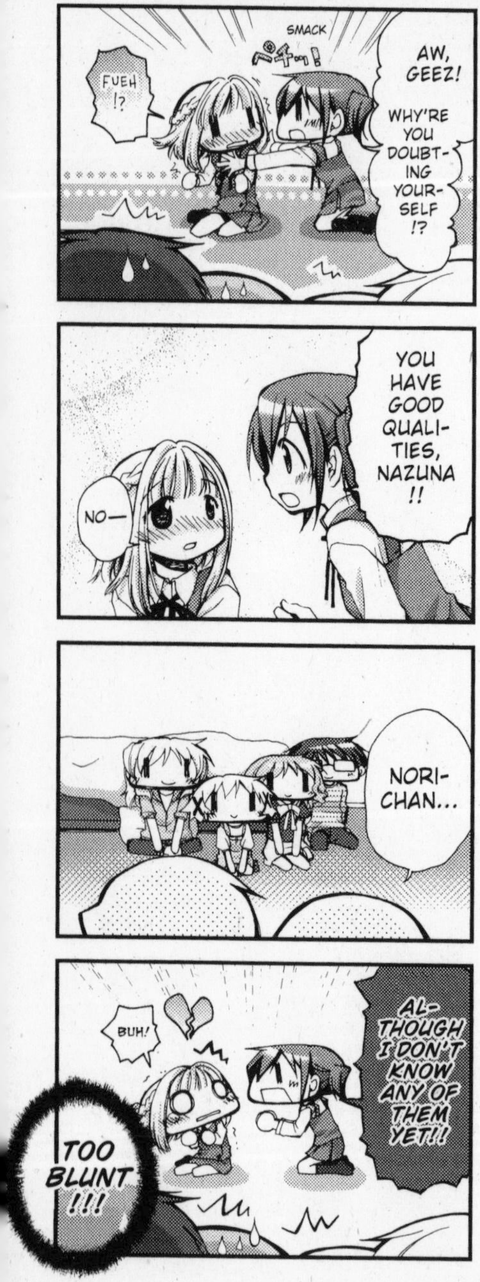
SMACK
AW, GEEZ!
WHY'RE YOU DOUBTING YOURSELF !?
FUEH !?
YOU HAVE GOOD QUALITIES, NAZUNA !!
NO—
NORI-CHAN...
ALTHOUGH I DON'T KNOW ANY OF THEM YET!!
BUH!
TOO BLUNT !!!

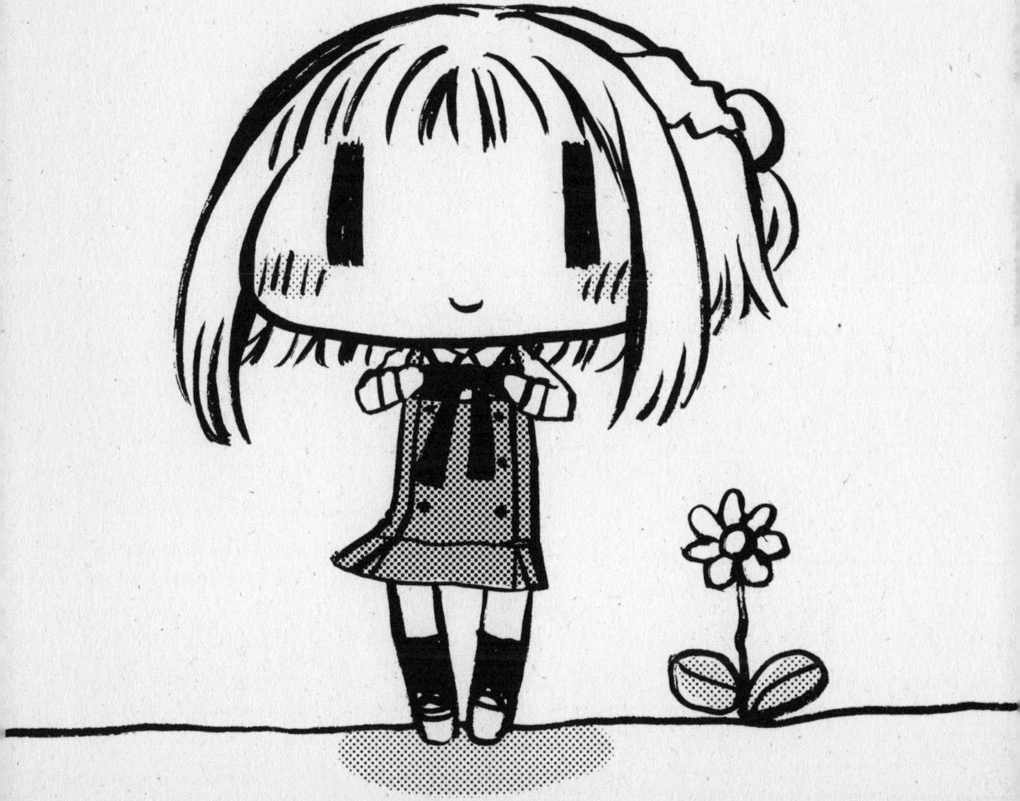

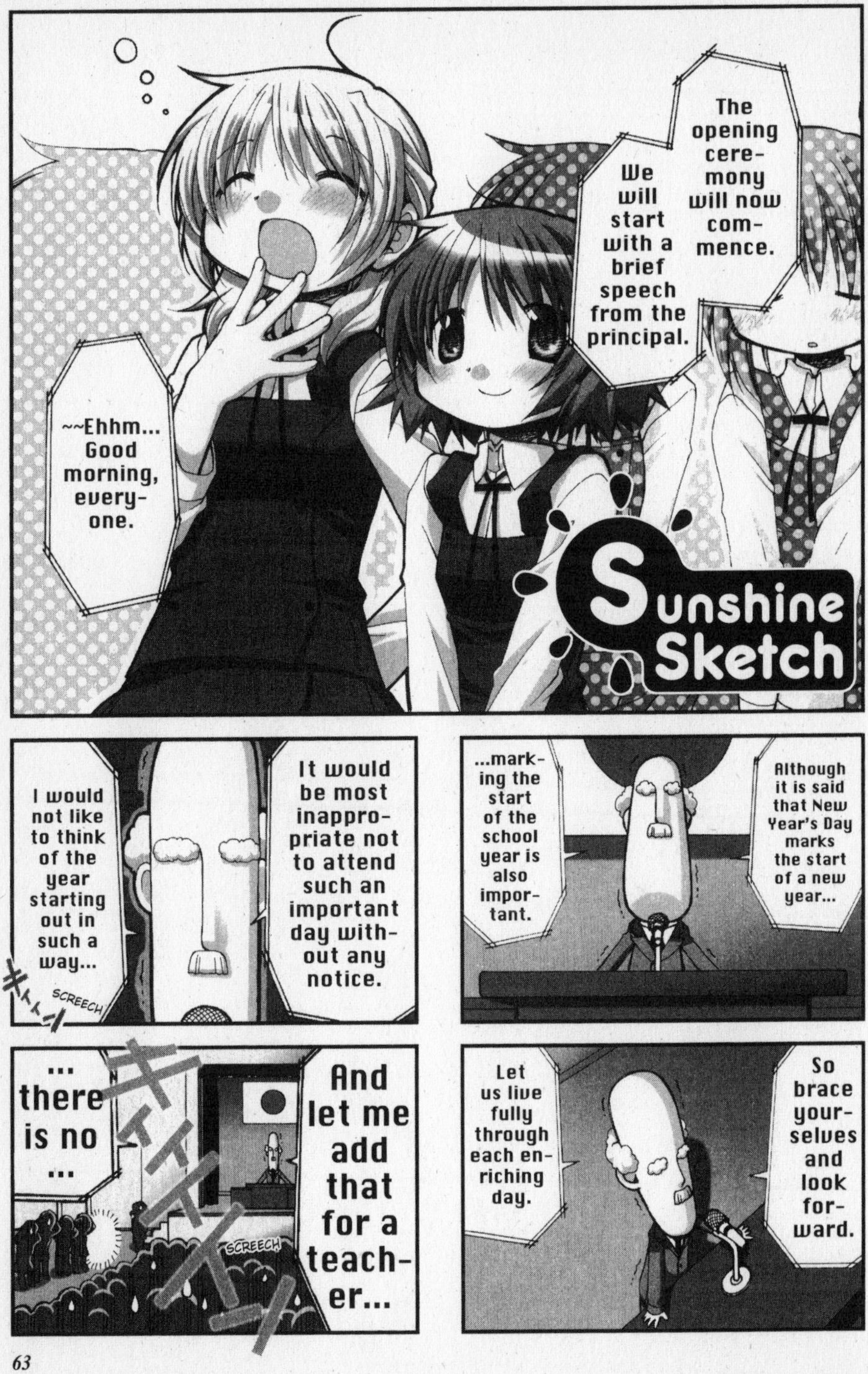
The opening ceremony will now commence.
We will start with a brief speech from the principal.
~~Ehhm... Good morning, everyone.
Sunshine Sketch
Although it is said that New Year's Day marks the start of a new year...
...marking the start of the school year is also important.
It would be most inappropriate not to attend such an important day without any notice.
I would not like to think of the year starting out in such a way...
SCREECH
So brace yourselves and look forward.
Let us live fully through each enriching day.
And let me add that for a teacher...
... there is no ...
SCREECH

FLYING BODY ATTACK

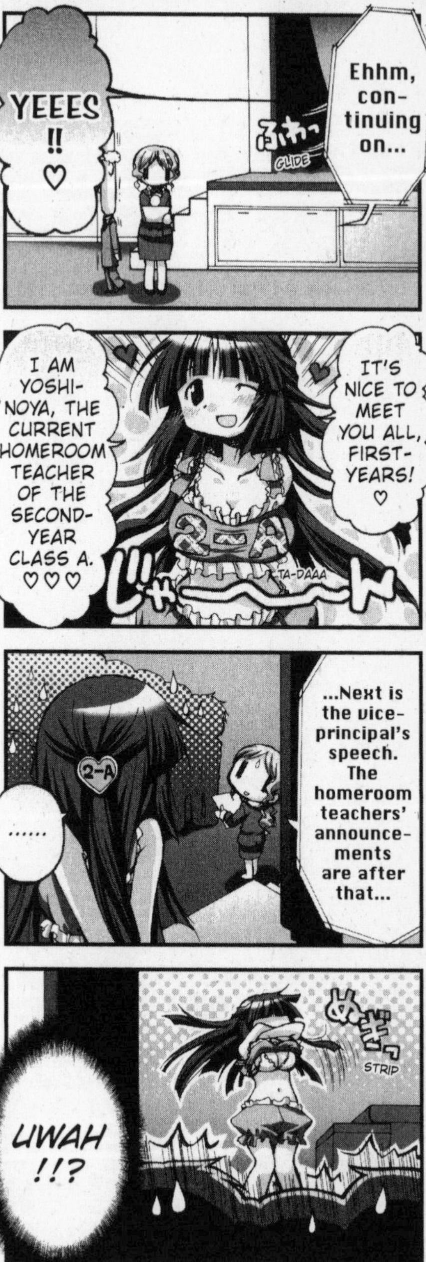
Ehhm, continuing on...
ふわっ
GLIDE
YEEES!! ♡
IT'S NICE TO MEET YOU ALL, FIRST-YEARS! ♡
I AM YOSHINOYA, THE CURRENT HOMEROOM TEACHER OF THE SECOND-YEAR CLASS A. ♡♡♡
じゃーーん
TA-DAAA
...Next is the vice-principal's speech. The homeroom teachers' announcements are after that...
2-A
......
めぎっ
STRIP
UWAH!!?

THE USUAL FLOOR

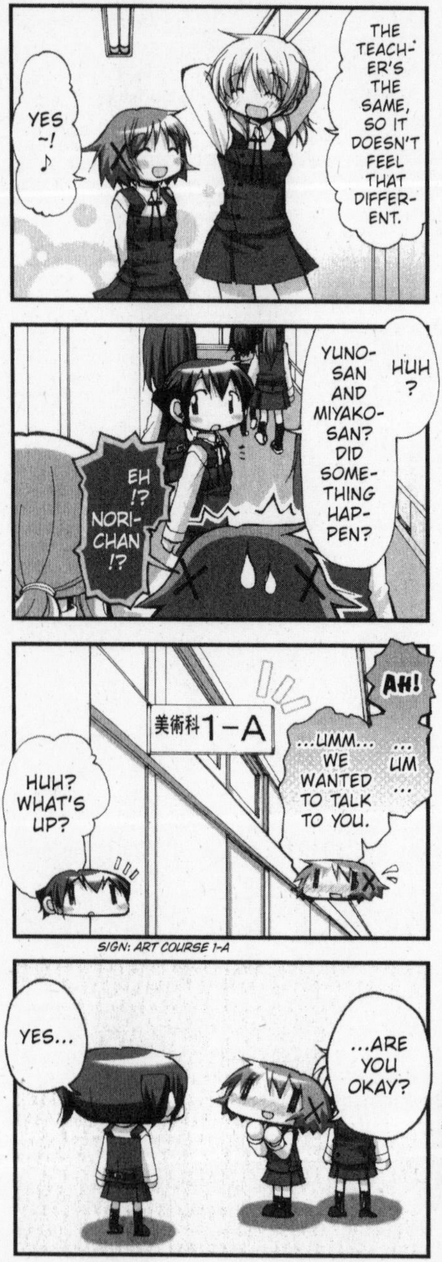
THE TEACHER'S THE SAME, SO IT DOESN'T FEEL THAT DIFFERENT.
YES~! ♪
HUH?
YUNO-SAN AND MIYAKO-SAN? DID SOMETHING HAPPEN?
EH!? NORI-CHAN!?
AH!
...UM...
...UMM... WE WANTED TO TALK TO YOU.
美術科1-A
HUH? WHAT'S UP?
SIGN: ART COURSE 1-A
...ARE YOU OKAY?
YES...

GIRLS GO WHEREVER

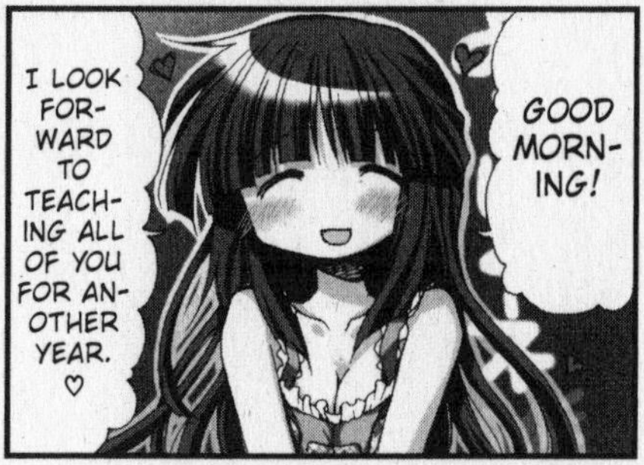
GOOD MORNING!
I LOOK FORWARD TO TEACHING ALL OF YOU FOR ANOTHER YEAR. ♡

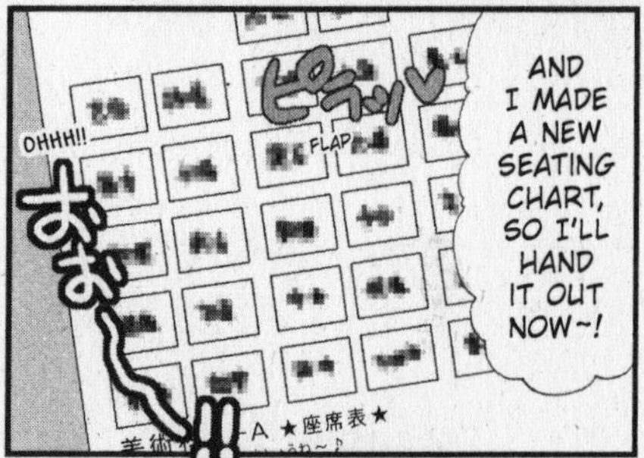
AND I MADE A NEW SEATING CHART, SO I'LL HAND IT OUT NOW~!
ピラッ♥
FLAP
OHHH!!
おぉ〜〜!!
★座席表★

TEXT: ☆ SEATING CHART ☆

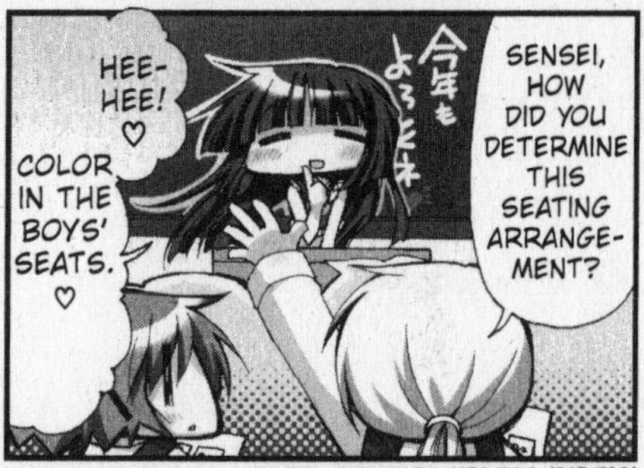
SENSEI, HOW DID YOU DETERMINE THIS SEATING ARRANGEMENT?
今年もよろしくネ
HEE-HEE! ♡
COLOR IN THE BOYS' SEATS. ♡

BOARD: LET'S WORK HARD THIS YEAR TOO!

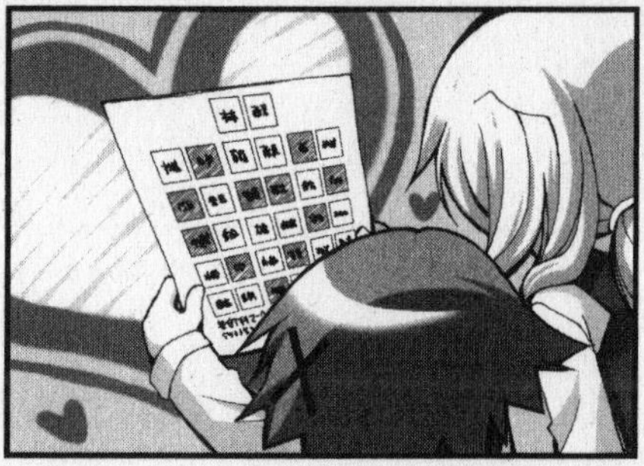

PARALLEL LINES

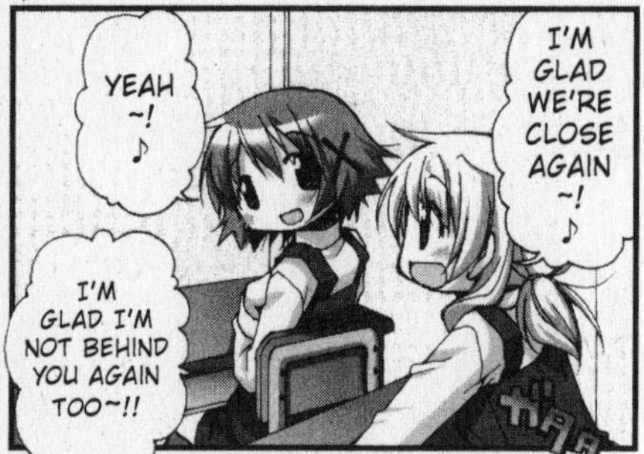
I'M GLAD WE'RE CLOSE AGAIN ~! ♪
YEAH ~! ♪
I'M GLAD I'M NOT BEHIND YOU AGAIN TOO~!!

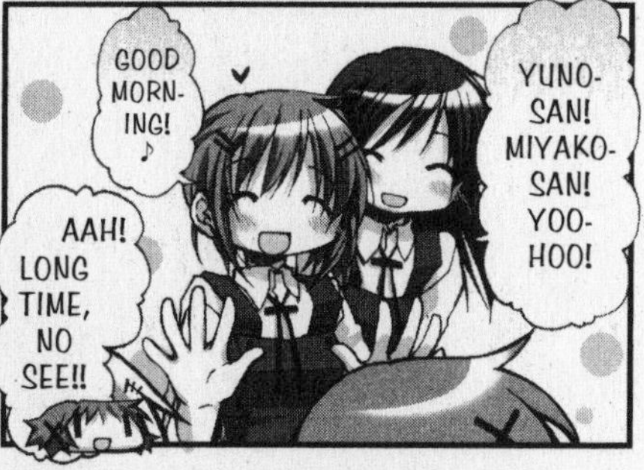
YUNO-SAN! MIYAKO-SAN! YOO-HOO!
GOOD MORNING! ♪
AAH! LONG TIME, NO SEE!!

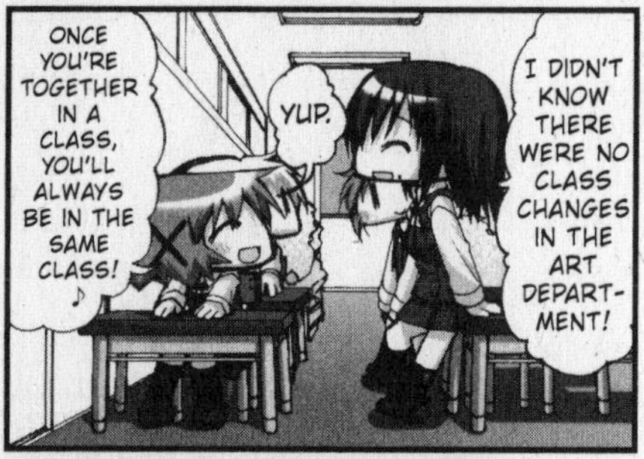
I DIDN'T KNOW THERE WERE NO CLASS CHANGES IN THE ART DEPARTMENT!
YUP.
ONCE YOU'RE TOGETHER IN A CLASS, YOU'LL ALWAYS BE IN THE SAME CLASS! ♪

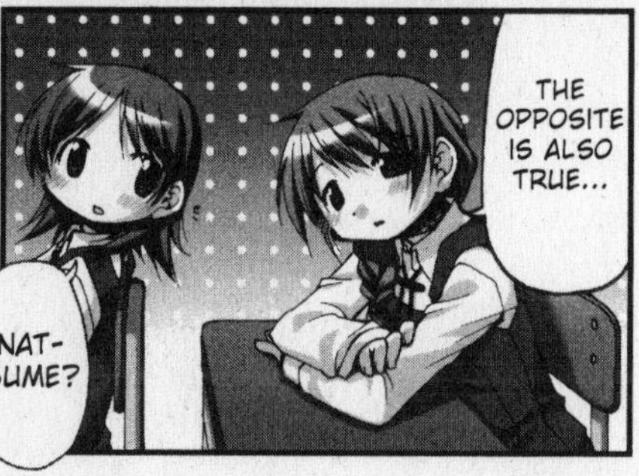
THE OPPOSITE IS ALSO TRUE...
NAT-SUME?

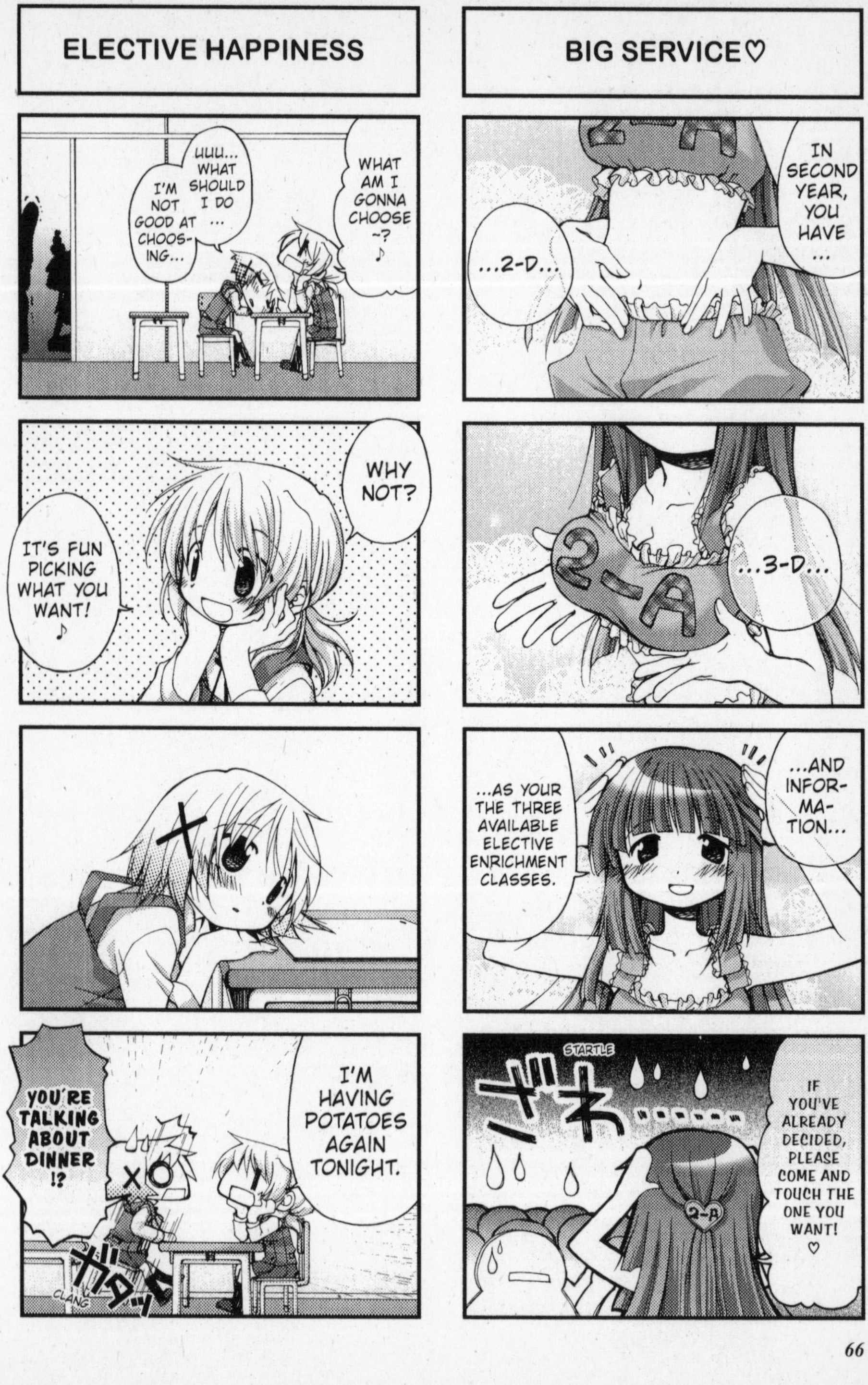
BIG SERVICE♡
IN SECOND YEAR, YOU HAVE ...
...2-D...
...3-D...
...AND INFOR-MA-TION...
...AS YOUR THE THREE AVAILABLE ELECTIVE ENRICHMENT CLASSES.
STARTLE
IF YOU'VE ALREADY DECIDED, PLEASE COME AND TOUCH THE ONE YOU WANT! ♡
2-A
ELECTIVE HAPPINESS
WHAT AM I GONNA CHOOSE ~? ♪
UUU... WHAT SHOULD I DO ...
I'M NOT GOOD AT CHOOS-ING...
WHY NOT?
IT'S FUN PICKING WHAT YOU WANT! ♪
I'M HAVING POTATOES AGAIN TONIGHT.
YOU'RE TALKING ABOUT DINNER !?
CLANG

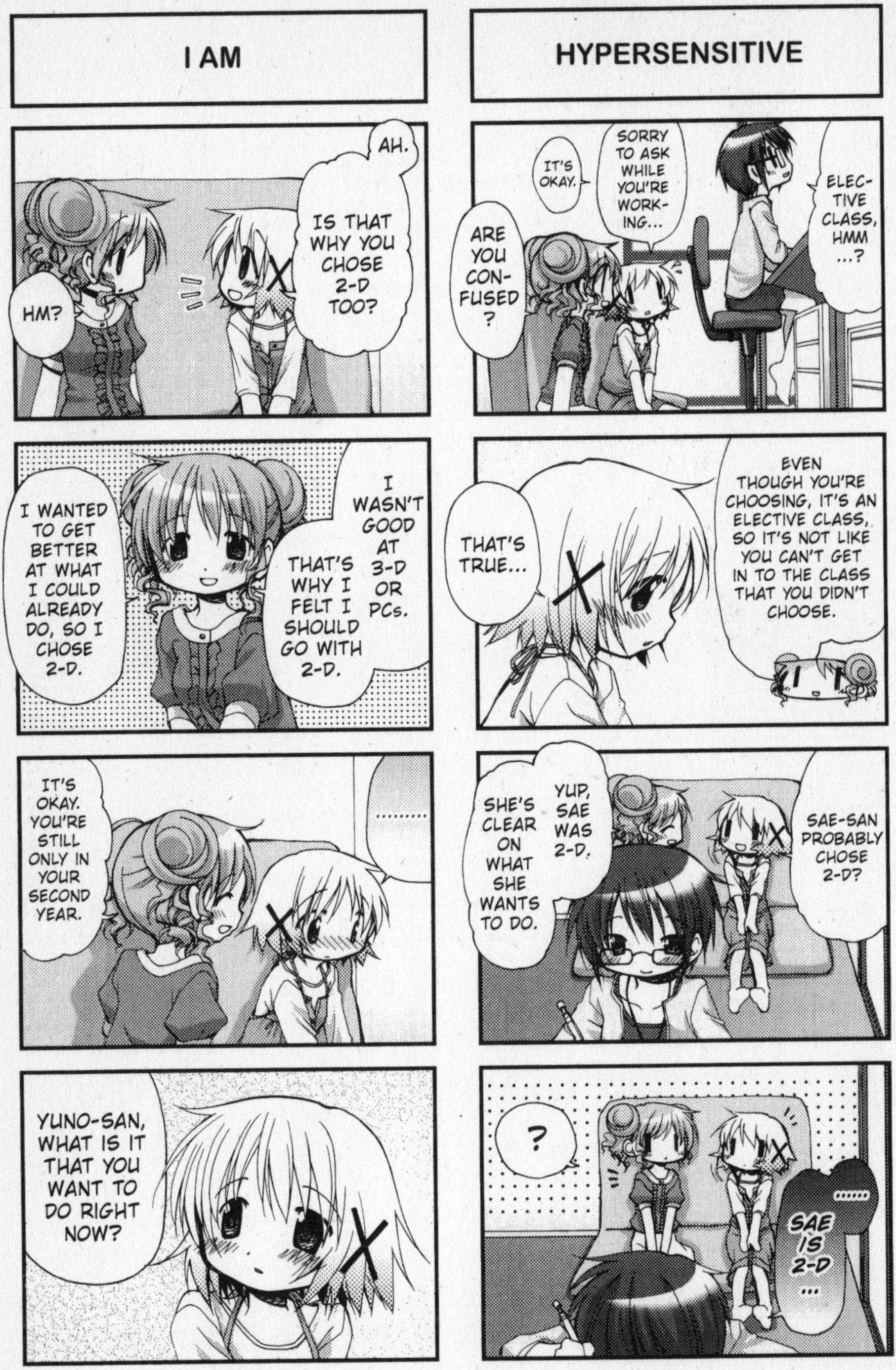
I AM HYPERSENSITIVE
ELECTIVE CLASS, HMM ...?
SORRY TO ASK WHILE YOU'RE WORKING...
IT'S OKAY.
ARE YOU CONFUSED?
EVEN THOUGH YOU'RE CHOOSING, IT'S AN ELECTIVE CLASS, SO IT'S NOT LIKE YOU CAN'T GET IN TO THE CLASS THAT YOU DIDN'T CHOOSE.
THAT'S TRUE...
SAE-SAN PROBABLY CHOSE 2-D?
YUP, SAE WAS 2-D.
SHE'S CLEAR ON WHAT SHE WANTS TO DO.
...... SAE IS 2-D ...
?
AH.
IS THAT WHY YOU CHOSE 2-D TOO?
HM?
I WASN'T GOOD AT 3-D OR PCs.
THAT'S WHY I FELT I SHOULD GO WITH 2-D.
I WANTED TO GET BETTER AT WHAT I COULD ALREADY DO, SO I CHOSE 2-D.
......
IT'S OKAY. YOU'RE STILL ONLY IN YOUR SECOND YEAR.
YUNO-SAN, WHAT IS IT THAT YOU WANT TO DO RIGHT NOW?

STILL ANXIOUS

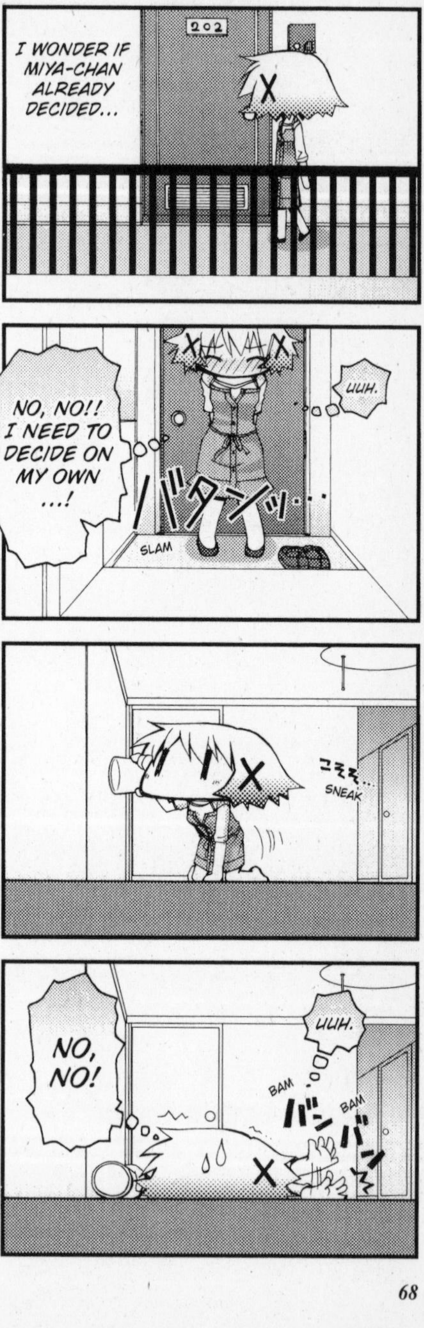
I WONDER IF MIYA-CHAN ALREADY DECIDED...
UUH.
NO, NO!! I NEED TO DECIDE ON MY OWN ...!
バタンッ…
SLAM
こそそ…
SNEAK
UUH.
NO, NO!
BAM
バンバン
BAM

COMMOTION

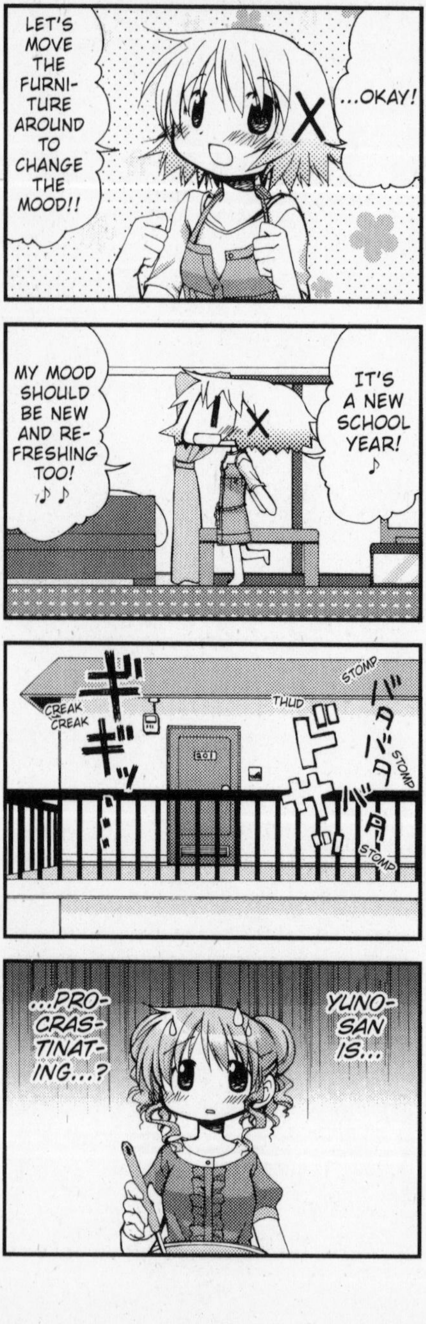
LET'S MOVE THE FURNI- TURE AROUND TO CHANGE THE MOOD!!
...OKAY!
IT'S A NEW SCHOOL YEAR! ♪
MY MOOD SHOULD BE NEW AND RE- FRESHING TOO! ♪♪
STOMP
THUD
CREAK CREAK
STOMP
STOMP
YUNO- SAN IS...
...PRO- CRAS- TINAT- ING...?

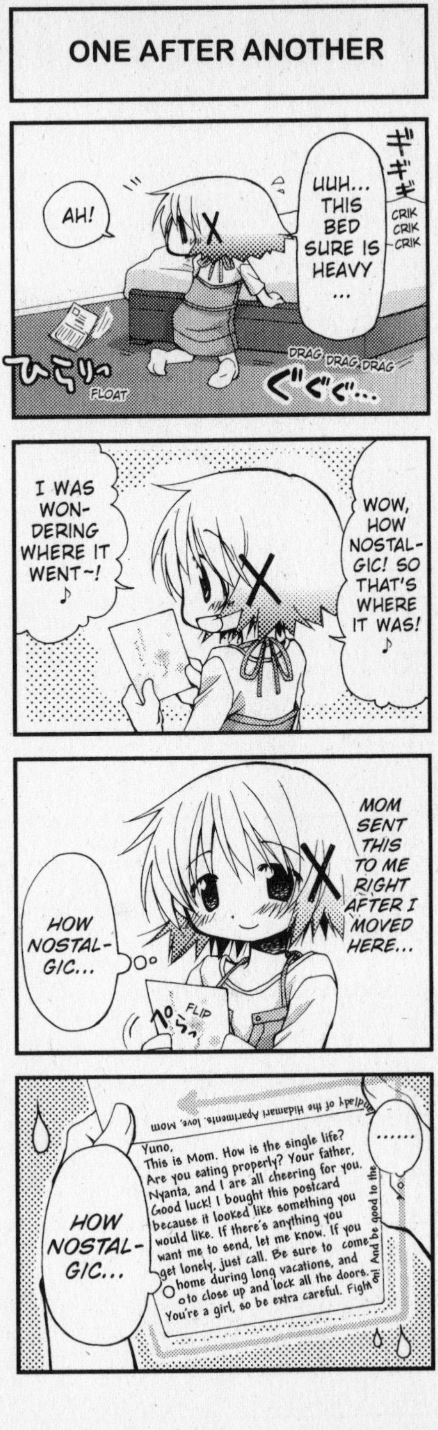
ONE AFTER ANOTHER
UUH... THIS BED SURE IS HEAVY ...
ギギギ
CRIK CRIK CRIK
AH!
ひらりっ
FLOAT
ぐぐぐ…
DRAG DRAG DRAG
WOW, HOW NOSTALGIC! SO THAT'S WHERE IT WAS! ♪
I WAS WONDERING WHERE IT WENT~! ♪
MOM SENT THIS TO ME RIGHT AFTER I MOVED HERE...
HOW NOSTALGIC...
FLIP
......
Yuno, This is Mom. How is the single life? Are you eating properly? Your father, Nyanta, and I are all cheering for you. Good luck! I bought this postcard because it looked like something you would like. If there's anything you want me to send, let me know. If you get lonely, just call. Be sure to come home during long vacations, and to close up and lock all the doors. You're a girl, so be extra careful. Fight on! And be good to the
dlady of the Hidamari Apartments. love, Mom
HOW NOSTALGIC...

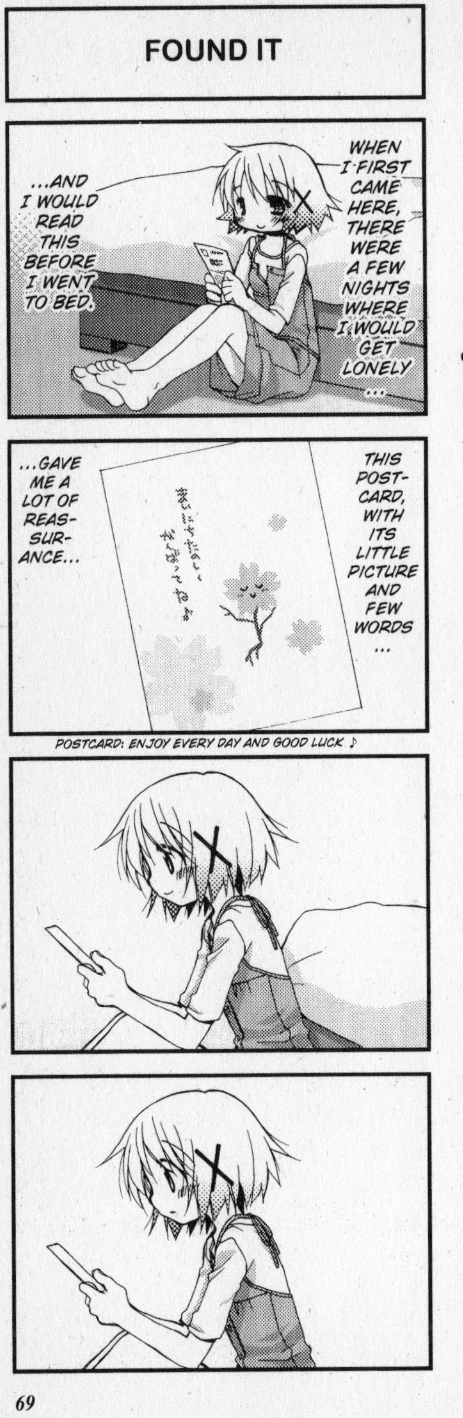
FOUND IT
WHEN I FIRST CAME HERE, THERE WERE A FEW NIGHTS WHERE I WOULD GET LONELY ...
...AND I WOULD READ THIS BEFORE I WENT TO BED.
THIS POSTCARD, WITH ITS LITTLE PICTURE AND FEW WORDS ...
...GAVE ME A LOT OF REASSURANCE...

POSTCARD: ENJOY EVERY DAY AND GOOD LUCK ♪

ARRIVED AT CONCLUSION

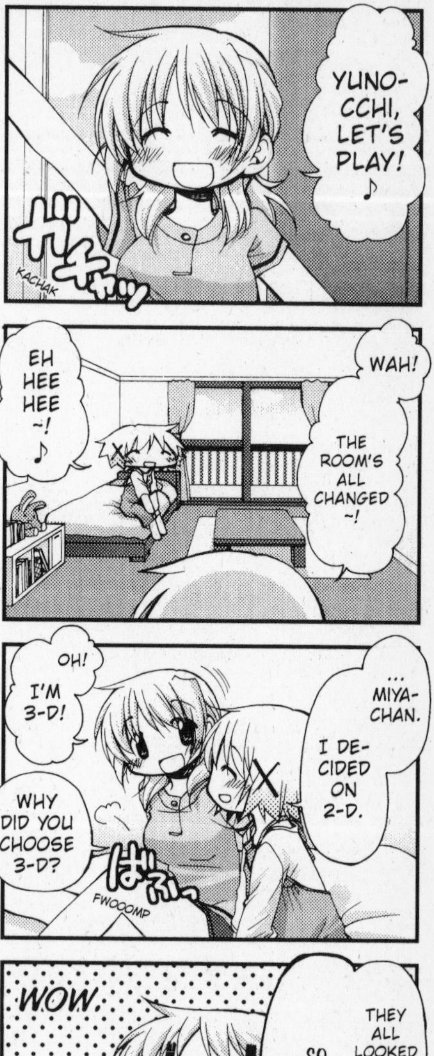
YUNO-CCHI, LET'S PLAY! ♪
KACHAK
WAH!
THE ROOM'S ALL CHANGED ~!
EH HEE HEE ~! ♪
... MIYA-CHAN.
I DECIDED ON 2-D.
OH! I'M 3-D!
WHY DID YOU CHOOSE 3-D?
FWOOOMP
THEY ALL LOOKED INTER-EST-ING...
...SO I DECIDED BY DRAWING STRAWS.
WOW.

NEW MORNING

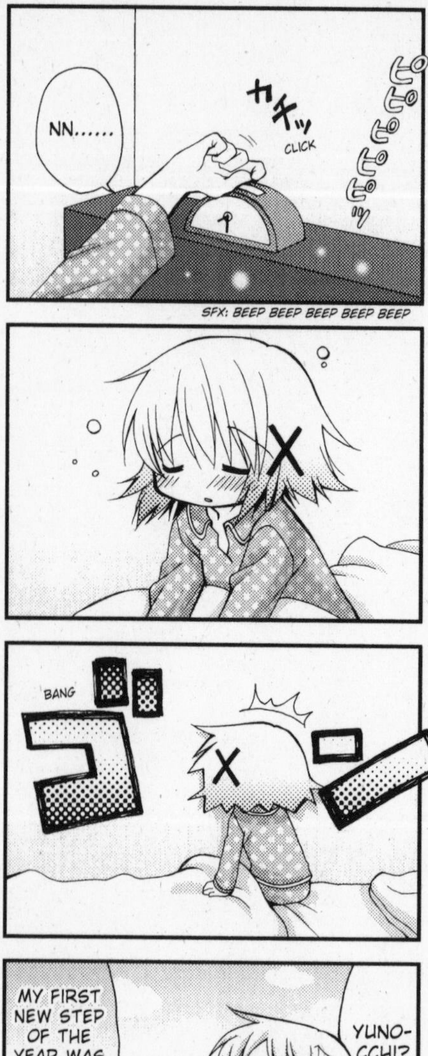
CLICK
NN......
BANG
YUNO-CCHI?
MY FIRST NEW STEP OF THE YEAR WAS A FAILURE ...
?

SFX: BEEP BEEP BEEP BEEP BEEP

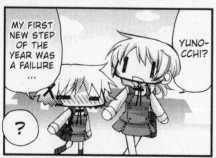

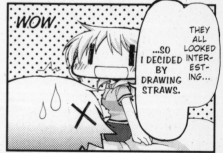

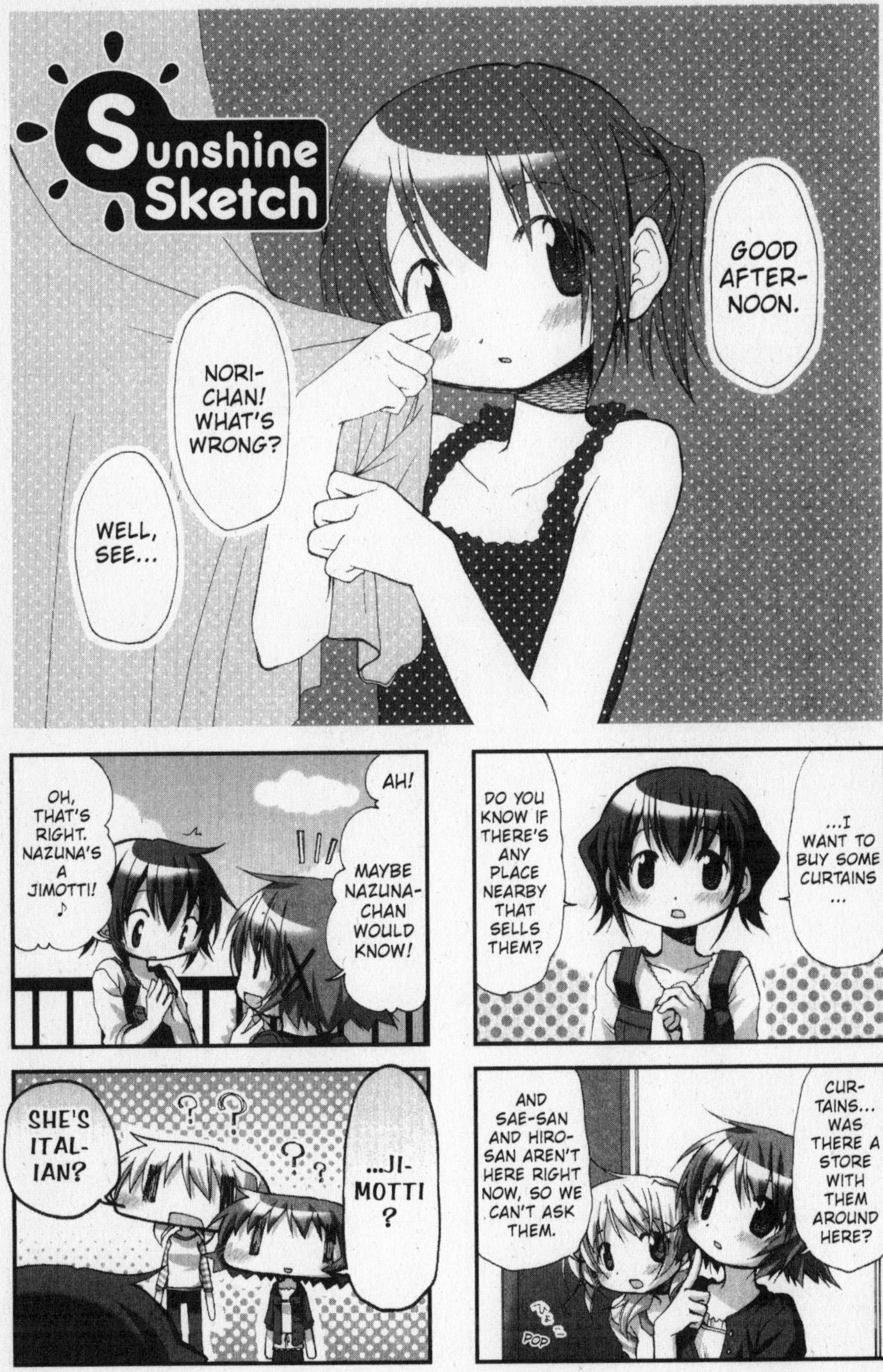
Sunshine Sketch
GOOD AFTERNOON.
NORI-CHAN! WHAT'S WRONG?
WELL, SEE...
...I WANT TO BUY SOME CURTAINS ...
DO YOU KNOW IF THERE'S ANY PLACE NEARBY THAT SELLS THEM?
AH!
MAYBE NAZUNA-CHAN WOULD KNOW!
OH, THAT'S RIGHT. NAZUNA'S A JIMOTTI! ♪
CURTAINS... WAS THERE A STORE WITH THEM AROUND HERE?
AND SAE-SAN AND HIRO-SAN AREN'T HERE RIGHT NOW, SO WE CAN'T ASK THEM.
POP
...JIMOTTI?
SHE'S ITALIAN?

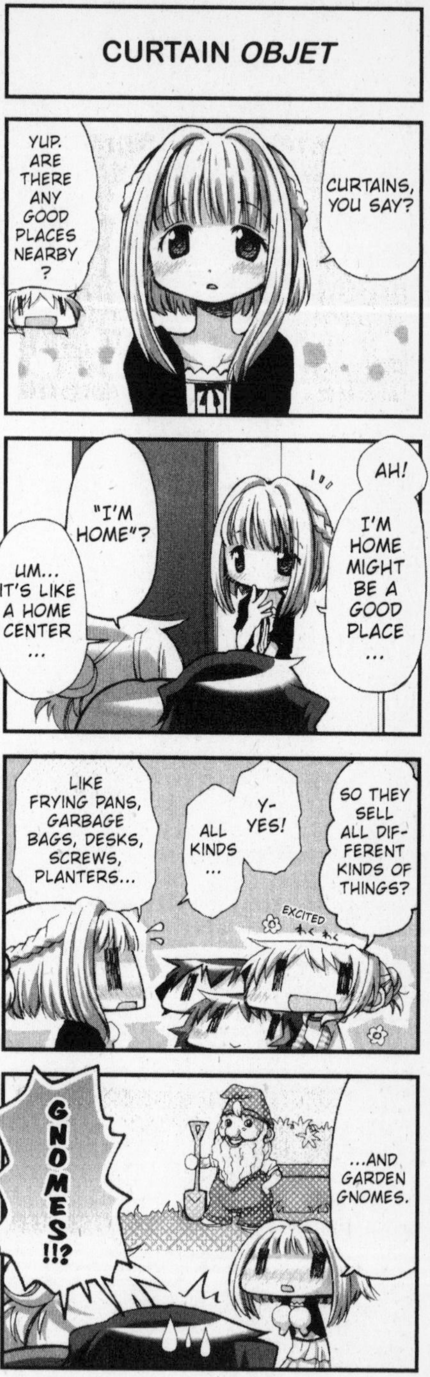
CURTAIN OBJET
CURTAINS, YOU SAY?
YUP. ARE THERE ANY GOOD PLACES NEARBY?
AH! I'M HOME MIGHT BE A GOOD PLACE...
"I'M HOME"?
UM... IT'S LIKE A HOME CENTER...
SO THEY SELL ALL DIF-FERENT KINDS OF THINGS?
Y-YES!
ALL KINDS...
LIKE FRYING PANS, GARBAGE BAGS, DESKS, SCREWS, PLANTERS...
EXCITED
...AND GARDEN GNOMES.
GNOMES!!?

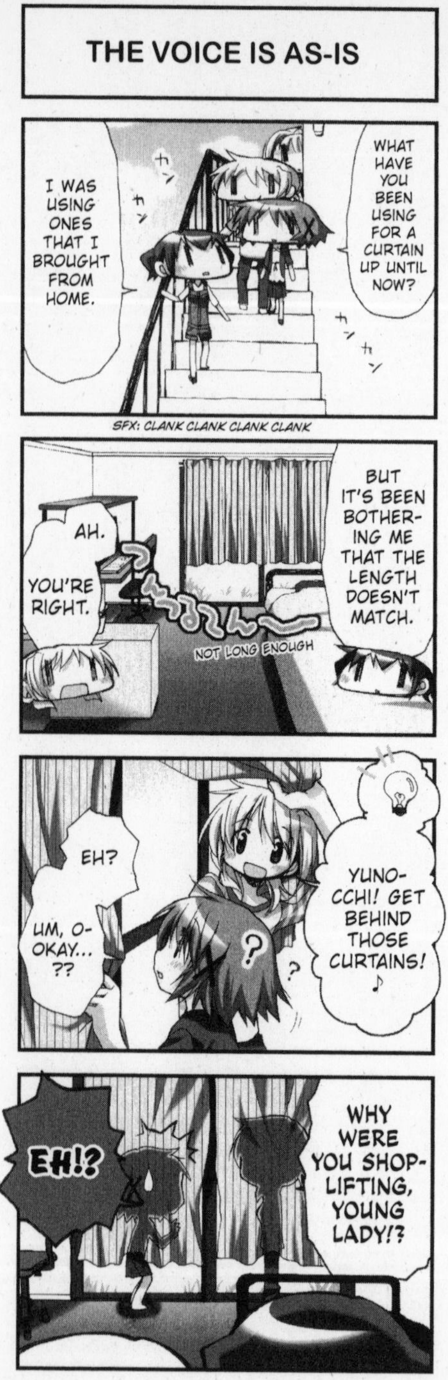
THE VOICE IS AS-IS
WHAT HAVE YOU BEEN USING FOR A CURTAIN UP UNTIL NOW?
I WAS USING ONES THAT I BROUGHT FROM HOME.
SFX: CLANK CLANK CLANK CLANK
BUT IT'S BEEN BOTHER-ING ME THAT THE LENGTH DOESN'T MATCH.
AH.
YOU'RE RIGHT.
NOT LONG ENOUGH
YUNO-CCHI! GET BEHIND THOSE CURTAINS! ♪
EH?
UM, O-OKAY... ??
WHY WERE YOU SHOP-LIFTING, YOUNG LADY!?
EH!?

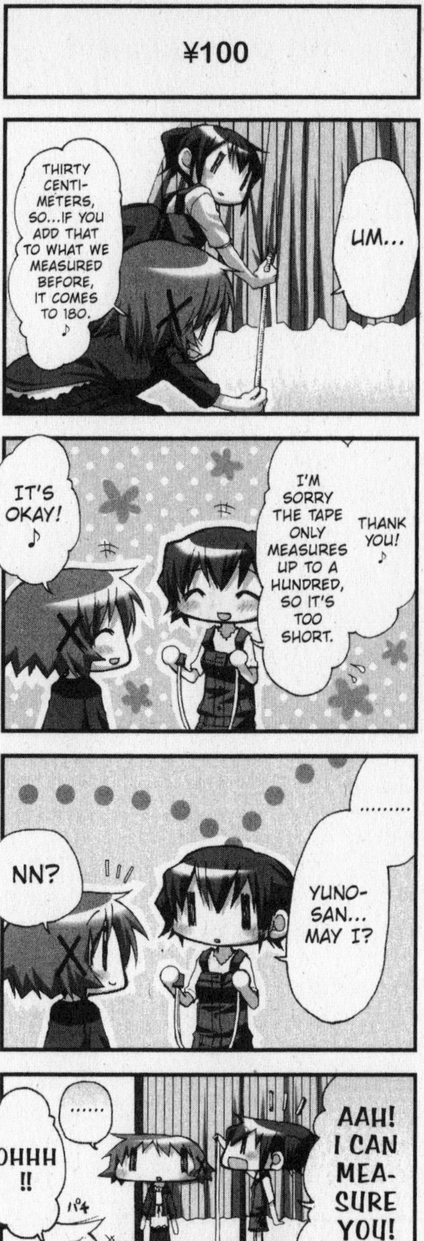
¥100
UM...
THIRTY CENTIMETERS, SO...IF YOU ADD THAT TO WHAT WE MEASURED BEFORE, IT COMES TO 180. ♪
I'M SORRY THE TAPE ONLY MEASURES UP TO A HUNDRED, SO IT'S TOO SHORT.
THANK YOU! ♪
IT'S OKAY! ♪
....
YUNO-SAN... MAY I?
NN?
AAH! I CAN MEASURE YOU! AMAZING!
......
OHHH!!
SFX: CLAP CLAP CLAP CLAP

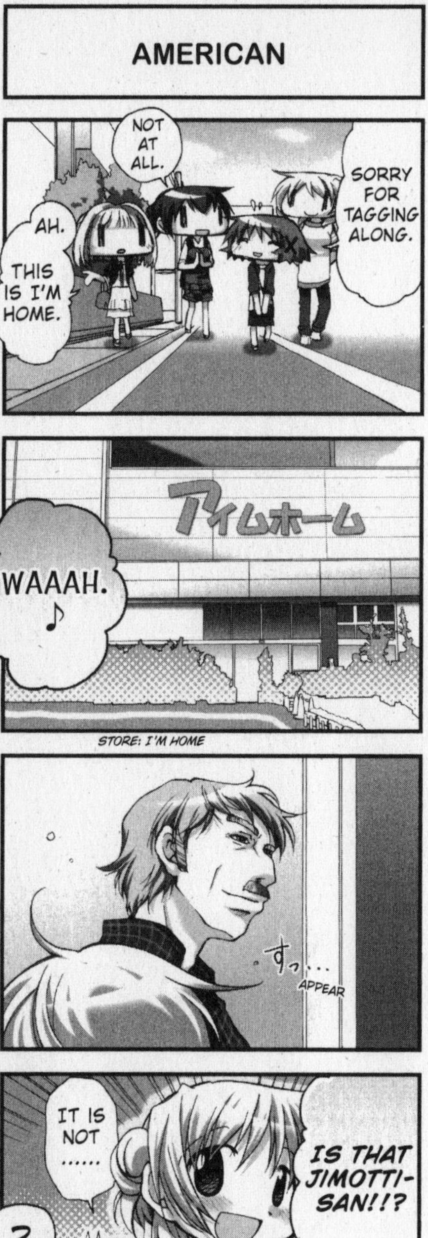
AMERICAN
SORRY FOR TAGGING ALONG.
NOT AT ALL.
AH.
THIS IS I'M HOME.
アイムホーム
WAAAH. ♪
STORE: I'M HOME
APPEAR
IS THAT JIMOTTI-SAN!!?
IT IS NOT ......
?

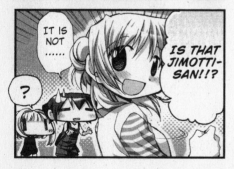

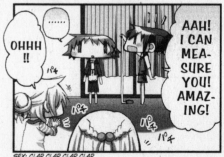

ART SUBJECT AND NORMAL SUBJECT

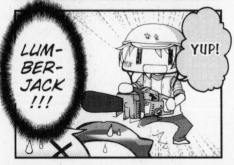

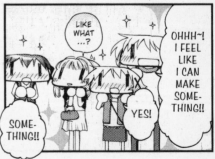

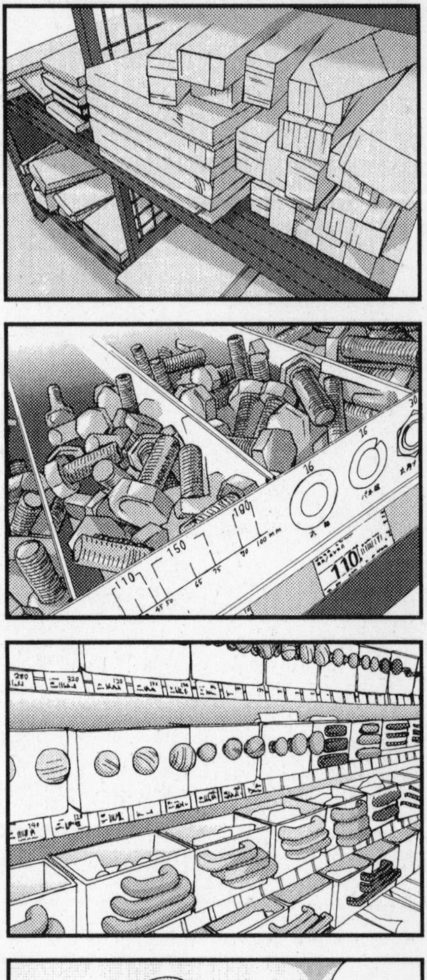
OHHH~! I FEEL LIKE I CAN MAKE SOMETHING!!
LIKE WHAT ...?
YES!
SOMETHING!!

COMPLETE SET

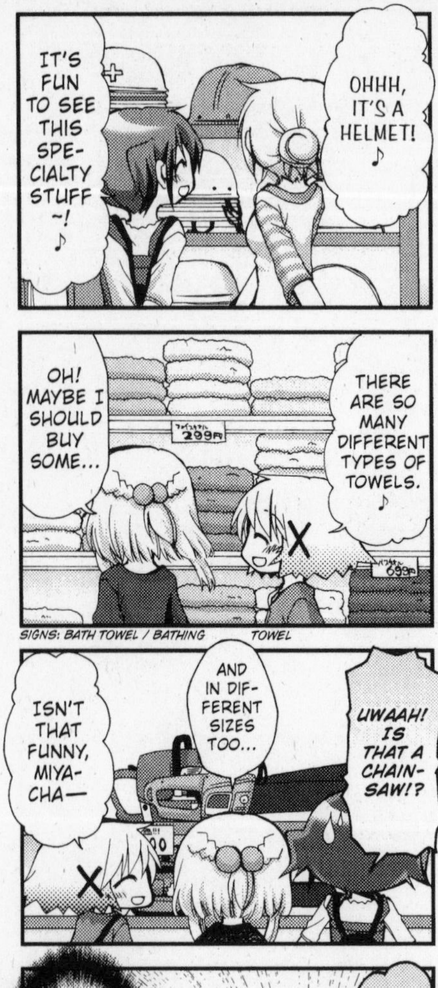
OHHH, IT'S A HELMET! ♪
IT'S FUN TO SEE THIS SPECIALTY STUFF~! ♪
THERE ARE SO MANY DIFFERENT TYPES OF TOWELS. ♪
OH! MAYBE I SHOULD BUY SOME...
UWAAH! IS THAT A CHAINSAW!?
AND IN DIFFERENT SIZES TOO...
ISN'T THAT FUNNY, MIYA-CHA—
YUP!
LUMBERJACK!!!

SIGNS: BATH TOWEL / BATHING TOWEL

WORDS NOT NECESSARY?

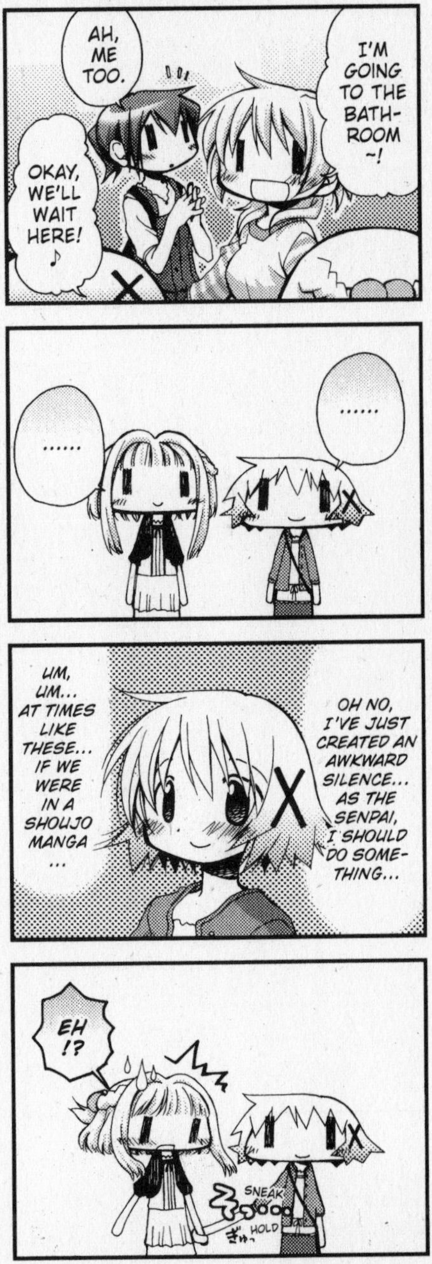
I'M GOING TO THE BATH-ROOM ~!
AH, ME TOO.
OKAY, WE'LL WAIT HERE! ♪
......
......
OH NO, I'VE JUST CREATED AN AWKWARD SILENCE... AS THE SENPAI, I SHOULD DO SOME-THING...
UM, UM... AT TIMES LIKE THESE... IF WE WERE IN A SHOUJO MANGA ...
EH !?
SNEAK
HOLD ぎゅっ

WATCHING

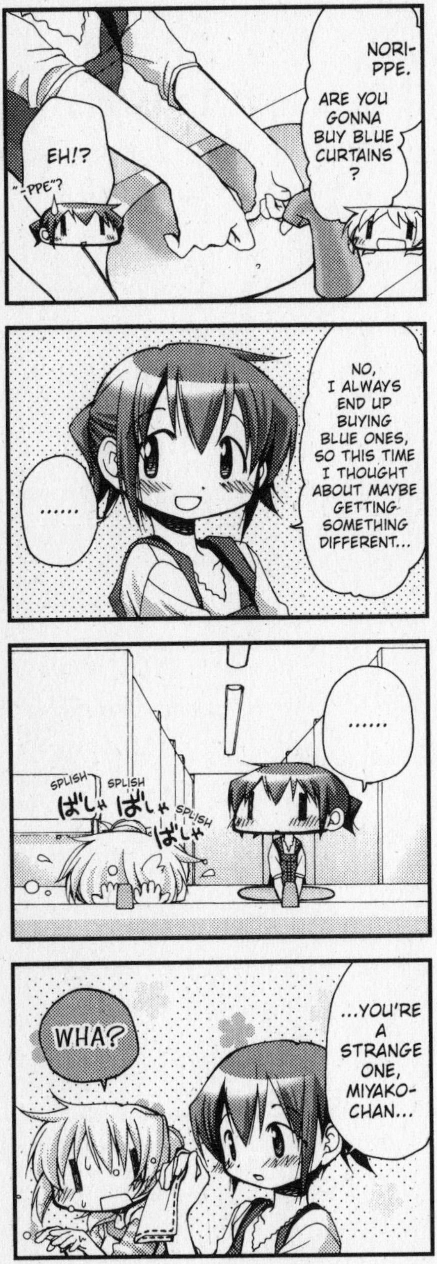
NORI-PPE.
ARE YOU GONNA BUY BLUE CURTAINS ?
EH!?
"-PPE"?
NO, I ALWAYS END UP BUYING BLUE ONES, SO THIS TIME I THOUGHT ABOUT MAYBE GETTING SOMETHING DIFFERENT...
......
......
SPLISH ばしゃ
SPLISH ばしゃ
SPLISH ばしゃ
...YOU'RE A STRANGE ONE, MIYAKO-CHAN...
WHA?

NAZUNA-SAN

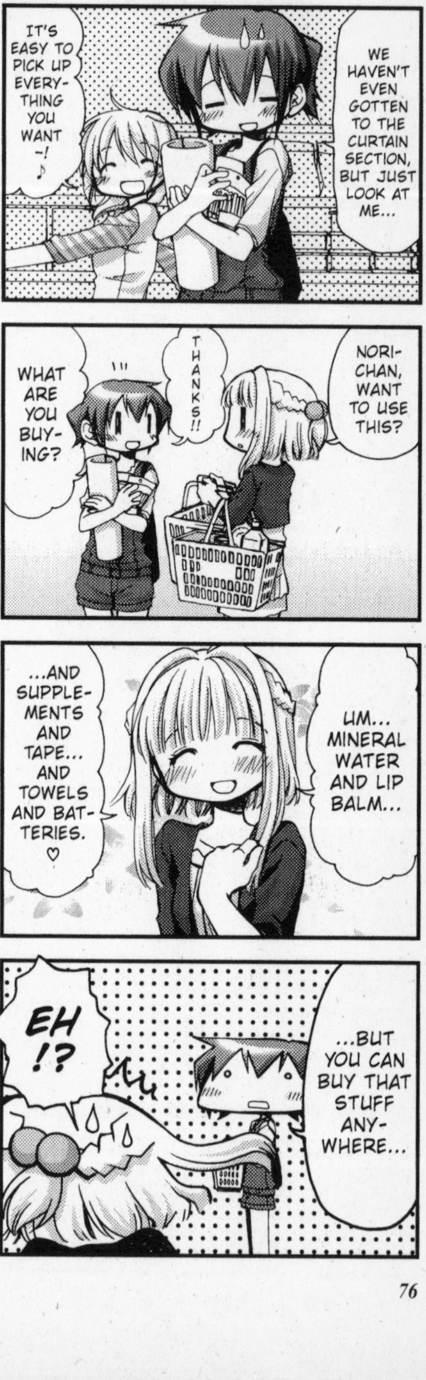
WE HAVEN'T EVEN GOTTEN TO THE CURTAIN SECTION, BUT JUST LOOK AT ME...
IT'S EASY TO PICK UP EVERYTHING YOU WANT~! ♪
NORI-CHAN, WANT TO USE THIS?
THANKS!!
WHAT ARE YOU BUYING?
UM... MINERAL WATER AND LIP BALM...
...AND SUPPLEMENTS AND TAPE... AND TOWELS AND BATTERIES. ♡
...BUT YOU CAN BUY THAT STUFF ANYWHERE...
EH!?

BRIDE BRIDE

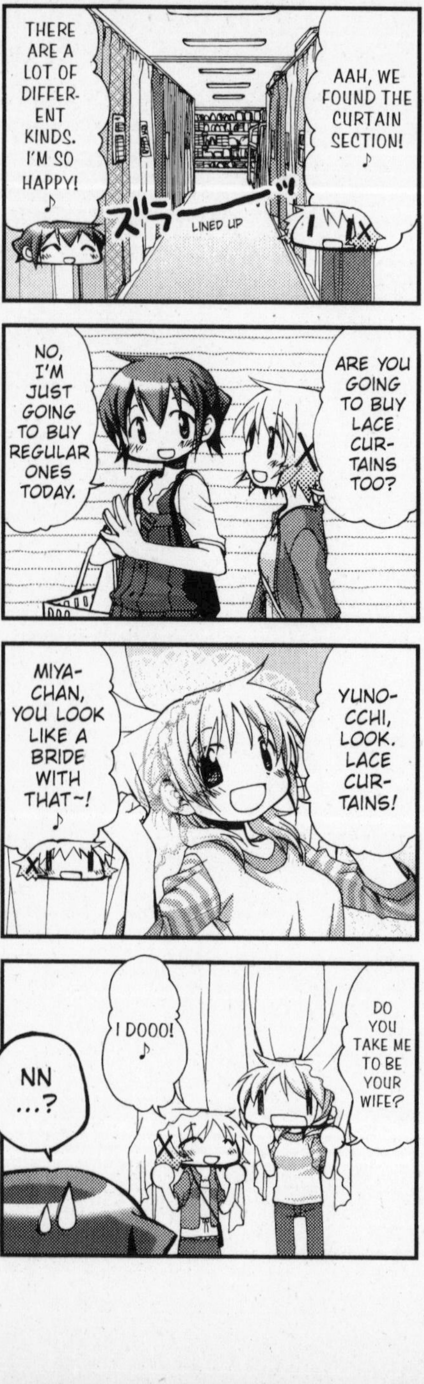
AAH, WE FOUND THE CURTAIN SECTION! ♪
THERE ARE A LOT OF DIFFERENT KINDS. I'M SO HAPPY! ♪
ズラーーッ
LINED UP
ARE YOU GOING TO BUY LACE CURTAINS TOO?
NO, I'M JUST GOING TO BUY REGULAR ONES TODAY.
YUNOCCHI, LOOK. LACE CURTAINS!
MIYA-CHAN, YOU LOOK LIKE A BRIDE WITH THAT~! ♪
DO YOU TAKE ME TO BE YOUR WIFE?
I DOOO! ♪
NN ...?

THE DISTANT CONSENTS

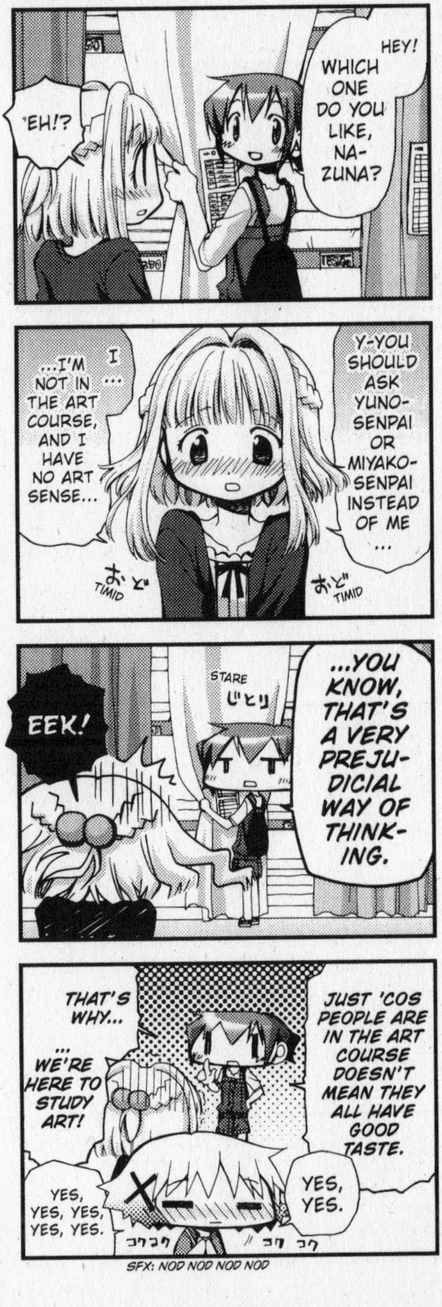
HEY!
WHICH ONE DO YOU LIKE, NA-ZUNA?
EH!?
Y-YOU SHOULD ASK YUNO-SENPAI OR MIYAKO-SENPAI INSTEAD OF ME...
I...
...I'M NOT IN THE ART COURSE, AND I HAVE NO ART SENSE...
おど TIMID
おど TIMID
...YOU KNOW, THAT'S A VERY PREJU-DICIAL WAY OF THINK-ING.
STARE じとり
EEK!
JUST 'COS PEOPLE ARE IN THE ART COURSE DOESN'T MEAN THEY ALL HAVE GOOD TASTE.
THAT'S WHY...
...WE'RE HERE TO STUDY ART!
YES, YES.
YES, YES, YES, YES, YES.
コクコク
コク コク
SFX: NOD NOD NOD NOD

RESOLUTION

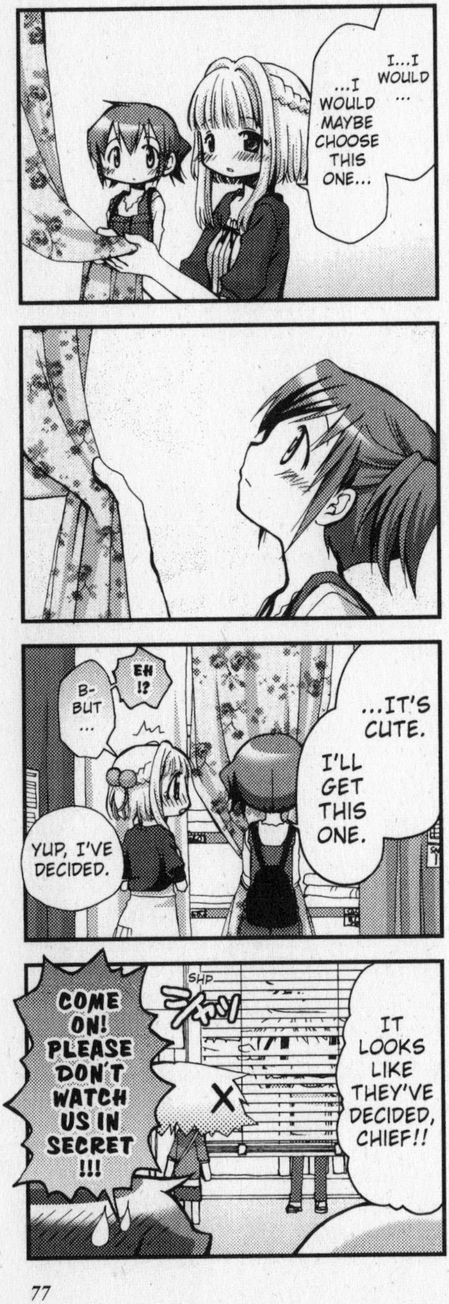
I...I WOULD...
...I WOULD MAYBE CHOOSE THIS ONE...
...IT'S CUTE.
I'LL GET THIS ONE.
EH!?
B-BUT...
YUP, I'VE DECIDED.
IT LOOKS LIKE THEY'VE DECIDED, CHIEF!!
SHP シャッ
COME ON! PLEASE DON'T WATCH US IN SECRET!!!

PLENTY OF SUN

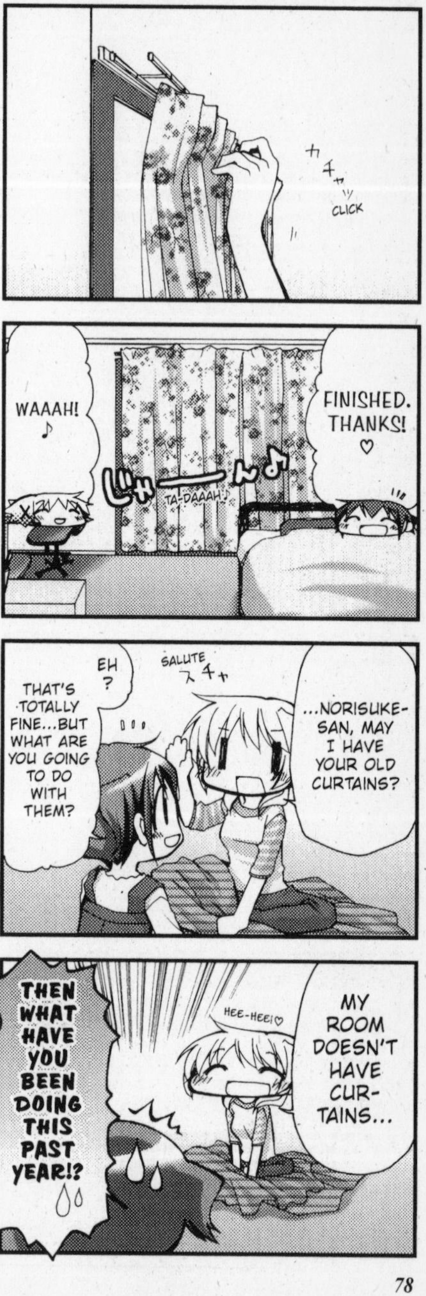
カチャッ
CLICK
FINISHED. THANKS! ♡
WAAAH! ♪
じゃーん♪
TA-DAAAH!♪
...NORISUKE-SAN, MAY I HAVE YOUR OLD CURTAINS?
SALUTE
スチャ
EH?
THAT'S TOTALLY FINE...BUT WHAT ARE YOU GOING TO DO WITH THEM?
MY ROOM DOESN'T HAVE CURTAINS...
HEE-HEE!♡
THEN WHAT HAVE YOU BEEN DOING THIS PAST YEAR!?

CUTE

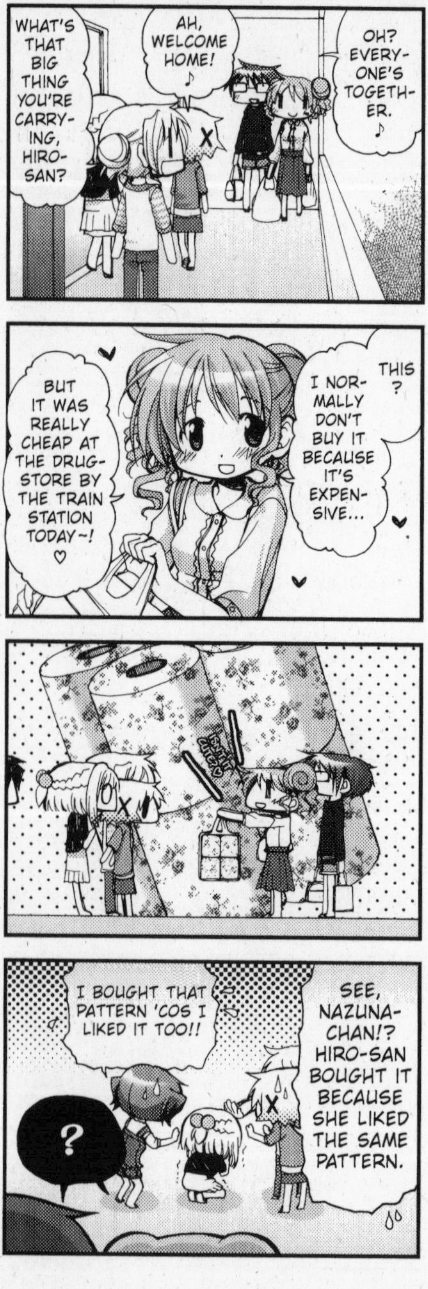
OH? EVERYONE'S TOGETHER. ♪
AH, WELCOME HOME! ♪
WHAT'S THAT BIG THING YOU'RE CARRYING, HIRO-SAN?
THIS?
I NORMALLY DON'T BUY IT BECAUSE IT'S EXPENSIVE...
BUT IT WAS REALLY CHEAP AT THE DRUGSTORE BY THE TRAIN STATION TODAY~! ♡
ISN'T IT CUTE?♡
SEE, NAZUNA-CHAN!? HIRO-SAN BOUGHT IT BECAUSE SHE LIKED THE SAME PATTERN.
I BOUGHT THAT PATTERN 'COS I LIKED IT TOO!!
?

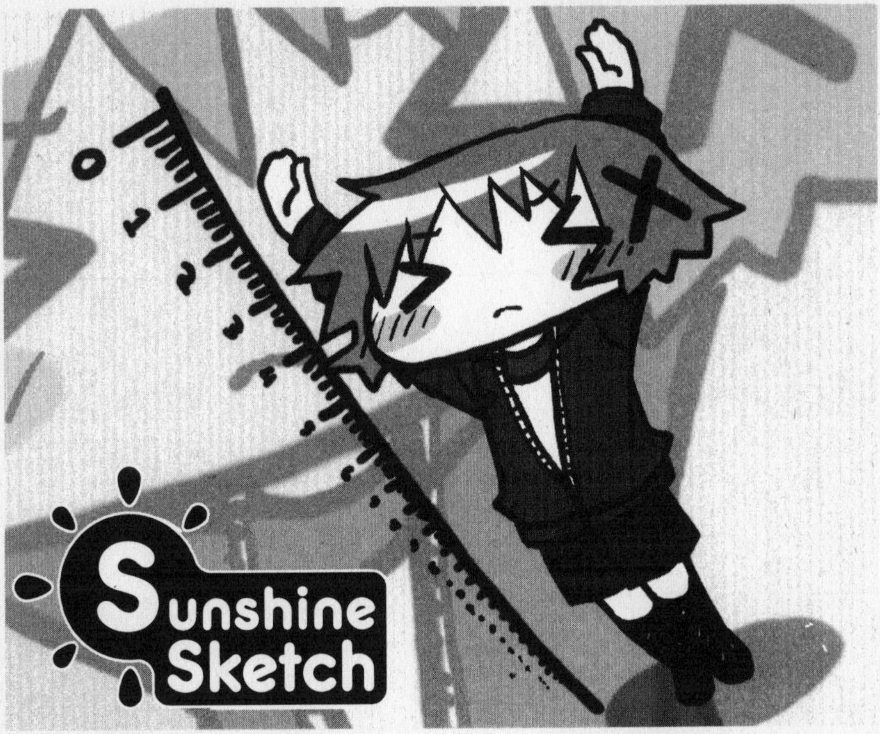
Sunshine Sketch

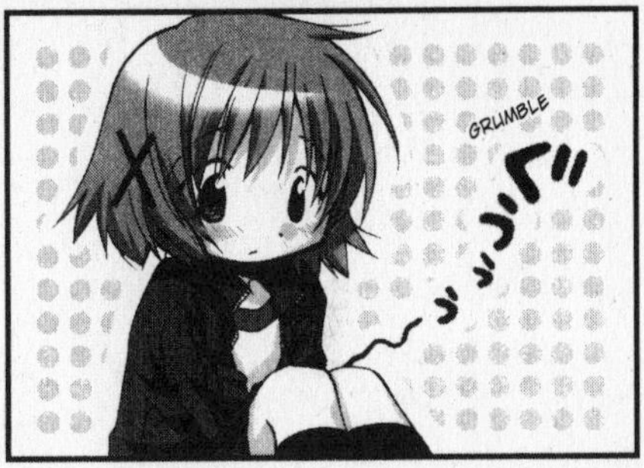
GRUMBLE

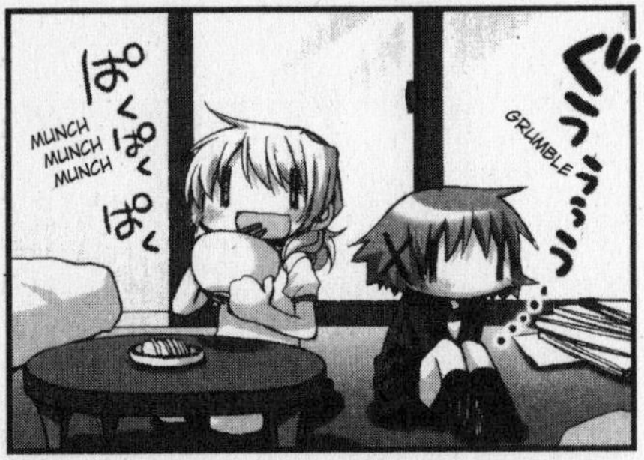
ぱくぱくぱく
MUNCH MUNCH MUNCH
GRUMBLE

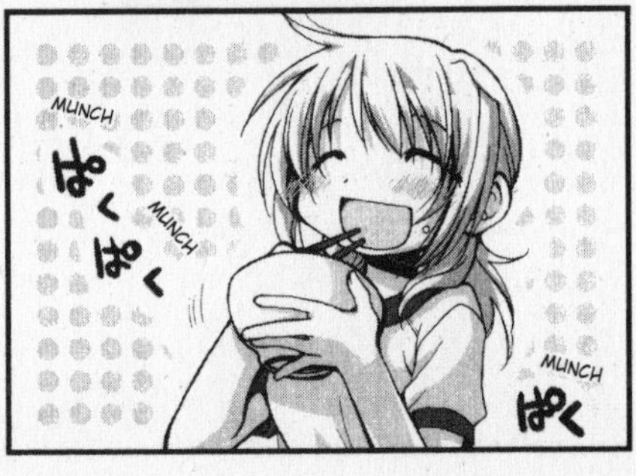
MUNCH
ぱく
MUNCH
ぱく
MUNCH
ぱく

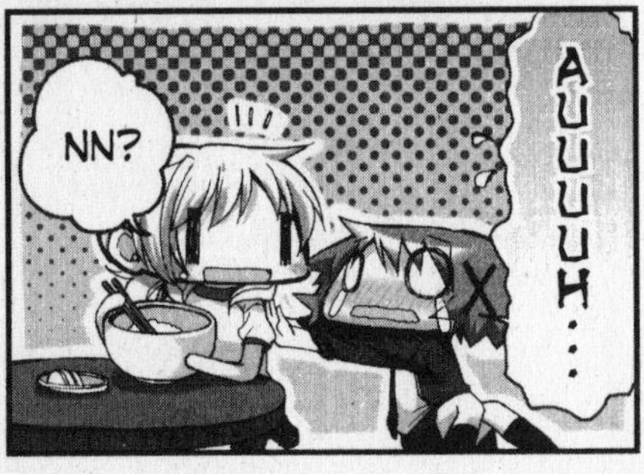
NN?
AUUUUH...

RESISTANCE IS FUTILE

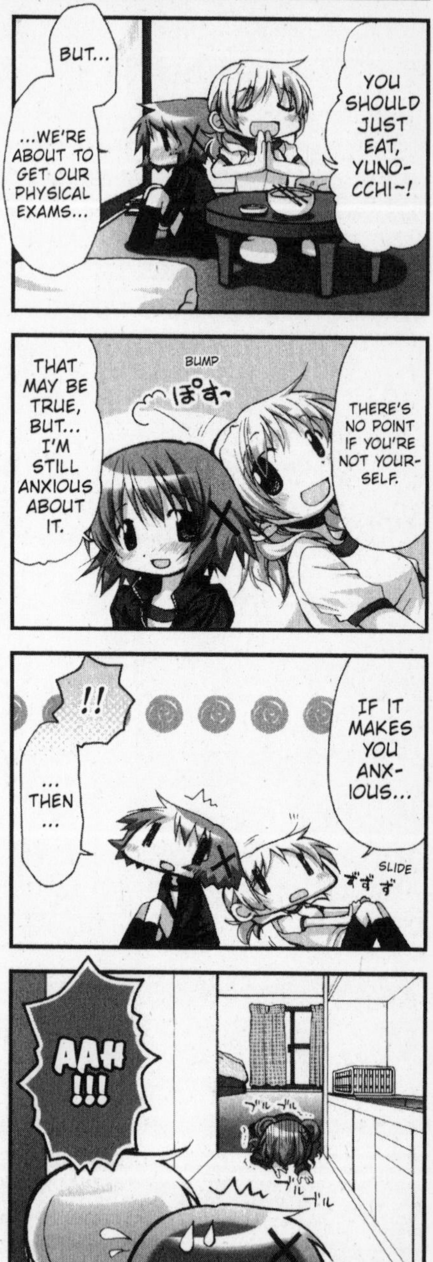
YOU SHOULD JUST EAT, YUNO-CCHI~!
BUT...
...WE'RE ABOUT TO GET OUR PHYSICAL EXAMS...
THERE'S NO POINT IF YOU'RE NOT YOURSELF.
BUMP
THAT MAY BE TRUE, BUT... I'M STILL ANXIOUS ABOUT IT.
IF IT MAKES YOU ANXIOUS...
SLIDE
!!
...THEN...
AAH!!!

SFX: SHAKE SHAKE SHAKE SHAKE

QUICK FIX

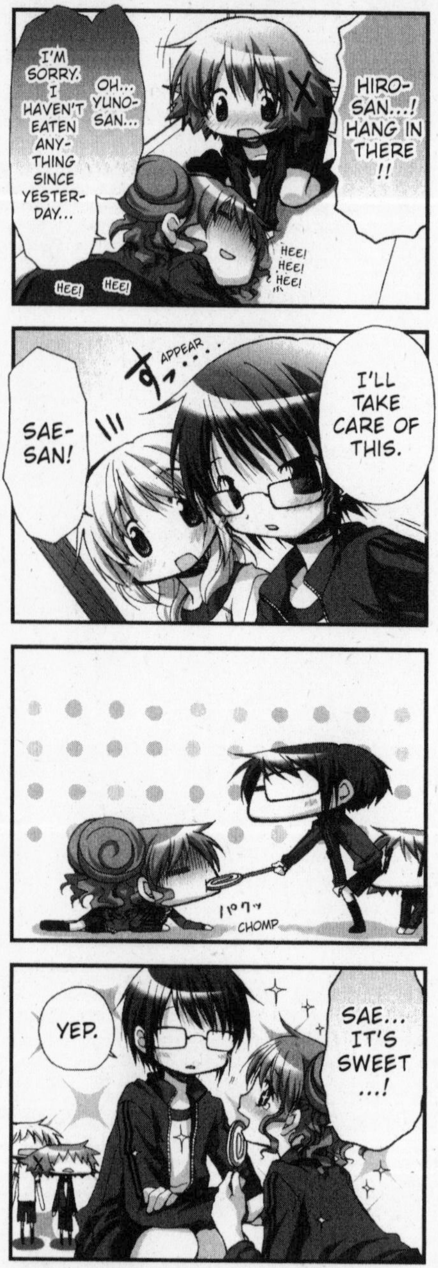
HIRO-SAN...! HANG IN THERE!!
OH... YUNO-SAN...
I'M SORRY. I HAVEN'T EATEN ANYTHING SINCE YESTERDAY...
HEE! HEE! HEE!
HEE! HEE!
I'LL TAKE CARE OF THIS.
APPEAR
SAE-SAN!
CHOMP
SAE... IT'S SWEET...!
YEP.

LINE OF STENCH

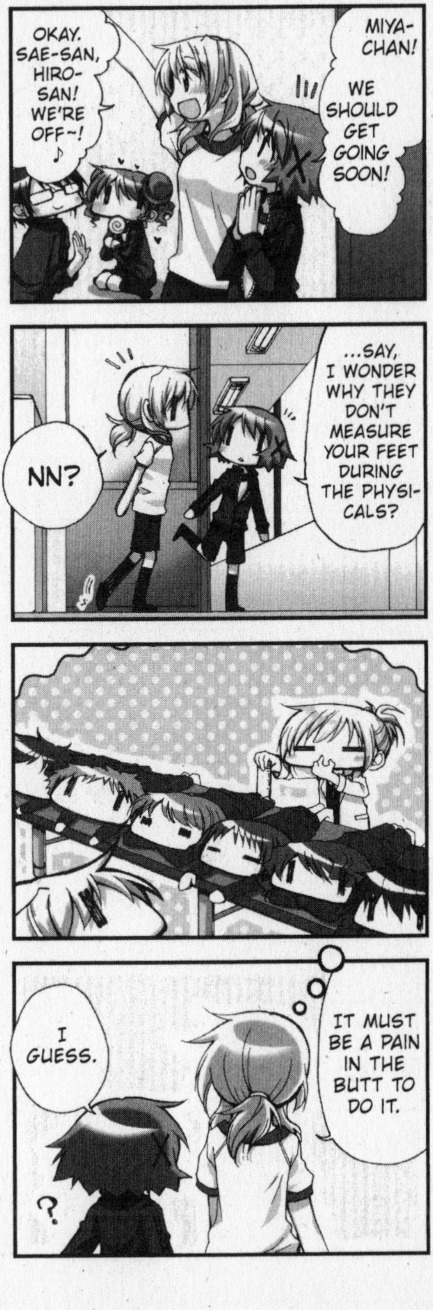
MIYA-CHAN!
WE SHOULD GET GOING SOON!
OKAY. SAE-SAN, HIRO-SAN! WE'RE OFF~! ♪
...SAY, I WONDER WHY THEY DON'T MEASURE YOUR FEET DURING THE PHYSICALS?
NN?
IT MUST BE A PAIN IN THE BUTT TO DO IT.
I GUESS.

OVERWHELMING HAPPINESS

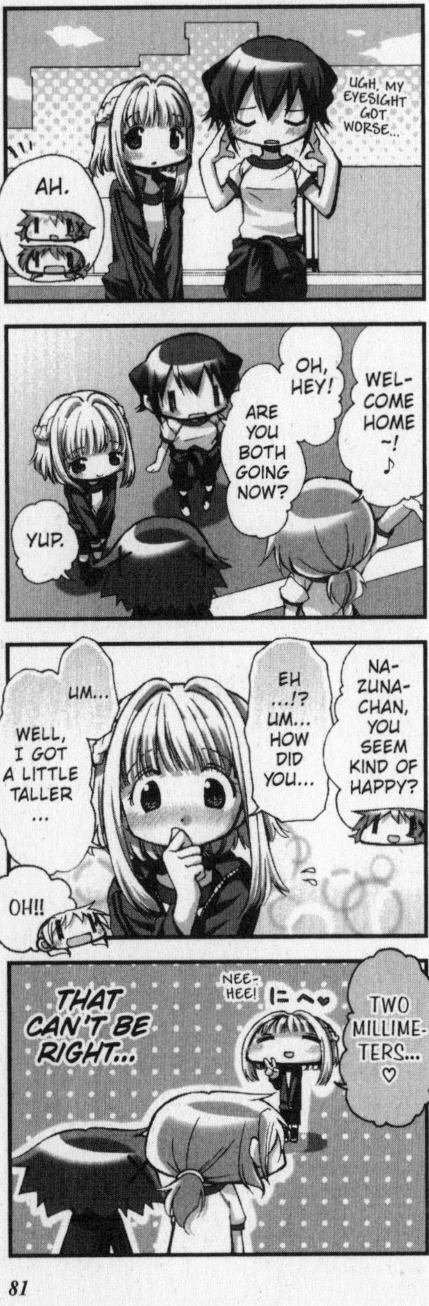
UGH, MY EYESIGHT GOT WORSE...
AH.
WEL-COME HOME ~! ♪
OH, HEY! ARE YOU BOTH GOING NOW?
YUP.
NA-ZUNA-CHAN, YOU SEEM KIND OF HAPPY?
EH ...!? UM... HOW DID YOU...
UM... WELL, I GOT A LITTLE TALLER ...
OH!!
TWO MILLIME-TERS... ♡
NEE-HEE!
に～❤
THAT CAN'T BE RIGHT...

LIGHT AND DARKNESS

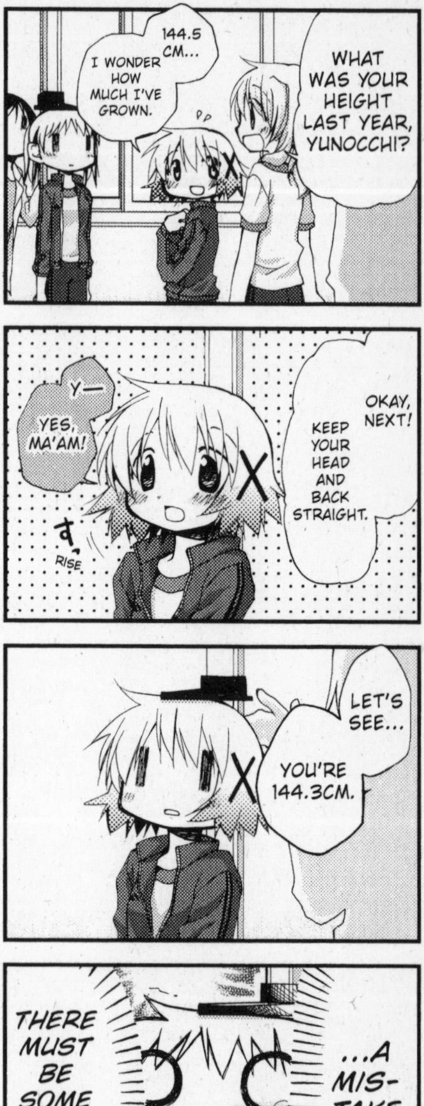
WHAT WAS YOUR HEIGHT LAST YEAR, YUNOCCHI?
144.5 CM...
I WONDER HOW MUCH I'VE GROWN.
OKAY, NEXT!
KEEP YOUR HEAD AND BACK STRAIGHT.
Y—
YES, MA'AM!
RISE
LET'S SEE...
YOU'RE 144.3CM.
...A MISTAKE!!
THERE MUST BE SOME MISTAKE!!

A GIRL'S FEELINGS

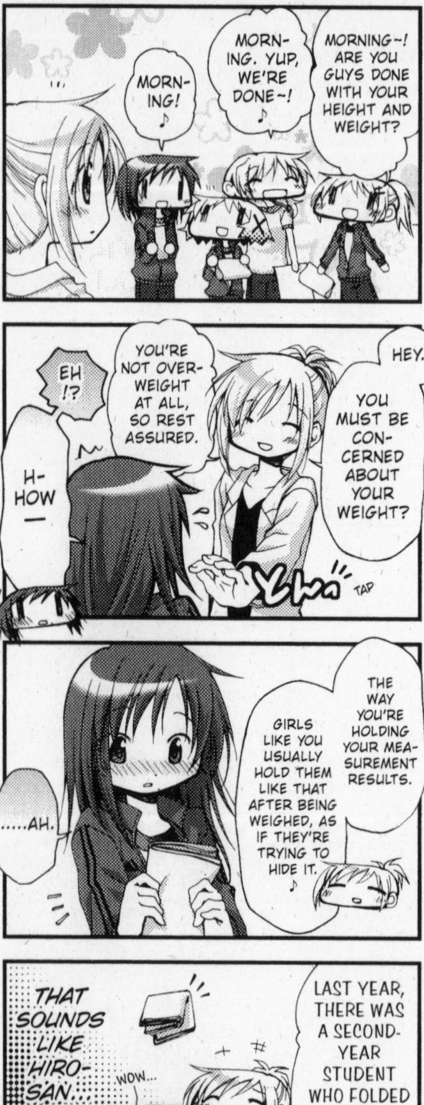
MORNING~! ARE YOU GUYS DONE WITH YOUR HEIGHT AND WEIGHT?
MORNING. YUP, WE'RE DONE~! ♪
MORNING! ♪
HEY.
YOU MUST BE CONCERNED ABOUT YOUR WEIGHT?
YOU'RE NOT OVERWEIGHT AT ALL, SO REST ASSURED.
EH!?
H-HOW—
TAP
THE WAY YOU'RE HOLDING YOUR MEASUREMENT RESULTS.
GIRLS LIKE YOU USUALLY HOLD THEM LIKE THAT AFTER BEING WEIGHED, AS IF THEY'RE TRYING TO HIDE IT. ♪
......AH.
LAST YEAR, THERE WAS A SECOND-YEAR STUDENT WHO FOLDED HERS UNTIL SHE COULDN'T FOLD IT ANYMORE.
WOW...
THAT SOUNDS LIKE HIRO-SAN...

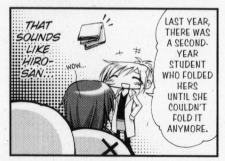

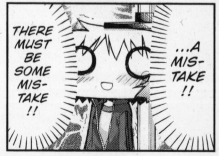

TOP DIAGONAL

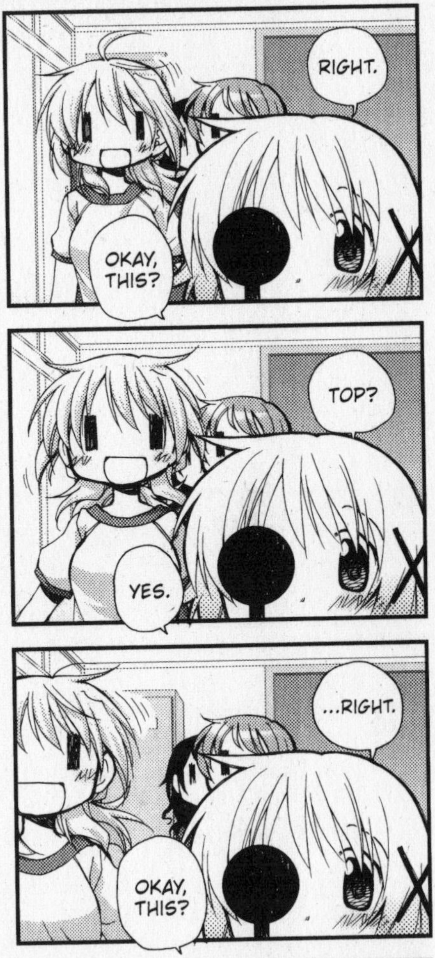
RIGHT.
OKAY, THIS?
TOP?
YES.
...RIGHT.
OKAY, THIS?
RIGHT.
ガンッ
BANG

USE YOUR IMAGINATION

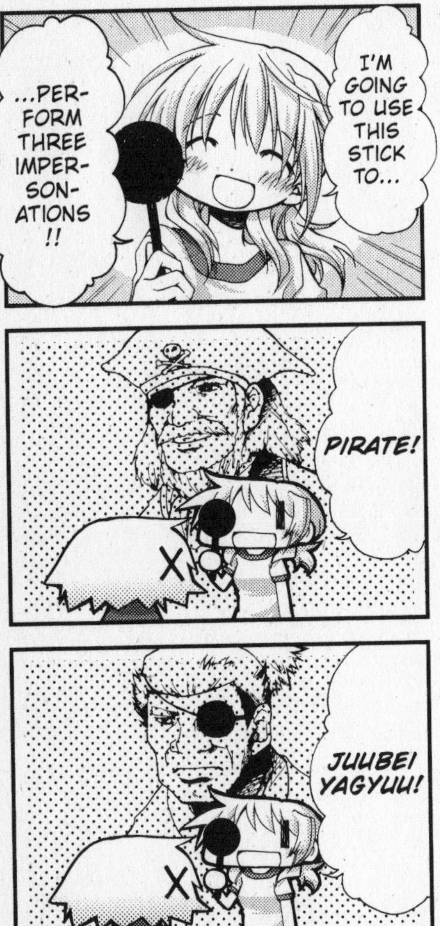
I'M GOING TO USE THIS STICK TO...
...PER-FORM THREE IMPER-SON-ATIONS!!
PIRATE!
JUUBEI YAGYUU!
DOKU-GAN-RYUU MASA-MUNE!
MIYA-CHAN, THEY ALL LOOK THE SAME...

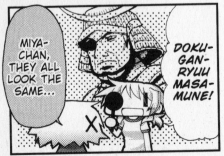

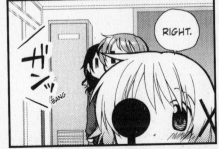

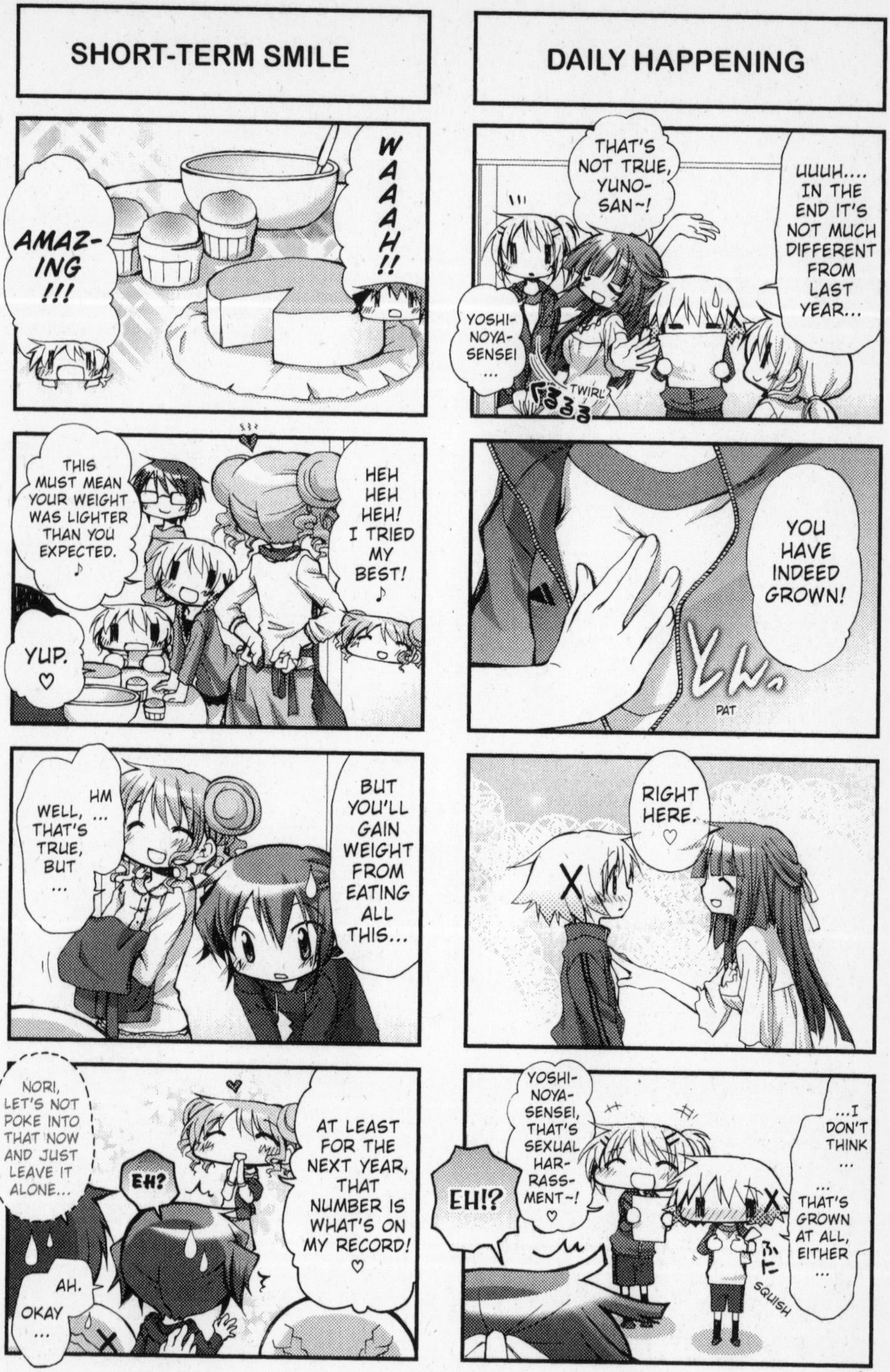
DAILY HAPPENING
UUUH.... IN THE END IT'S NOT MUCH DIFFERENT FROM LAST YEAR...
THAT'S NOT TRUE, YUNO-SAN~!
YOSHI-NOYA-SENSEI ...
TWIRL
YOU HAVE INDEED GROWN!
PAT
RIGHT HERE. ♡
...I DON'T THINK ... ... THAT'S GROWN AT ALL, EITHER ...
SQUISH
YOSHI-NOYA-SENSEI, THAT'S SEXUAL HAR-RASS-MENT~! ♡
EH!?
SHORT-TERM SMILE
WAAAAH!!
AMAZ-ING!!!
HEH HEH HEH! I TRIED MY BEST! ♪
THIS MUST MEAN YOUR WEIGHT WAS LIGHTER THAN YOU EXPECTED. ♪
YUP. ♡
BUT YOU'LL GAIN WEIGHT FROM EATING ALL THIS...
HM ... WELL, THAT'S TRUE, BUT ...
AT LEAST FOR THE NEXT YEAR, THAT NUMBER IS WHAT'S ON MY RECORD! ♡
EH?
NORI, LET'S NOT POKE INTO THAT NOW AND JUST LEAVE IT ALONE...
AH. OKAY ...

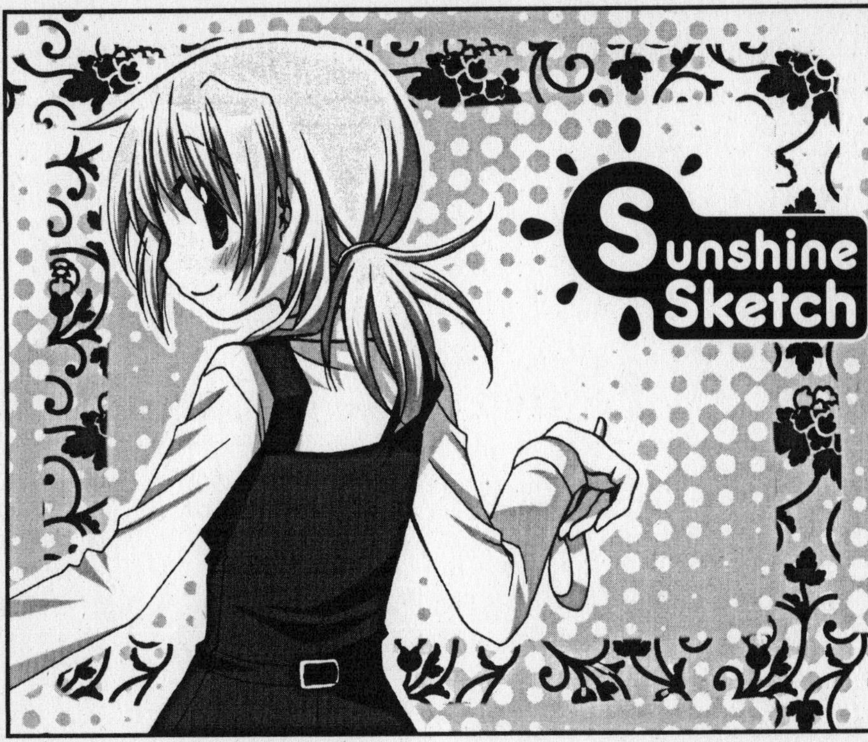
Sunshine Sketch

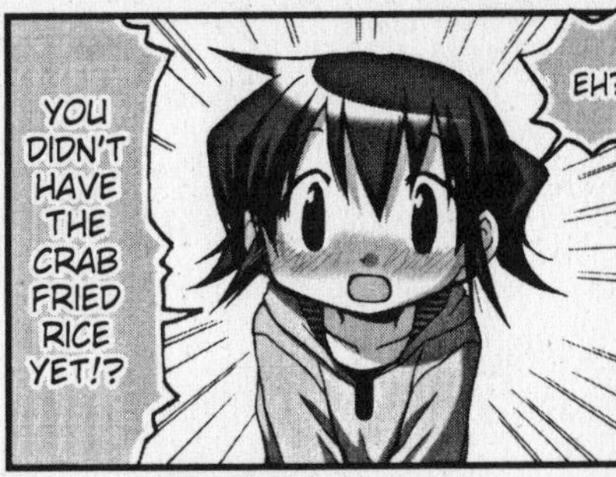
YOU DIDN'T HAVE THE CRAB FRIED RICE YET!?
EH?

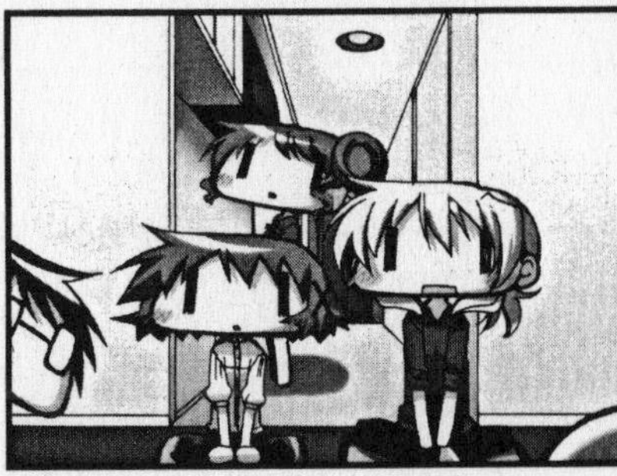

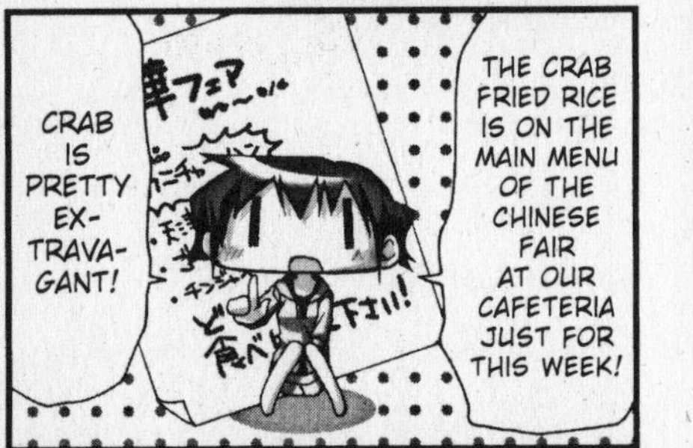
THE CRAB FRIED RICE IS ON THE MAIN MENU OF THE CHINESE FAIR AT OUR CAFETERIA JUST FOR THIS WEEK!
CRAB IS PRETTY EX-TRAVA-GANT!

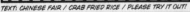

TEXT: CHINESE FAIR / CRAB FRIED RICE / PLEASE TRY IT OUT!

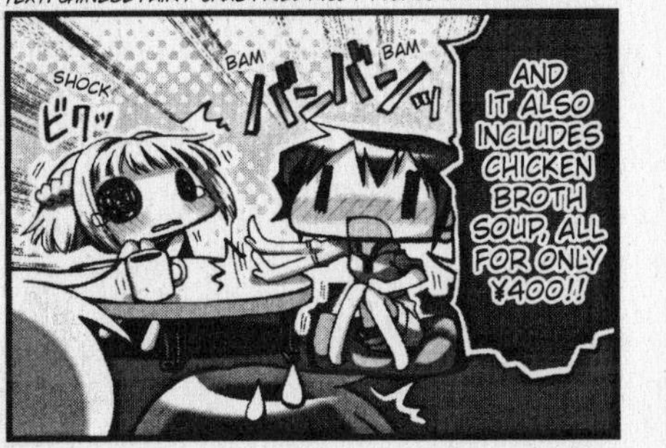
AND IT ALSO INCLUDES CHICKEN BROTH SOUP, ALL FOR ONLY ¥400!!
BAM
BAM
SHOCK

EFFORT

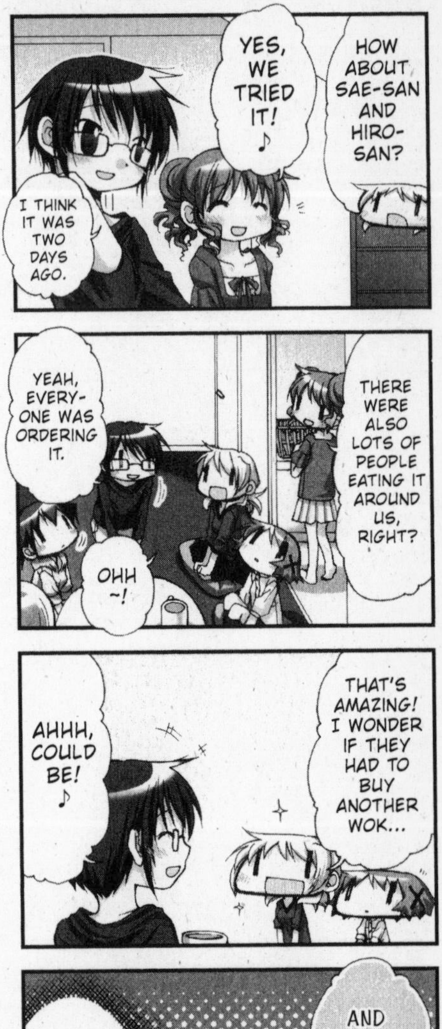
HOW ABOUT SAE-SAN AND HIRO-SAN?
YES, WE TRIED IT! ♪
I THINK IT WAS TWO DAYS AGO.
THERE WERE ALSO LOTS OF PEOPLE EATING IT AROUND US, RIGHT?
YEAH, EVERYONE WAS ORDERING IT.
OHH ~!
THAT'S AMAZING! I WONDER IF THEY HAD TO BUY ANOTHER WOK...
AHHH, COULD BE! ♪
AND A CRAB SPOON, MIYA-CHAN!
AREN'T YOU GETTING AHEAD OF YOURSELF THERE ...?

SHADOW PUPPETS

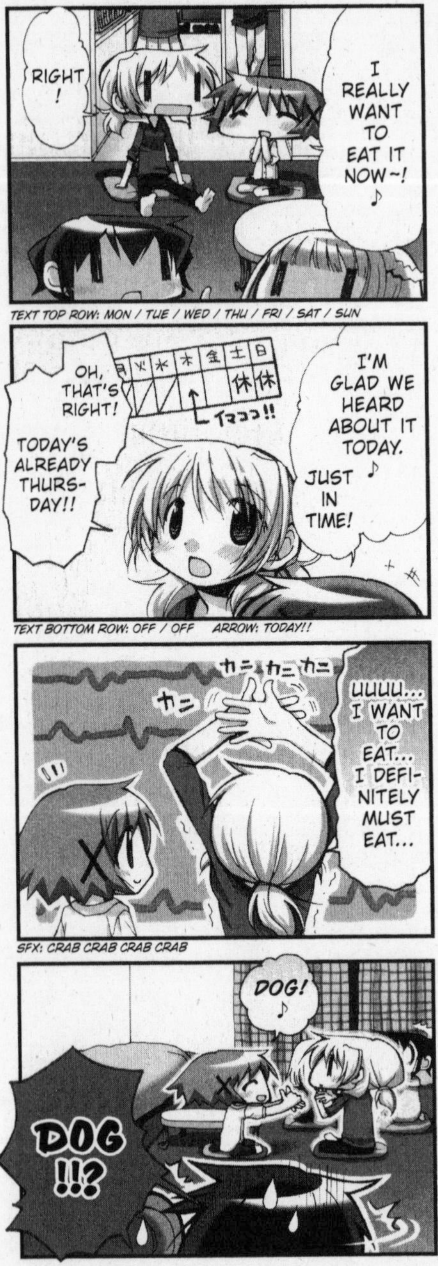
I REALLY WANT TO EAT IT NOW~! ♪
RIGHT!
I'M GLAD WE HEARD ABOUT IT TODAY. ♪
JUST IN TIME!
OH, THAT'S RIGHT!
TODAY'S ALREADY THURS-DAY!!
月 火 水 木 金 土 日
休 休
イマココ!!
カニ カニ カニ カニ
UUUU... I WANT TO EAT... I DEFINITELY MUST EAT...
DOG! ♪
DOG!!?

TEXT TOP ROW: MON / TUE / WED / THU / FRI / SAT / SUN

TEXT BOTTOM ROW: OFF / OFF ARROW: TODAY!!

SFX: CRAB CRAB CRAB CRAB

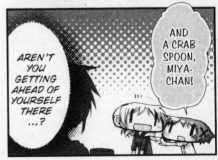

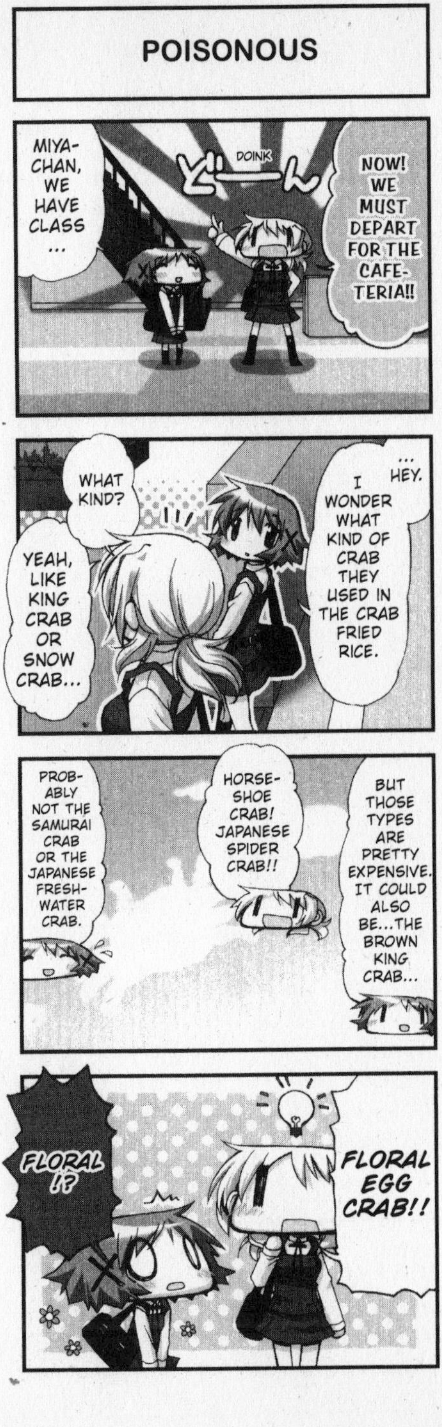
POISONOUS
NOW! WE MUST DEPART FOR THE CAFETERIA!!
DOINK
MIYA-CHAN, WE HAVE CLASS...
...HEY. I WONDER WHAT KIND OF CRAB THEY USED IN THE CRAB FRIED RICE.
WHAT KIND?
YEAH, LIKE KING CRAB OR SNOW CRAB...
BUT THOSE TYPES ARE PRETTY EXPENSIVE. IT COULD ALSO BE...THE BROWN KING CRAB...
HORSESHOE CRAB! JAPANESE SPIDER CRAB!!
PROBABLY NOT THE SAMURAI CRAB OR THE JAPANESE FRESHWATER CRAB.
FLORAL EGG CRAB!!
FLORAL!?

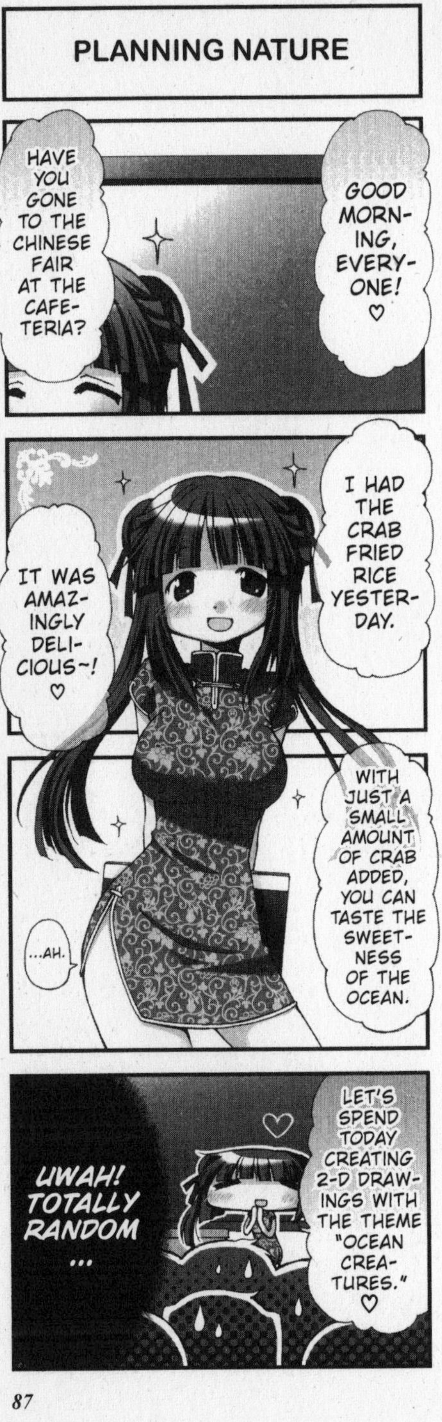
PLANNING NATURE
GOOD MORNING, EVERYONE! ♡
HAVE YOU GONE TO THE CHINESE FAIR AT THE CAFETERIA?
I HAD THE CRAB FRIED RICE YESTERDAY.
IT WAS AMAZINGLY DELICIOUS~! ♡
WITH JUST A SMALL AMOUNT OF CRAB ADDED, YOU CAN TASTE THE SWEETNESS OF THE OCEAN.
...AH.
LET'S SPEND TODAY CREATING 2-D DRAWINGS WITH THE THEME "OCEAN CREATURES." ♡
UWAH! TOTALLY RANDOM...

A STAR'S BACKSIDE

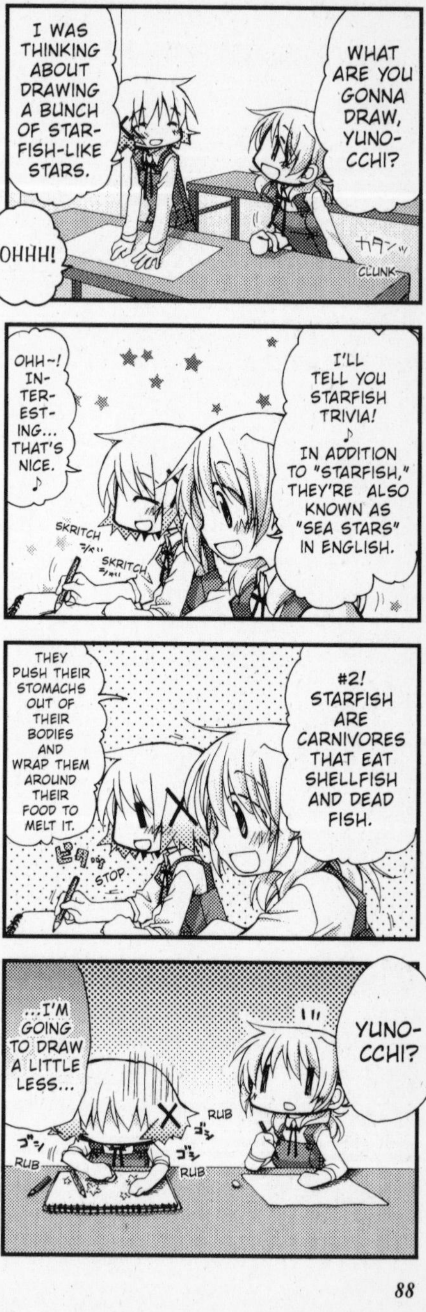
WHAT ARE YOU GONNA DRAW, YUNOCCHI?
CLUNK
I WAS THINKING ABOUT DRAWING A BUNCH OF STARFISH-LIKE STARS.
OHHH!
I'LL TELL YOU STARFISH TRIVIA! ♪ IN ADDITION TO "STARFISH," THEY'RE ALSO KNOWN AS "SEA STARS" IN ENGLISH.
OHH~! INTERESTING... THAT'S NICE. ♪
SKRITCH
SKRITCH
#2! STARFISH ARE CARNIVORES THAT EAT SHELLFISH AND DEAD FISH.
THEY PUSH THEIR STOMACHS OUT OF THEIR BODIES AND WRAP THEM AROUND THEIR FOOD TO MELT IT.
STOP
YUNO-CCHI?
...I'M GOING TO DRAW A LITTLE LESS...
RUB
RUB
RUB

DURING CLASS

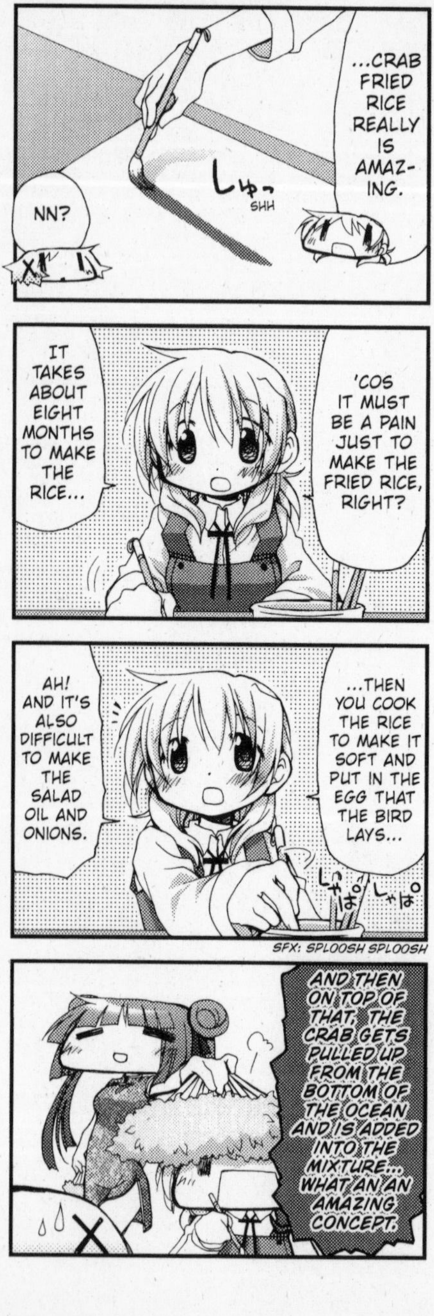
...CRAB FRIED RICE REALLY IS AMAZING.
SHH
NN?
'COS IT MUST BE A PAIN JUST TO MAKE THE FRIED RICE, RIGHT?
IT TAKES ABOUT EIGHT MONTHS TO MAKE THE RICE...
...THEN YOU COOK THE RICE TO MAKE IT SOFT AND PUT IN THE EGG THAT THE BIRD LAYS...
AH! AND IT'S ALSO DIFFICULT TO MAKE THE SALAD OIL AND ONIONS.
SFX: SPLOOSH SPLOOSH
AND THEN ON TOP OF THAT, THE CRAB GETS PULLED UP FROM THE BOTTOM OF THE OCEAN AND IS ADDED INTO THE MIXTURE... WHAT AN AN AMAZING CONCEPT.

TO EL DORADO

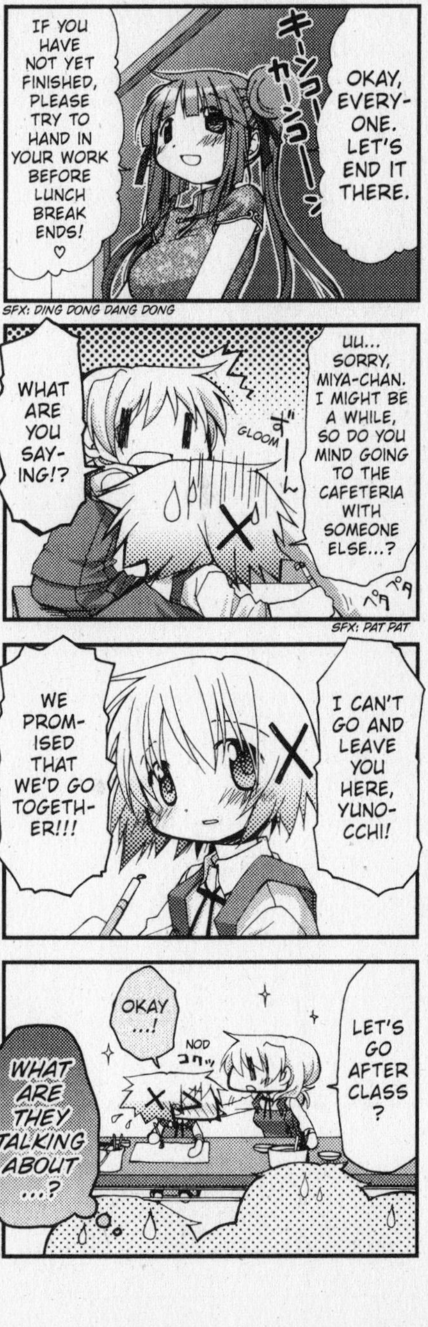
OKAY, EVERYONE. LET'S END IT THERE.
IF YOU HAVE NOT YET FINISHED, PLEASE TRY TO HAND IN YOUR WORK BEFORE LUNCH BREAK ENDS! ♡
SFX: DING DONG DANG DONG
UU... SORRY, MIYA-CHAN. I MIGHT BE A WHILE, SO DO YOU MIND GOING TO THE CAFETERIA WITH SOMEONE ELSE...?
GLOOM
WHAT ARE YOU SAYING!?
SFX: PAT PAT
I CAN'T GO AND LEAVE YOU HERE, YUNOCCHI!
WE PROMISED THAT WE'D GO TOGETHER!!!
LET'S GO AFTER CLASS?
OKAY ...!
NOD
WHAT ARE THEY TALKING ABOUT ...?

THREE SECOND CHARGE

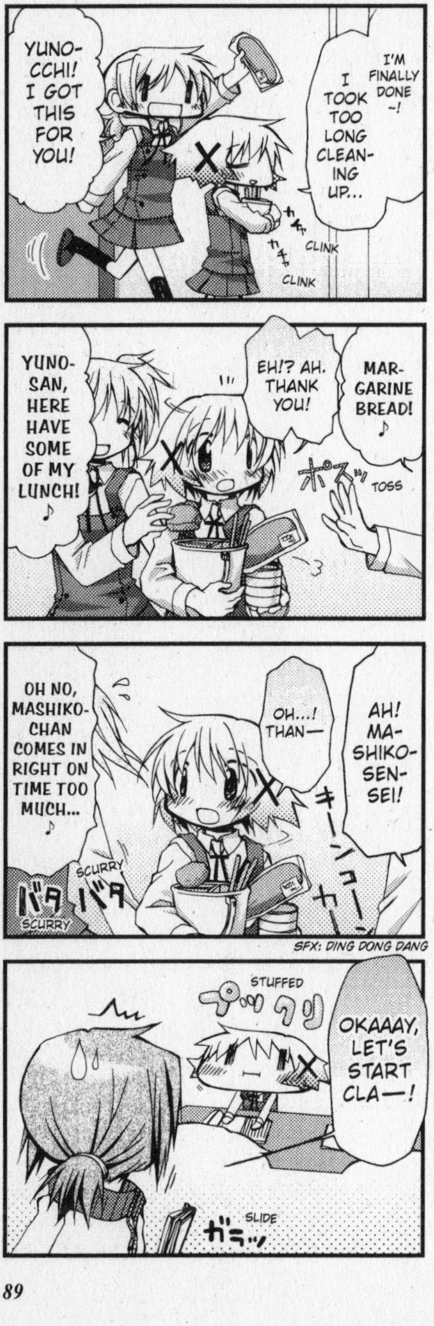
I'M FINALLY DONE ~!
I TOOK TOO LONG CLEANING UP...
YUNOCCHI! I GOT THIS FOR YOU!
CLINK
CLINK
MARGARINE BREAD! ♪
TOSS
EH!? AH. THANK YOU!
YUNO-SAN, HERE HAVE SOME OF MY LUNCH! ♪
AH! MASHIKO-SENSEI!
OH...! THAN—
OH NO, MASHIKO-CHAN COMES IN RIGHT ON TIME TOO MUCH... ♪
SCURRY
SCURRY
SFX: DING DONG DANG
OKAAAY, LET'S START CLA—!
STUFFED
SLIDE

DEMISE

YUNO-CCHI, RUN FASTER!
'KAY!
I'M SO HUNGRY ~!
SFX: DING DONG DANG DONG
I'M SORRY! WE'VE ALREADY SOLD OUT.
SINCE IT WAS THE LAST DAY OF THE FAIR, WE DIDN'T MAKE THAT MUCH.
IT'S OVER... IT'S ALL OVER...
DEVASTATED
MIYA-CHAN, I'VE...DONE SOMETHING FOR WHICH I CAN NEVER ATONE...
WHAT ARE THEY TALKING ABOUT ...?

CARING

AW!
SO YOU DIDN'T GET TO TRY THE CRAB FRIED RICE?
YES, THAT'S RIGHT ...
AND IT WAS ALL MY FAULT. I HOPE THEY HAVE ANOTHER CHINESE FAIR...
DROOP
NO PROB !!
......
ALL RIGHT! ♡
EVERYONE COME TO MY PLACE TODAY, AND WE'LL HAVE A FEAST! ♪
OH NO! YOU DON'T NEED TO GO OUT OF YOUR WAY!
IT WOULD BE WRONG TO DRAG YOU INTO THIS, HIRO-SAN!
SAE... THEY WOULD RATHER I NOT DO ANYTHING ...
N-NO !?
SFX: SHAKE SHAKE SHAKE

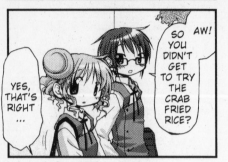

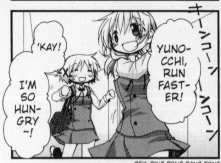

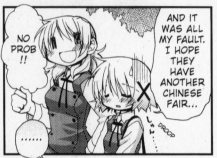

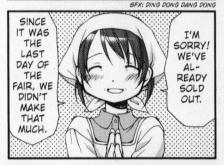

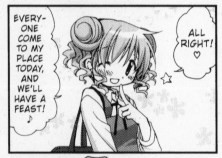

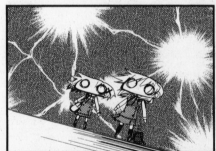

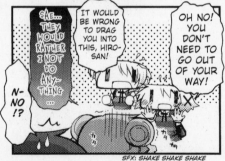

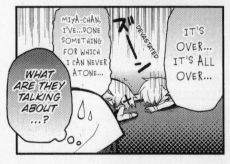

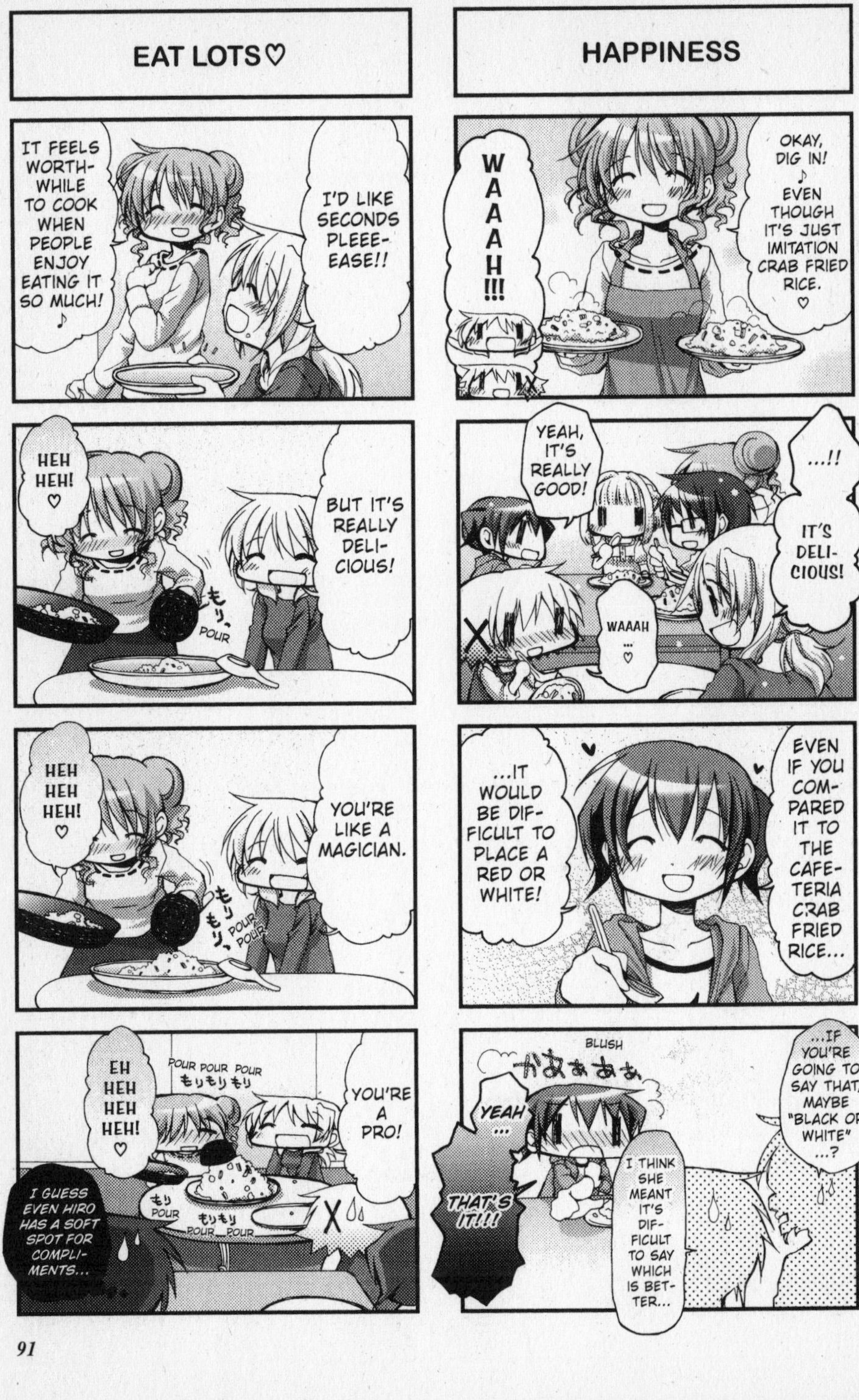
HAPPINESS
OKAY, DIG IN! ♪ EVEN THOUGH IT'S JUST IMITATION CRAB FRIED RICE. ♡
WAAAAH!!!
...!!
IT'S DELICIOUS!
YEAH, IT'S REALLY GOOD!
WAAAH... ♡
EVEN IF YOU COMPARED IT TO THE CAFETERIA CRAB FRIED RICE...
...IT WOULD BE DIFFICULT TO PLACE A RED OR WHITE!
...IF YOU'RE GOING TO SAY THAT, MAYBE "BLACK OR WHITE" ...?
BLUSH
がぁぁぁぁ
YEAH...
I THINK SHE MEANT IT'S DIFFICULT TO SAY WHICH IS BETTER...
THAT'S IT!!!
EAT LOTS♡
I'D LIKE SECONDS PLEEEEASE!!
IT FEELS WORTH-WHILE TO COOK WHEN PEOPLE ENJOY EATING IT SO MUCH! ♪
BUT IT'S REALLY DELICIOUS!
HEH HEH! ♡
もり、 POUR
YOU'RE LIKE A MAGICIAN.
HEH HEH HEH! ♡
もりもり、 POUR POUR
YOU'RE A PRO!
POUR POUR POUR もりもりもり
EH HEH HEH HEH! ♡
もり POUR もりもり POUR POUR
I GUESS EVEN HIRO HAS A SOFT SPOT FOR COMPLIMENTS...

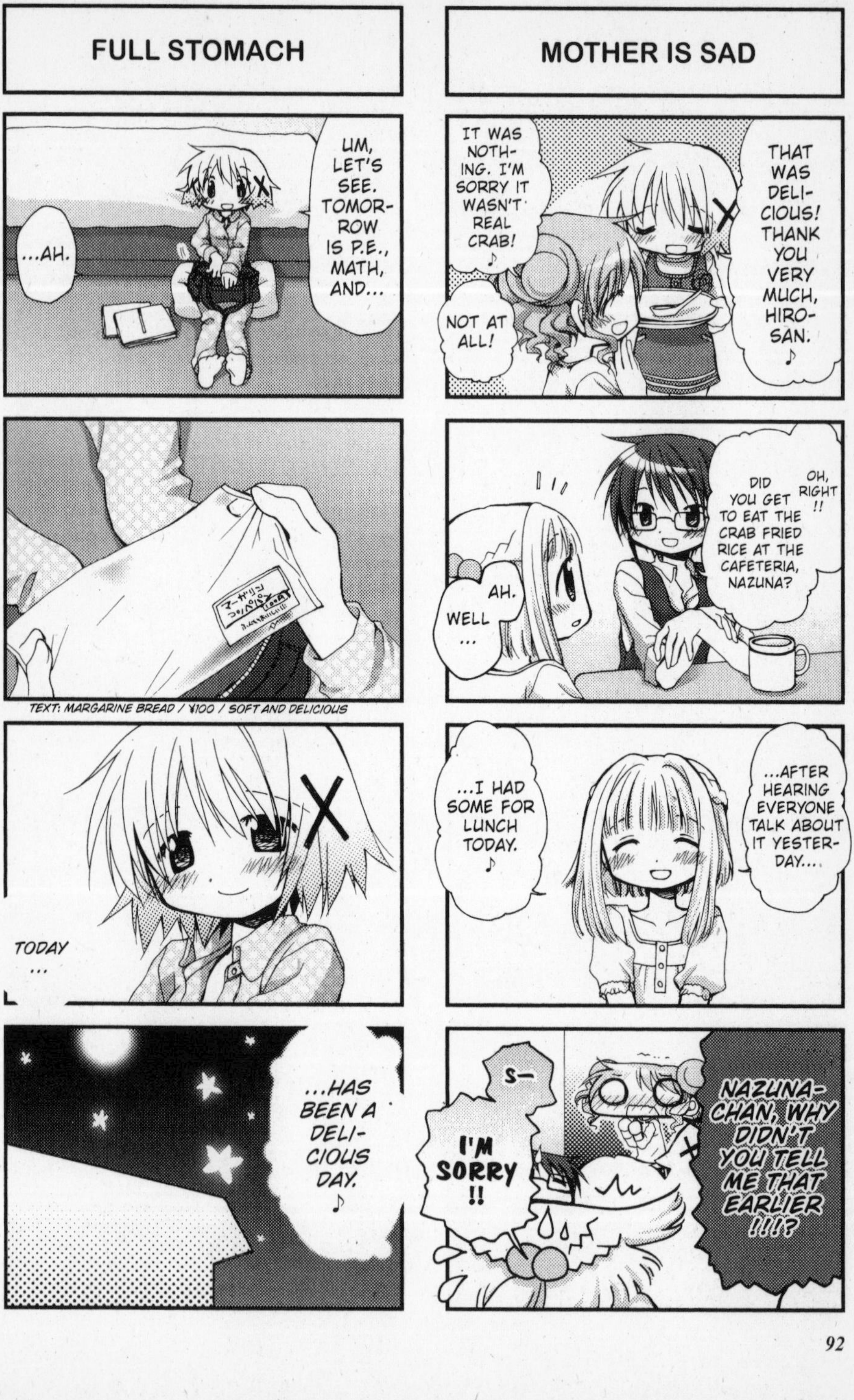
MOTHER IS SAD
THAT WAS DELI-CIOUS! THANK YOU VERY MUCH, HIRO-SAN. ♪
IT WAS NOTH-ING. I'M SORRY IT WASN'T REAL CRAB! ♪
NOT AT ALL!
OH, RIGHT !!
DID YOU GET TO EAT THE CRAB FRIED RICE AT THE CAFETERIA, NAZUNA?
AH. WELL ...
...AFTER HEARING EVERYONE TALK ABOUT IT YESTER-DAY....
...I HAD SOME FOR LUNCH TODAY. ♪
NAZUNA-CHAN, WHY DIDN'T YOU TELL ME THAT EARLIER !!!?
S—
I'M SORRY !!
FULL STOMACH
UM, LET'S SEE. TOMOR-ROW IS P.E., MATH, AND...
...AH.
TEXT: MARGARINE BREAD / ¥100 / SOFT AND DELICIOUS
TODAY ...
...HAS BEEN A DELI-CIOUS DAY. ♪

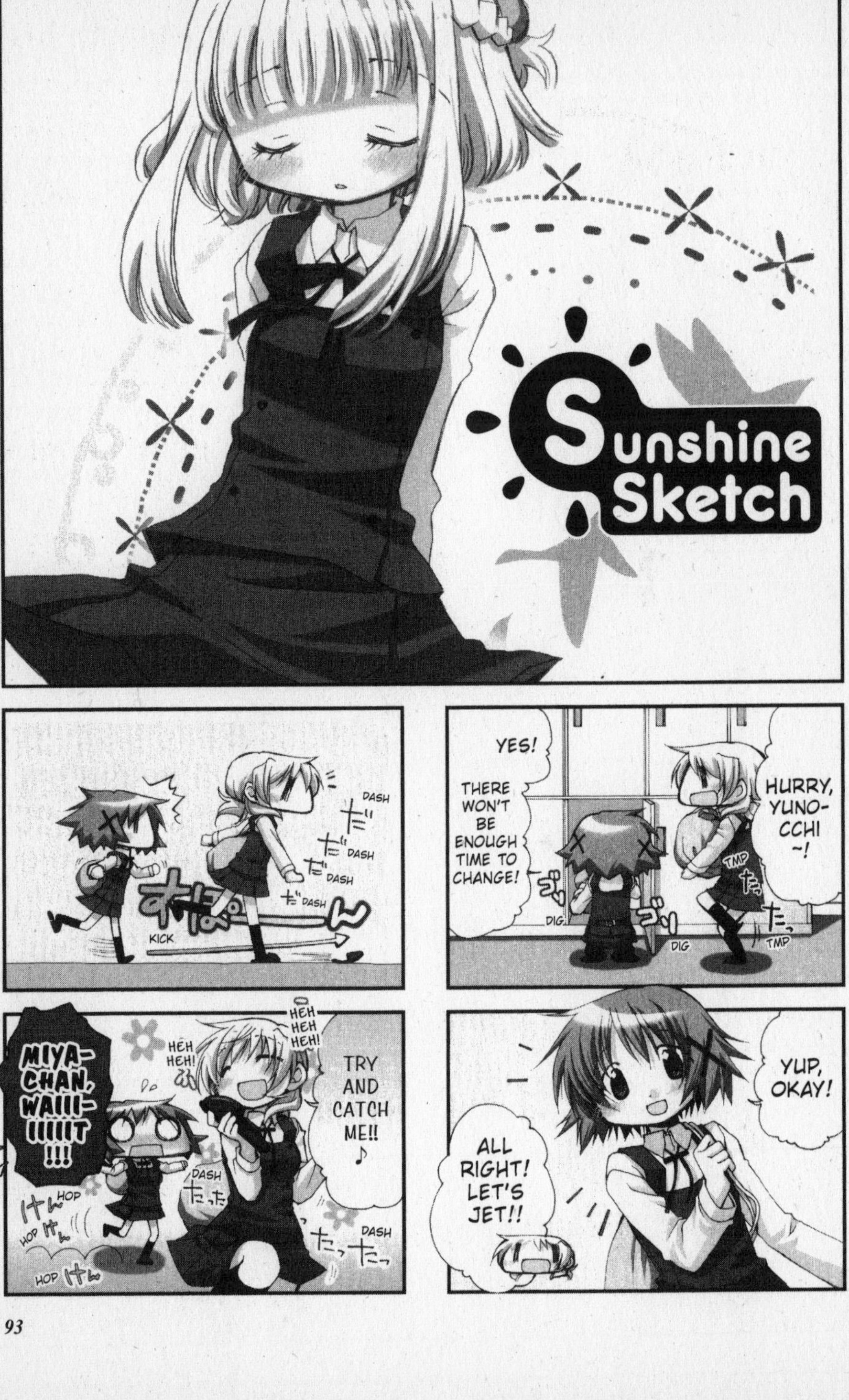
Sunshine Sketch
HURRY, YUNO-CCHI ~!
TMP
TMP
YES! THERE WON'T BE ENOUGH TIME TO CHANGE!
DIG
DIG
DASH
DASH
DASH
DASH
KICK
YUP, OKAY!
ALL RIGHT! LET'S JET!!
HEH HEH HEH!
TRY AND CATCH ME!! ♪
HEH HEH!
DASH
DASH
MIYA-CHAN, WAIIII-IIIIIIT!!!!
HOP
HOP
HOP

SECOND-YEAR STUDENT VIEWPOINT

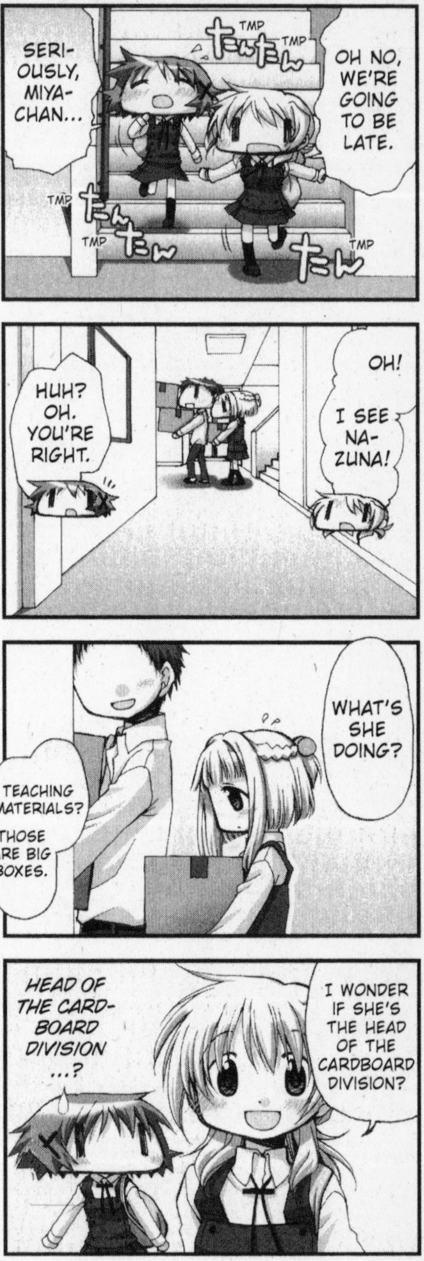
TMP
TMP
OH NO, WE'RE GOING TO BE LATE.
SERIOUSLY, MIYA-CHAN...
TMP
TMP
TMP
OH!
I SEE NAZUNA!
HUH? OH. YOU'RE RIGHT.
WHAT'S SHE DOING?
TEACHING MATERIALS?
THOSE ARE BIG BOXES.
I WONDER IF SHE'S THE HEAD OF THE CARDBOARD DIVISION?
HEAD OF THE CARDBOARD DIVISION ...?

CATCHBALL

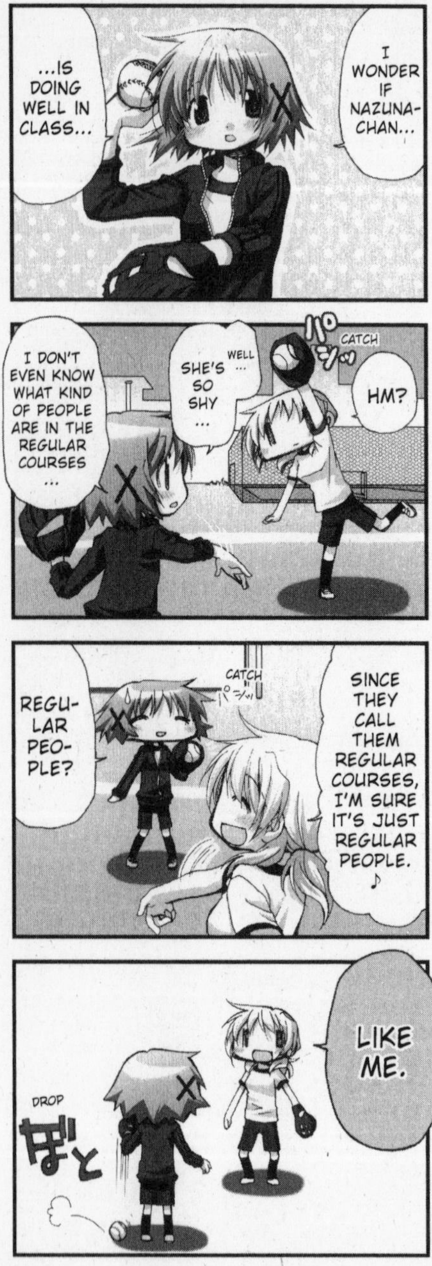
I WONDER IF NAZUNA-CHAN...
...IS DOING WELL IN CLASS...
CATCH
HM?
WELL ...
SHE'S SO SHY ...
I DON'T EVEN KNOW WHAT KIND OF PEOPLE ARE IN THE REGULAR COURSES ...
SINCE THEY CALL THEM REGULAR COURSES, I'M SURE IT'S JUST REGULAR PEOPLE. ♪
CATCH
REGULAR PEOPLE?
LIKE ME.
DROP

THIRD-YEAR STUDENT VIEWPOINT

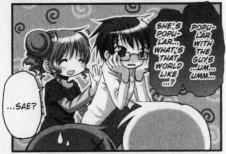

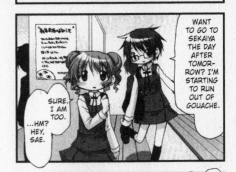

WANT TO GO TO SEKAIYA THE DAY AFTER TOMORROW? I'M STARTING TO RUN OUT OF GOUACHE.
SURE. I AM TOO.
...HM? HEY, SAE.
ISN'T ...
...THAT NAZUNA-CHAN?
EH? NAZUNA?
WAH!
HEY...
THAT GUY...
LOOKS LIKE HE'S INTERESTED, NO?
HEY, SAE?
...SAE?
どっきどっきどっきどっき

SFX: BADUM BADUM BADUM BADUM

LOVE SENIOR

WE SAW NAZUNA AND A GUY WALKING TOGETHER EARLIER!
AND IT SEEMED LIKE SHE WAS HAVING HIM CARRY HEAVY THINGS FOR HER.
ずずず
APPEAR
ずいっ
OH, WE SAW TOO, DURING BREAK.
WAS HE WEARING GLASSES?
NO, MORE TRIM AND SPORTY.
EH?
MAYBE NAZUNA-CHAN...
...IS PRETTY POPULAR WITH THE GUYS. ♪
EEH!?
POPULAR WITH THE GUYS UM... UMM...
SHE'S POPULAR... WHAT'S THAT WORLD LIKE...?
...SAE?

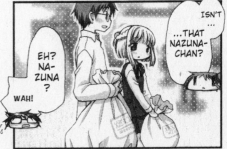

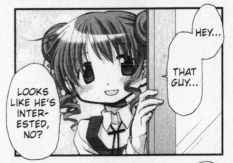

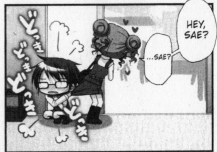

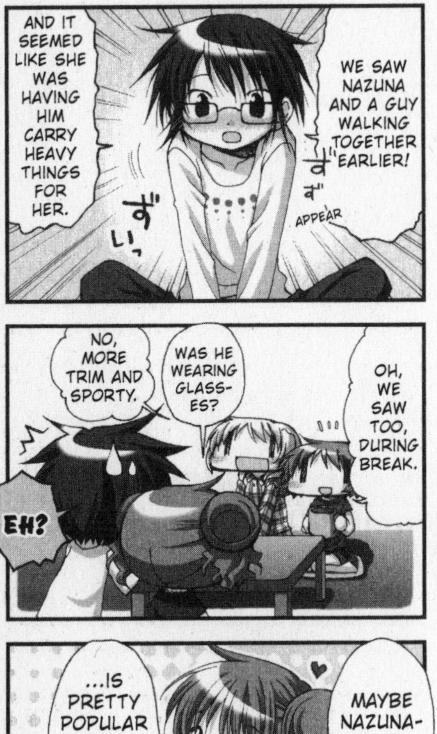

VERY POPULAR

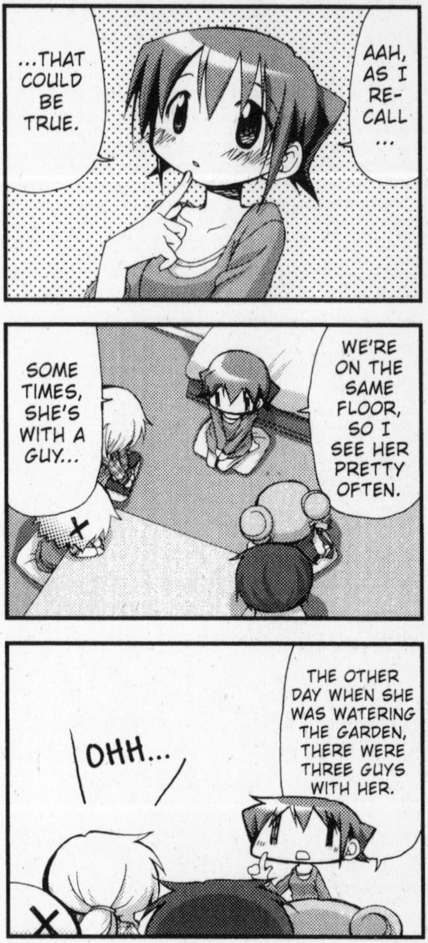
AAH, AS I RE-CALL...
...THAT COULD BE TRUE.
WE'RE ON THE SAME FLOOR, SO I SEE HER PRETTY OFTEN.
SOME TIMES, SHE'S WITH A GUY...
THE OTHER DAY WHEN SHE WAS WATERING THE GARDEN, THERE WERE THREE GUYS WITH HER.
OHH...
THEN AFTER THAT, THERE WERE FOUR LADYBUGS STUCK ON HER...
THAT DOESN'T SOUND RIGHT, BUT WOW...

OBSERVATION

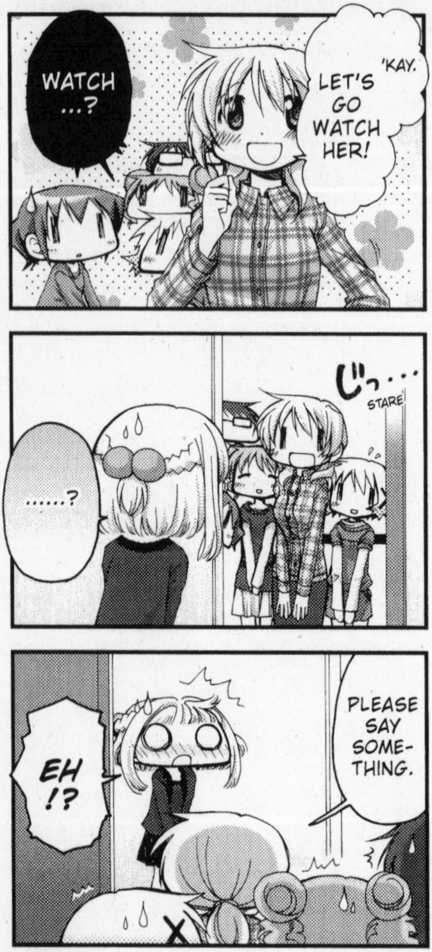
'KAY.
LET'S GO WATCH HER!
WATCH ...?
じっ...
STARE
......?
PLEASE SAY SOME-THING.
EH !?
UM, OKAY, HOW ABOUT SOME MOVE-MENT...
EEEH ...?

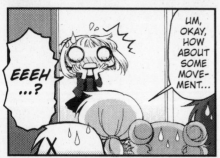

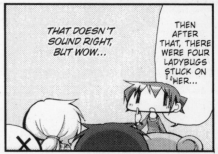

MISS PRECOCIOUS

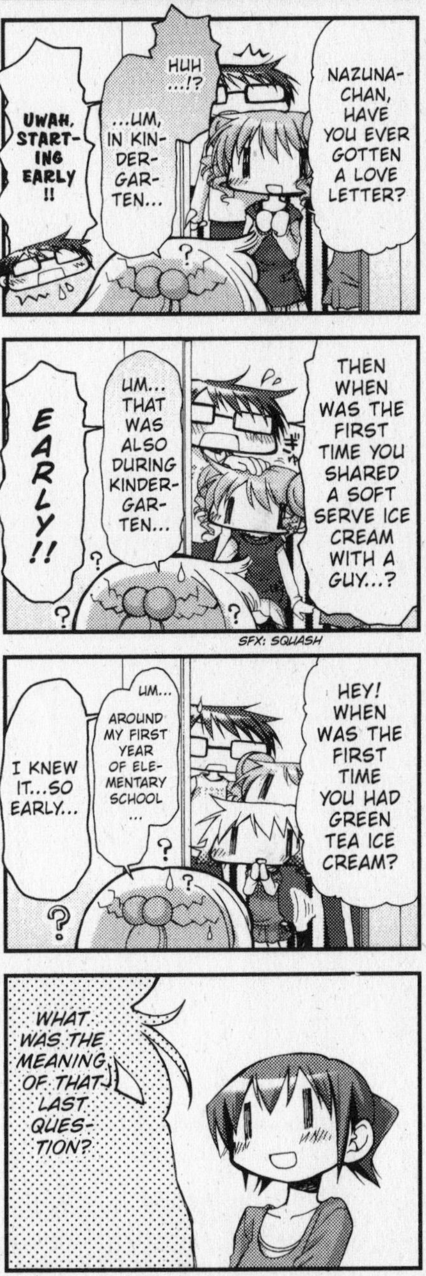
NAZUNA-CHAN, HAVE YOU EVER GOTTEN A LOVE LETTER?
HUH ...!?
...UM, IN KINDER-GARTEN...
UWAH, START-ING EARLY !!
THEN WHEN WAS THE FIRST TIME YOU SHARED A SOFT SERVE ICE CREAM WITH A GUY...?
UM... THAT WAS ALSO DURING KINDER-GARTEN...
EARLY!!
SFX: SQUASH
HEY! WHEN WAS THE FIRST TIME YOU HAD GREEN TEA ICE CREAM?
UM... AROUND MY FIRST YEAR OF ELE-MENTARY SCHOOL ...
I KNEW IT...SO EARLY...
WHAT WAS THE MEANING OF THAT LAST QUES-TION?

GO AROUND

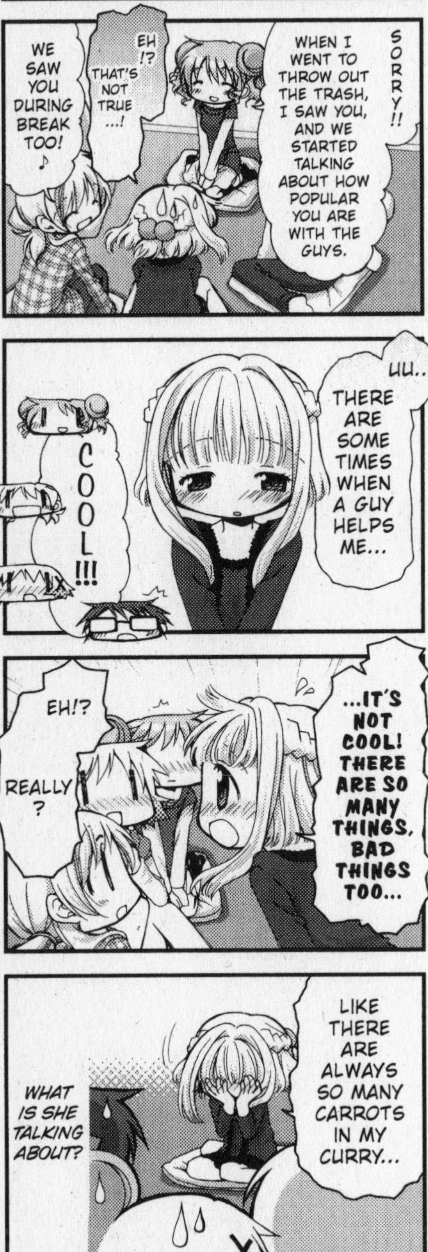
SORRY!!
WHEN I WENT TO THROW OUT THE TRASH, I SAW YOU, AND WE STARTED TALKING ABOUT HOW POPULAR YOU ARE WITH THE GUYS.
EH !? THAT'S NOT TRUE ...!
WE SAW YOU DURING BREAK TOO! ♪
UU... THERE ARE SOME TIMES WHEN A GUY HELPS ME...
COOL!!!
...IT'S NOT COOL! THERE ARE SO MANY THINGS, BAD THINGS TOO...
EH!? REALLY ?
LIKE THERE ARE ALWAYS SO MANY CARROTS IN MY CURRY...
WHAT IS SHE TALKING ABOUT?

—X—

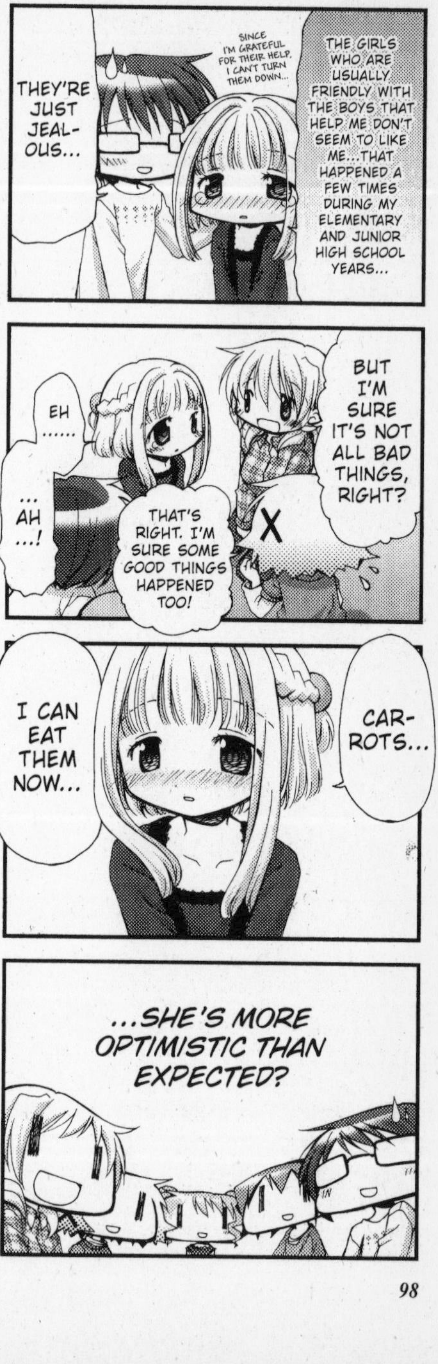
THE GIRLS WHO ARE USUALLY FRIENDLY WITH THE BOYS THAT HELP ME DON'T SEEM TO LIKE ME...THAT HAPPENED A FEW TIMES DURING MY ELEMENTARY AND JUNIOR HIGH SCHOOL YEARS...
SINCE I'M GRATEFUL FOR THEIR HELP, I CAN'T TURN THEM DOWN...
THEY'RE JUST JEALOUS...
BUT I'M SURE IT'S NOT ALL BAD THINGS, RIGHT?
X
THAT'S RIGHT. I'M SURE SOME GOOD THINGS HAPPENED TOO!
EH ......
...AH ...!
CARROTS...
I CAN EAT THEM NOW...
...SHE'S MORE OPTIMISTIC THAN EXPECTED?

HOT THOUGHT

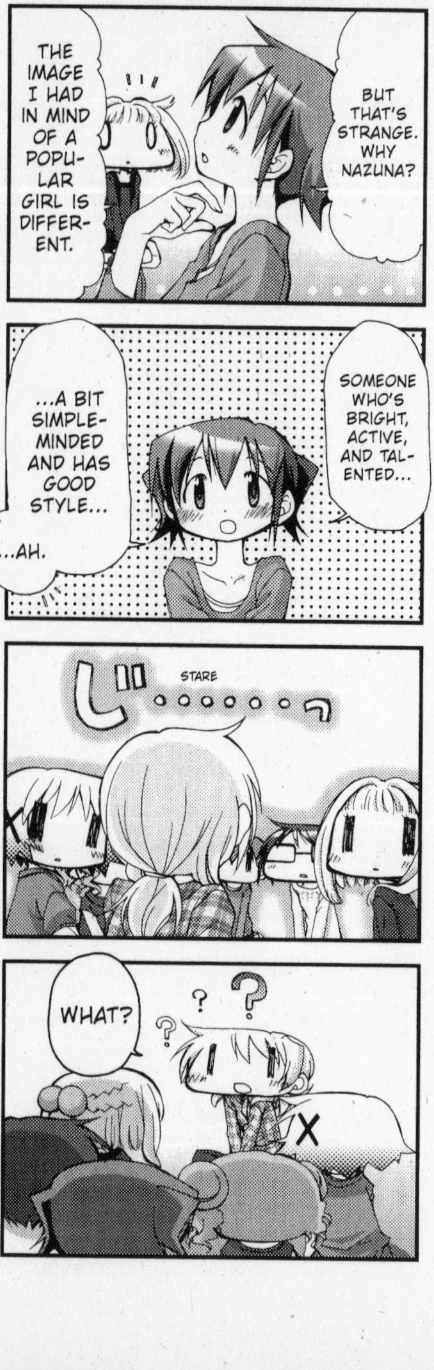
BUT THAT'S STRANGE. WHY NAZUNA?
THE IMAGE I HAD IN MIND OF A POPULAR GIRL IS DIFFERENT.
SOMEONE WHO'S BRIGHT, ACTIVE, AND TALENTED...
...A BIT SIMPLE-MINDED AND HAS GOOD STYLE...
...AH.
STARE
WHAT?
X

THAT'S IT

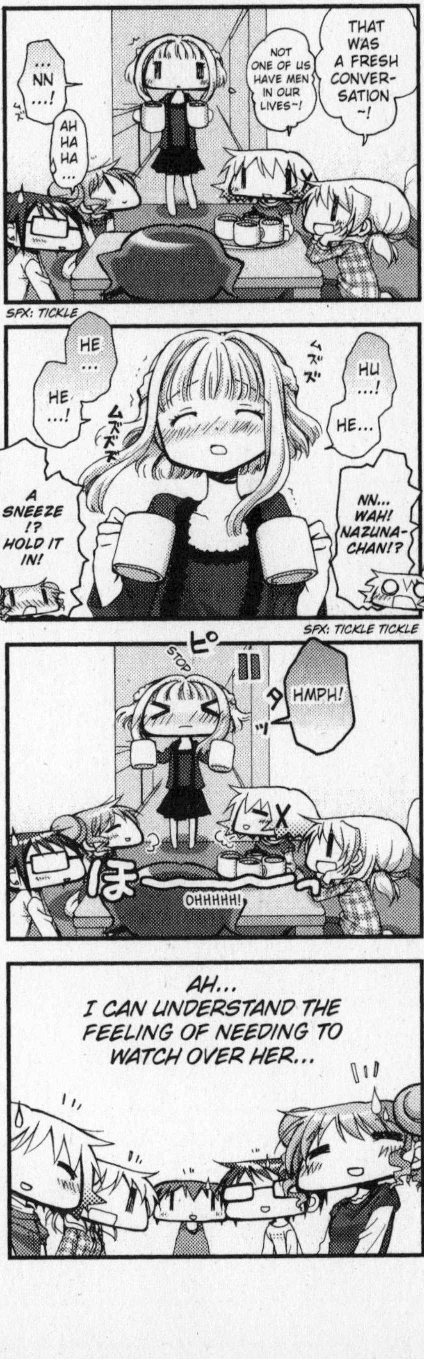
THAT WAS A FRESH CONVERSATION ~!
NOT ONE OF US HAVE MEN IN OUR LIVES~!
... NN ...!
AH HA HA ...
SFX: TICKLE
HU ...! HE...
HE ...
HE ...!
NN... WAH! NAZUNA-CHAN!?
A SNEEZE !? HOLD IT IN!
SFX: TICKLE TICKLE
STOP
HMPH!
OHHHHH!
AH... I CAN UNDERSTAND THE FEELING OF NEEDING TO WATCH OVER HER...

REMARK FROM TWO COLUMNS BACK

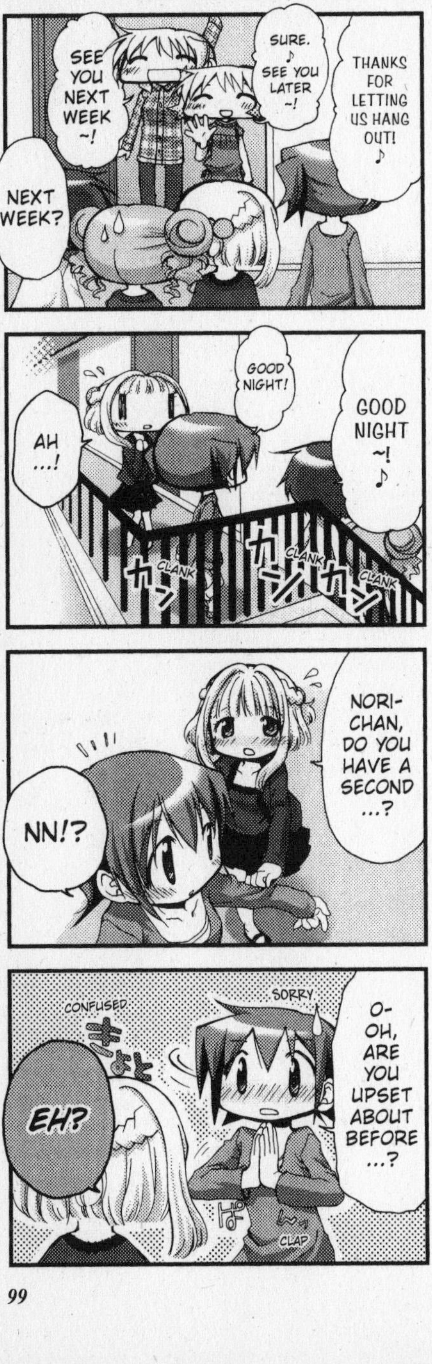
THANKS FOR LETTING US HANG OUT! ♪
SURE. ♪ SEE YOU LATER ~!
SEE YOU NEXT WEEK ~!
NEXT WEEK?
GOOD NIGHT ~! ♪
GOOD NIGHT!
AH ...!
CLANK
CLANK
CLANK
NORI-CHAN, DO YOU HAVE A SECOND ...?
NN!?
O-OH, ARE YOU UPSET ABOUT BEFORE ...?
SORRY
CONFUSED
EH?
CLAP

NAZUNA AND NORI

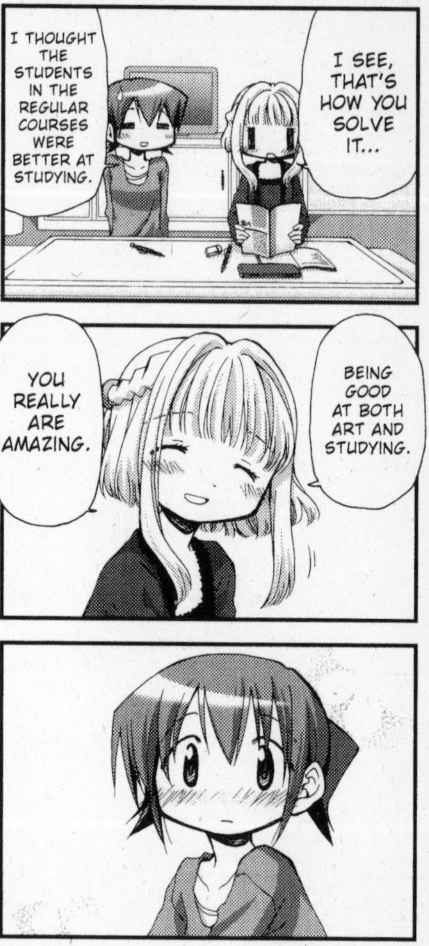
I SEE, THAT'S HOW YOU SOLVE IT...
I THOUGHT THE STUDENTS IN THE REGULAR COURSES WERE BETTER AT STUDYING.
BEING GOOD AT BOTH ART AND STUDYING.
YOU REALLY ARE AMAZING.
THAT'S NOT TRUE ...
IF IT'S ANYTHING THAT I UNDER-STAND, I CAN ALWAYS SHOW YOU...
REALLY? THANKS ~! ♪

YOSHINOYA RADAR

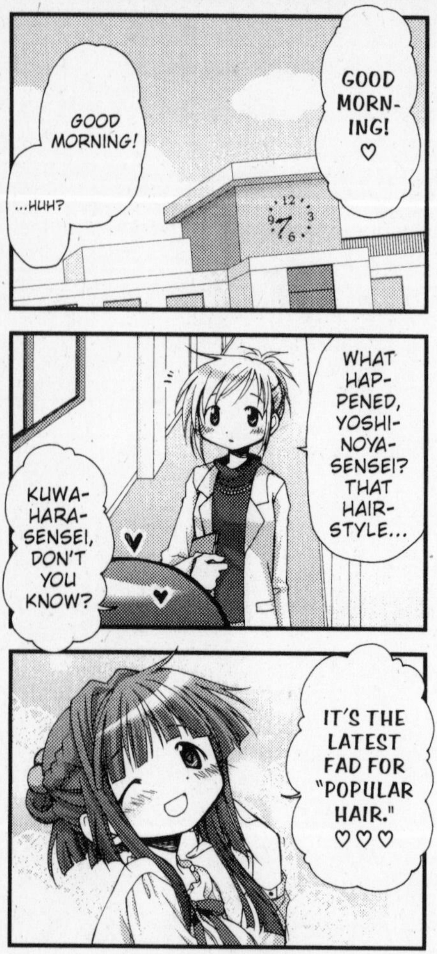
GOOD MORN-ING! ♡
GOOD MORNING!
...HUH?
WHAT HAP-PENED, YOSHI-NOYA-SENSEI? THAT HAIR-STYLE...
KUWA-HARA-SENSEI, DON'T YOU KNOW?
IT'S THE LATEST FAD FOR "POPULAR HAIR." ♡♡♡
POPULAR?
POPULAR ♡
WHERE DID SHE HEAR THAT ...?

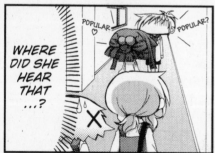

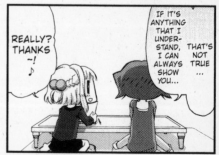

SUNSHINE SKETCH Extra Chapter "Until Natsume Became Natsume"

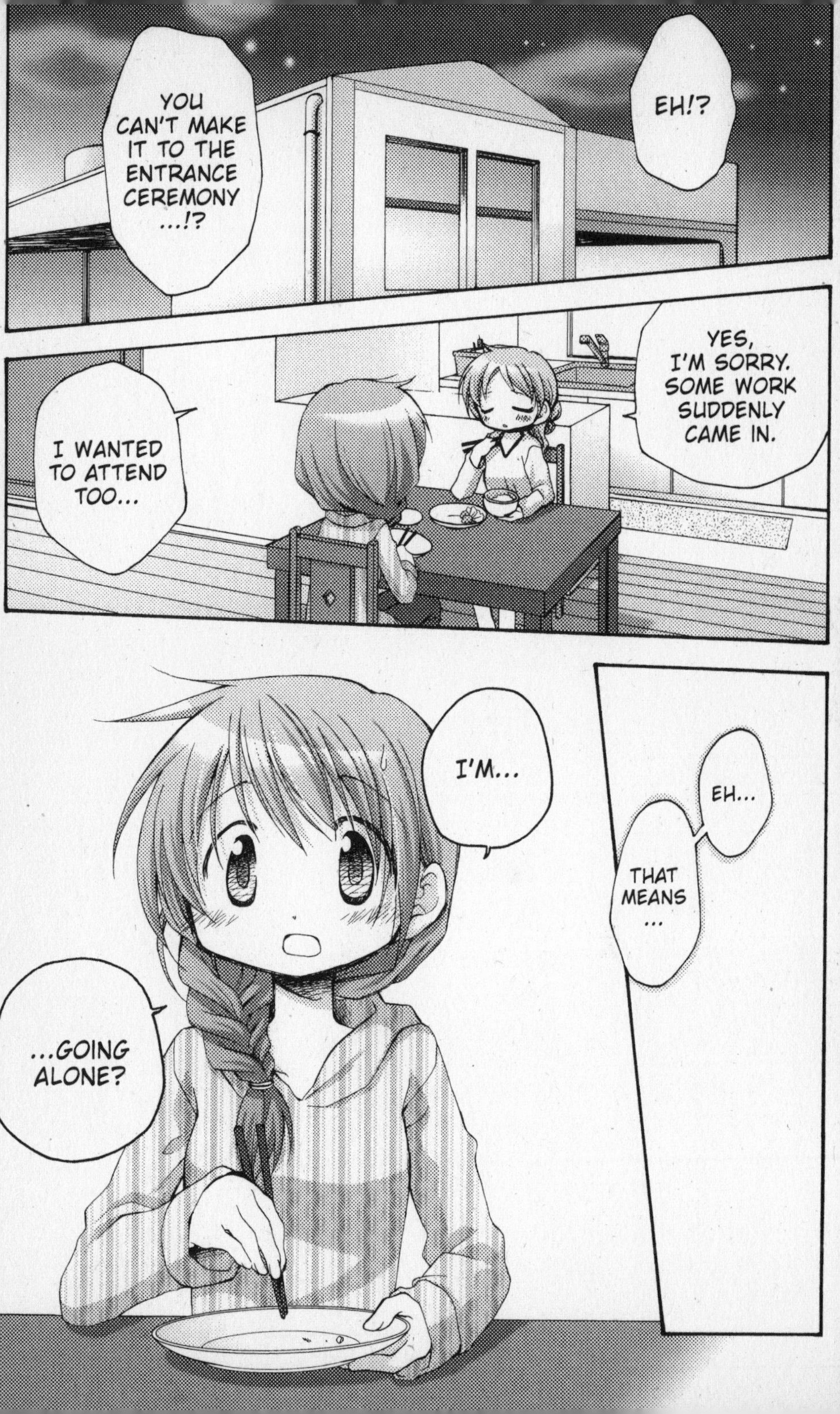
EH!?
YOU CAN'T MAKE IT TO THE ENTRANCE CEREMONY ...!?
YES, I'M SORRY. SOME WORK SUDDENLY CAME IN.
I WANTED TO ATTEND TOO...
EH...
THAT MEANS ...
I'M...
...GOING ALONE?

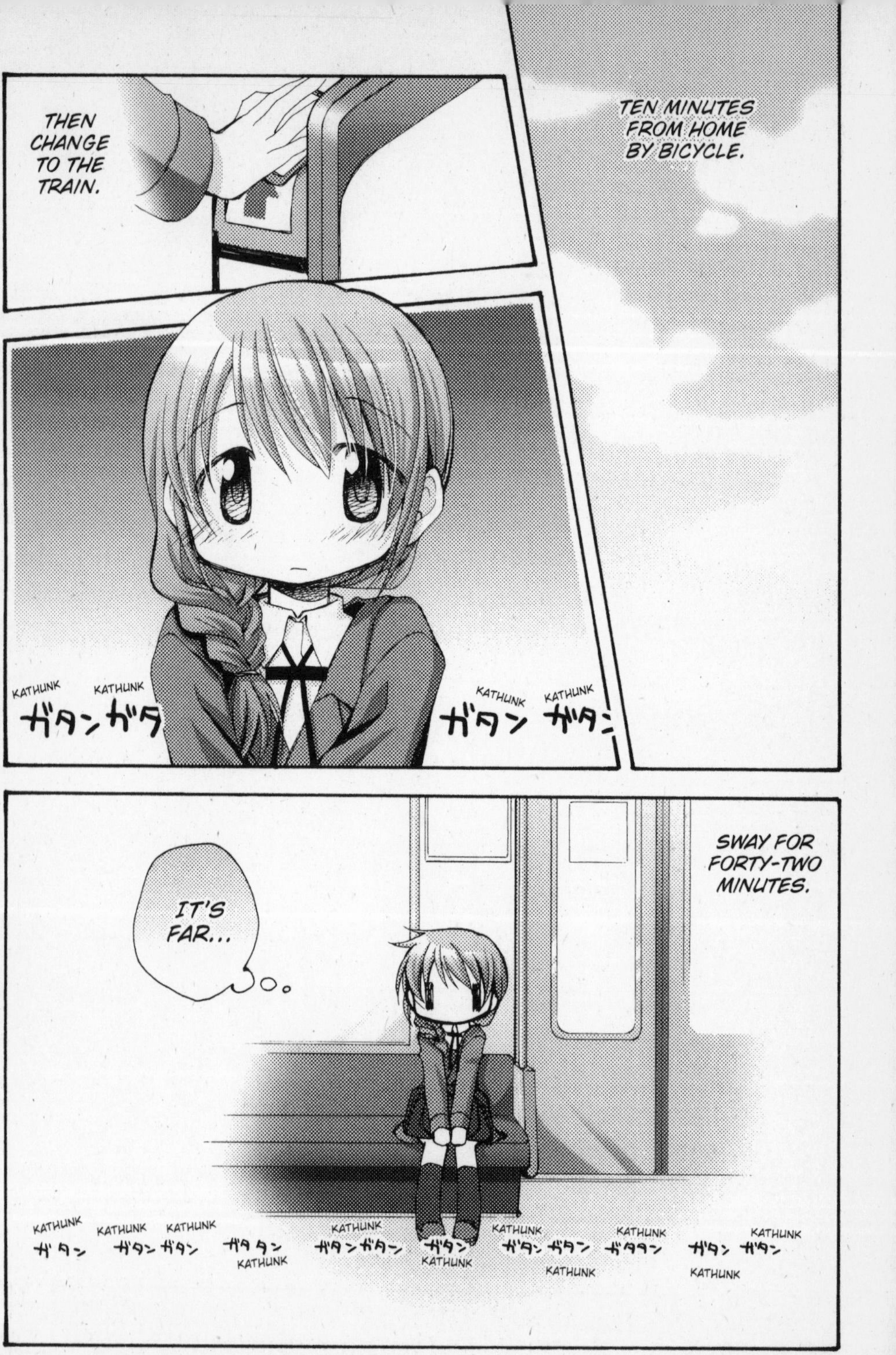
TEN MINUTES FROM HOME BY BICYCLE.
THEN CHANGE TO THE TRAIN.
KATHUNK KATHUNK
ガタン ガタン
KATHUNK KATHUNK
ガタンガタ
SWAY FOR FORTY-TWO MINUTES.
IT'S FAR...
KATHUNK KATHUNK KATHUNK KATHUNK KATHUNK KATHUNK KATHUNK KATHUNK KATHUNK KATHUNK KATHUNK KATHUNK KATHUNK

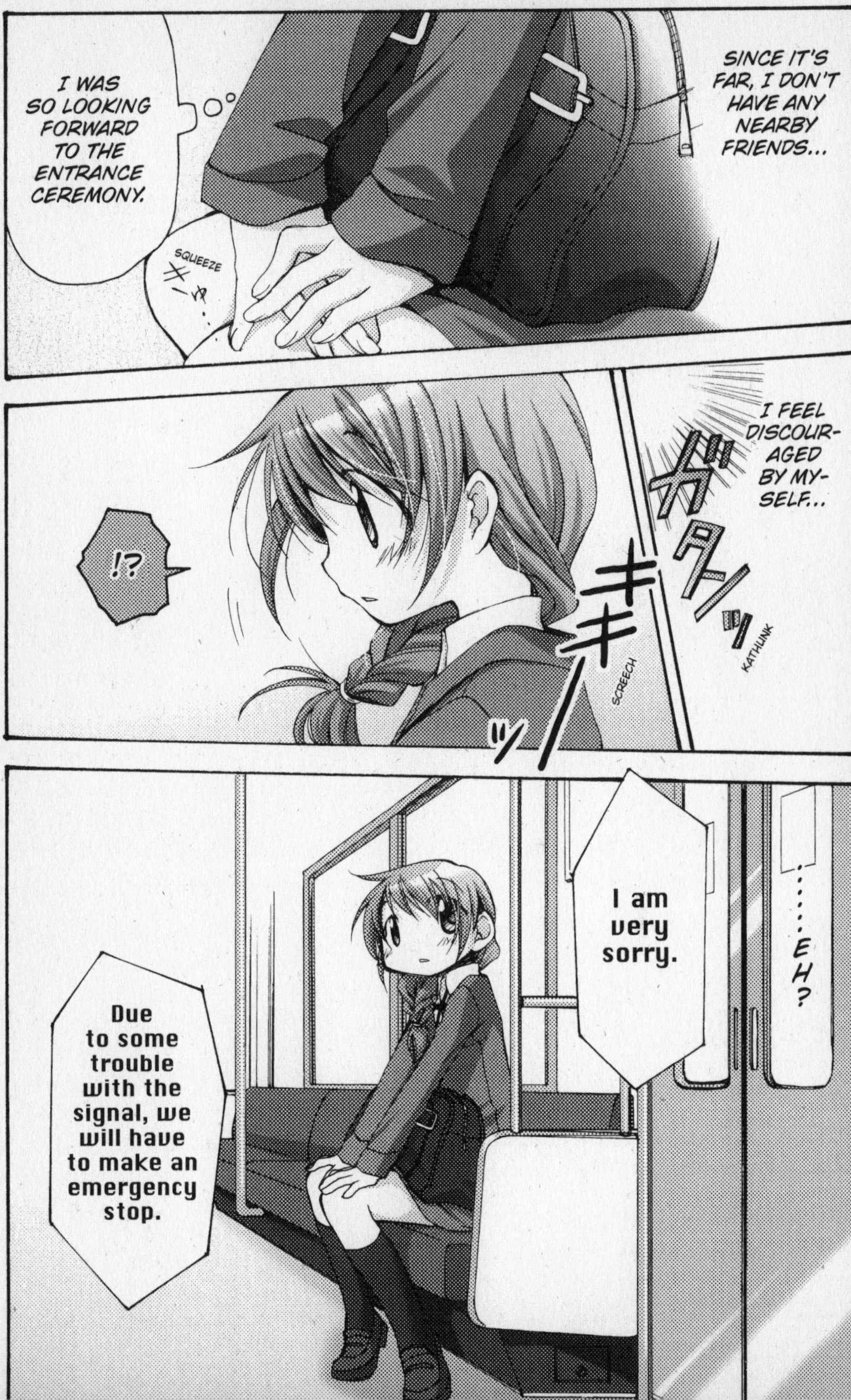
SINCE IT'S FAR, I DON'T HAVE ANY NEARBY FRIENDS...
I WAS SO LOOKING FORWARD TO THE ENTRANCE CEREMONY.
SQUEEZE
I FEEL DISCOURAGED BY MYSELF...
KATHUNK
SCREECH
!?
......EH?
I am very sorry.
Due to some trouble with the signal, we will have to make an emergency stop.

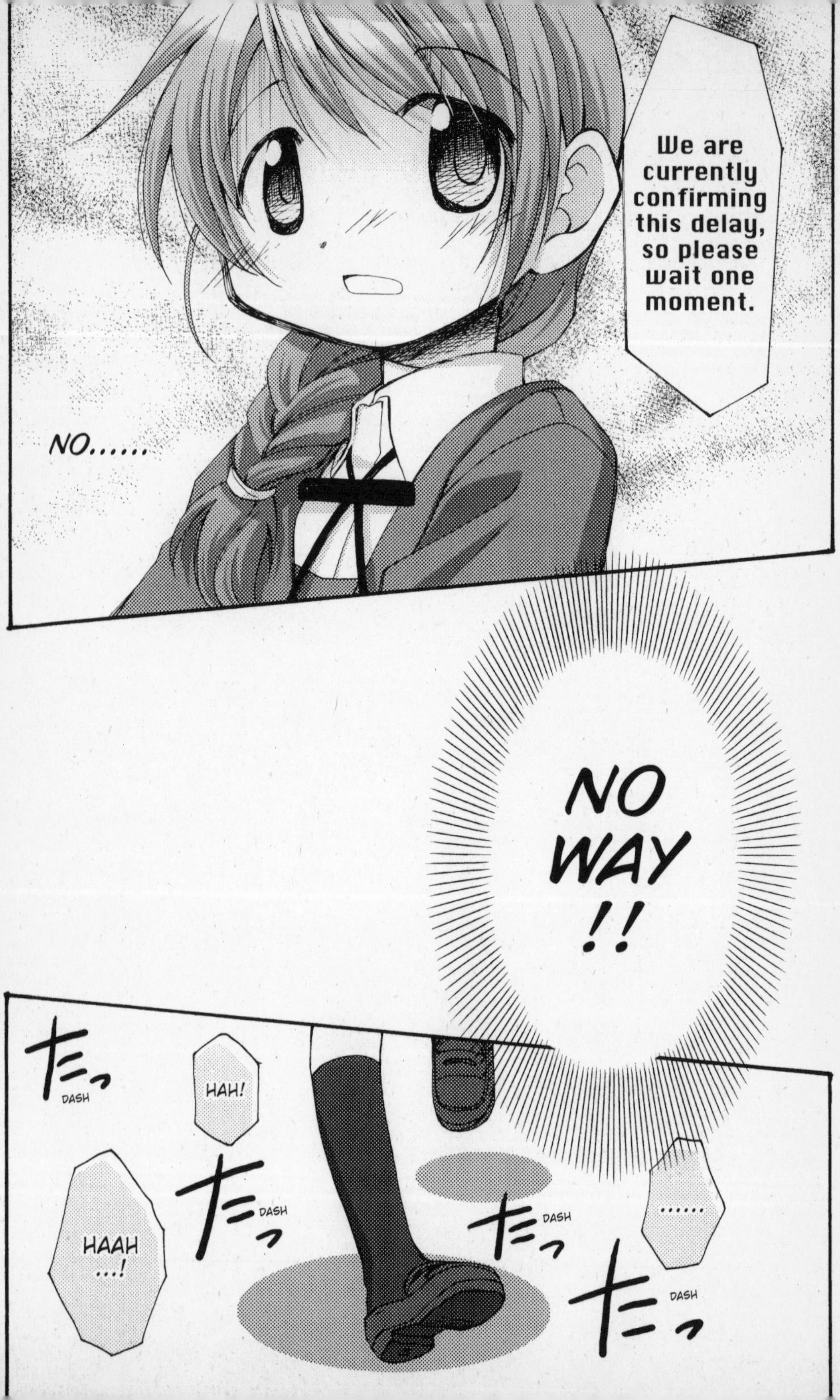

We are currently confirming this delay, so please wait one moment.
NO......
NO WAY !!
......
DASH
DASH
HAH!
DASH
DASH
HAAH ...!

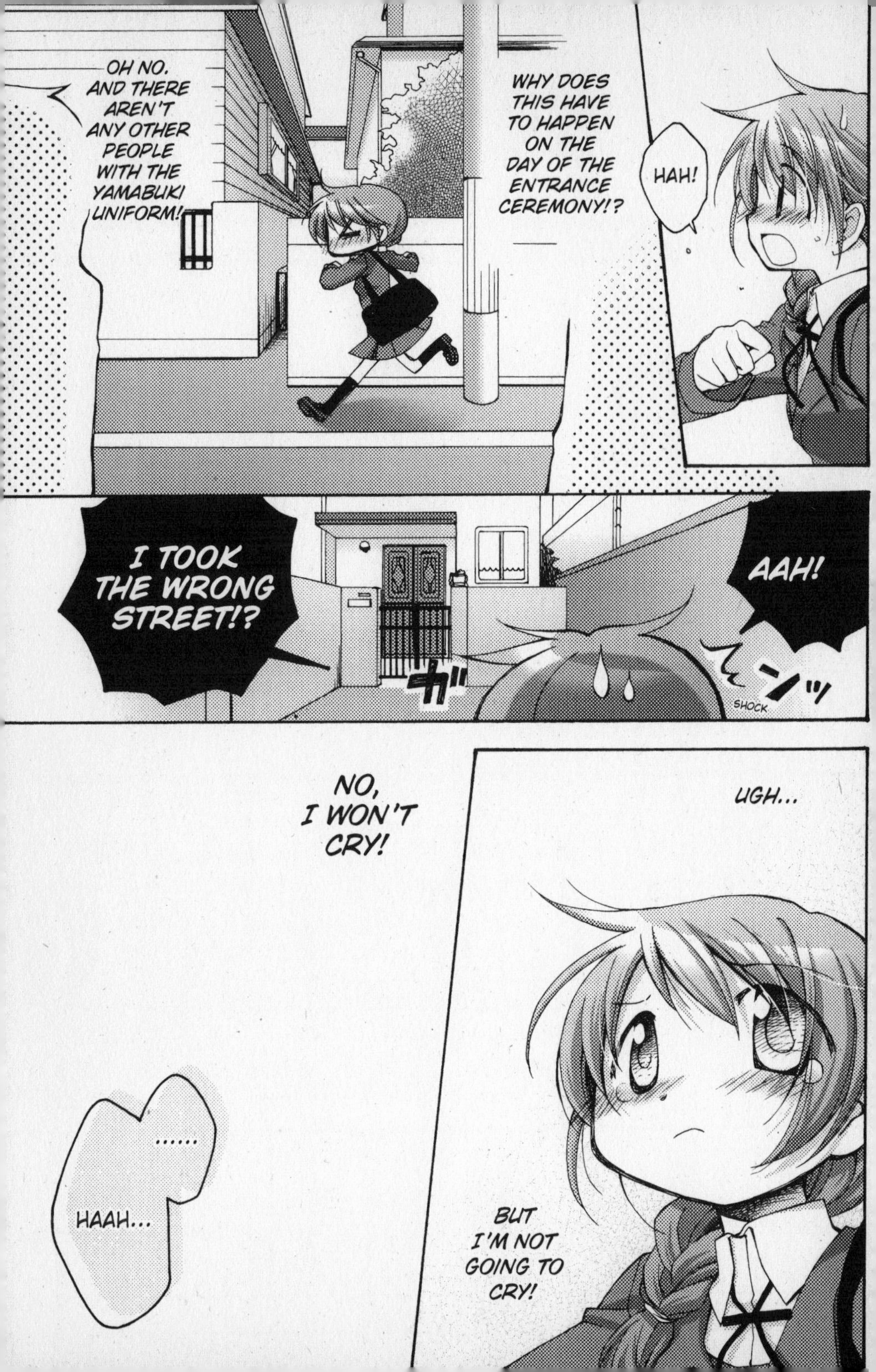
HAH!
WHY DOES THIS HAVE TO HAPPEN ON THE DAY OF THE ENTRANCE CEREMONY!?
OH NO. AND THERE AREN'T ANY OTHER PEOPLE WITH THE YAMABUKI UNIFORM!
AAH!
SHOCK
I TOOK THE WRONG STREET!?
UGH...
BUT I'M NOT GOING TO CRY!
NO, I WON'T CRY!
......
HAAH...

......
I'M FINALLY HERE...

UM, NATSU-ME... NATSU-ME...
...B18!

たっ DASH
たっ DASH
たっ DASH

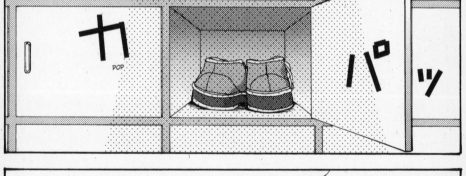

カ POP
パッ

EH!?

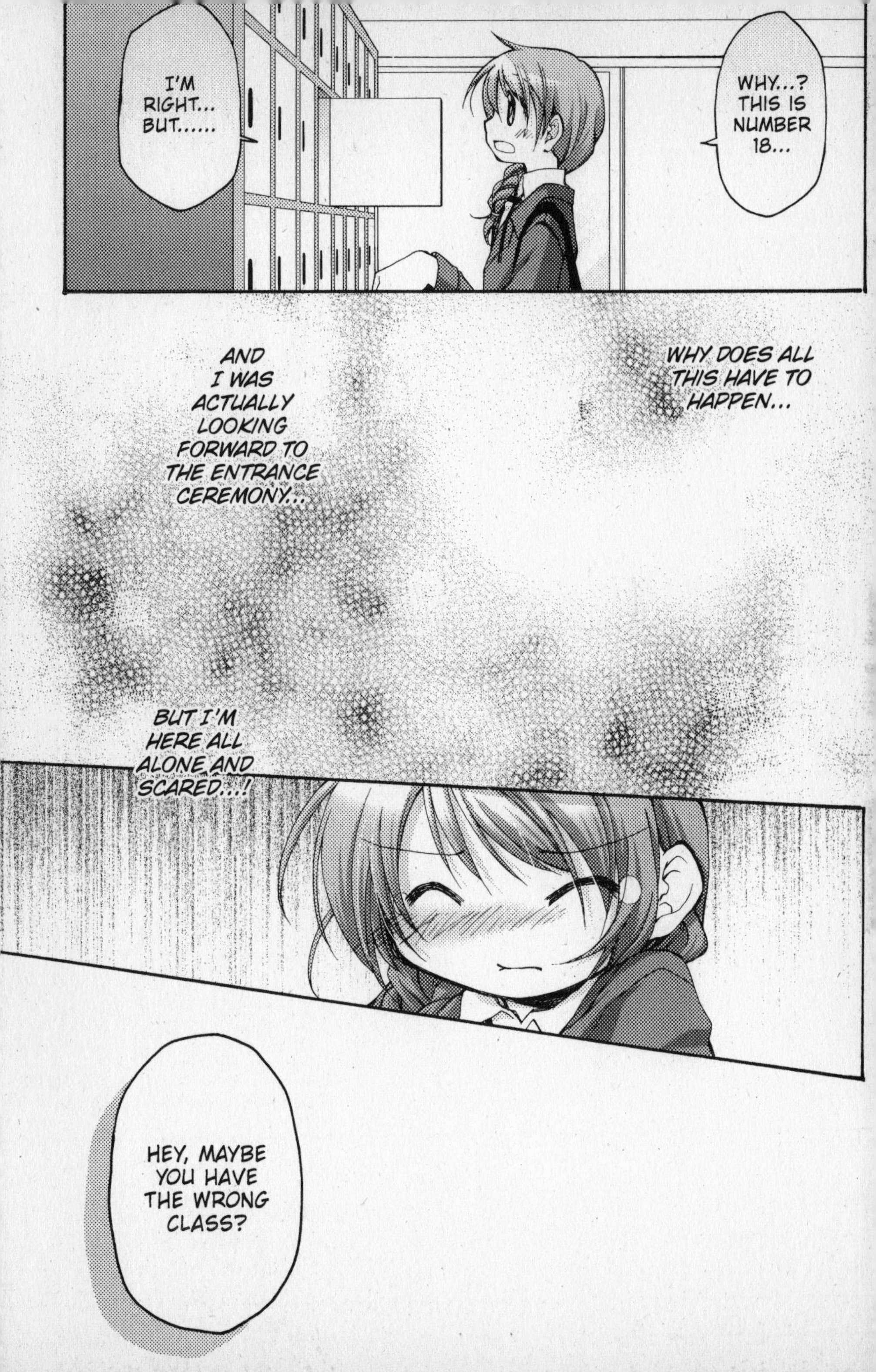
WHY...? THIS IS NUMBER 18...
I'M RIGHT... BUT......
WHY DOES ALL THIS HAVE TO HAPPEN...
AND I WAS ACTUALLY LOOKING FORWARD TO THE ENTRANCE CEREMONY...
BUT I'M HERE ALL ALONE AND SCARED...!
HEY, MAYBE YOU HAVE THE WRONG CLASS?

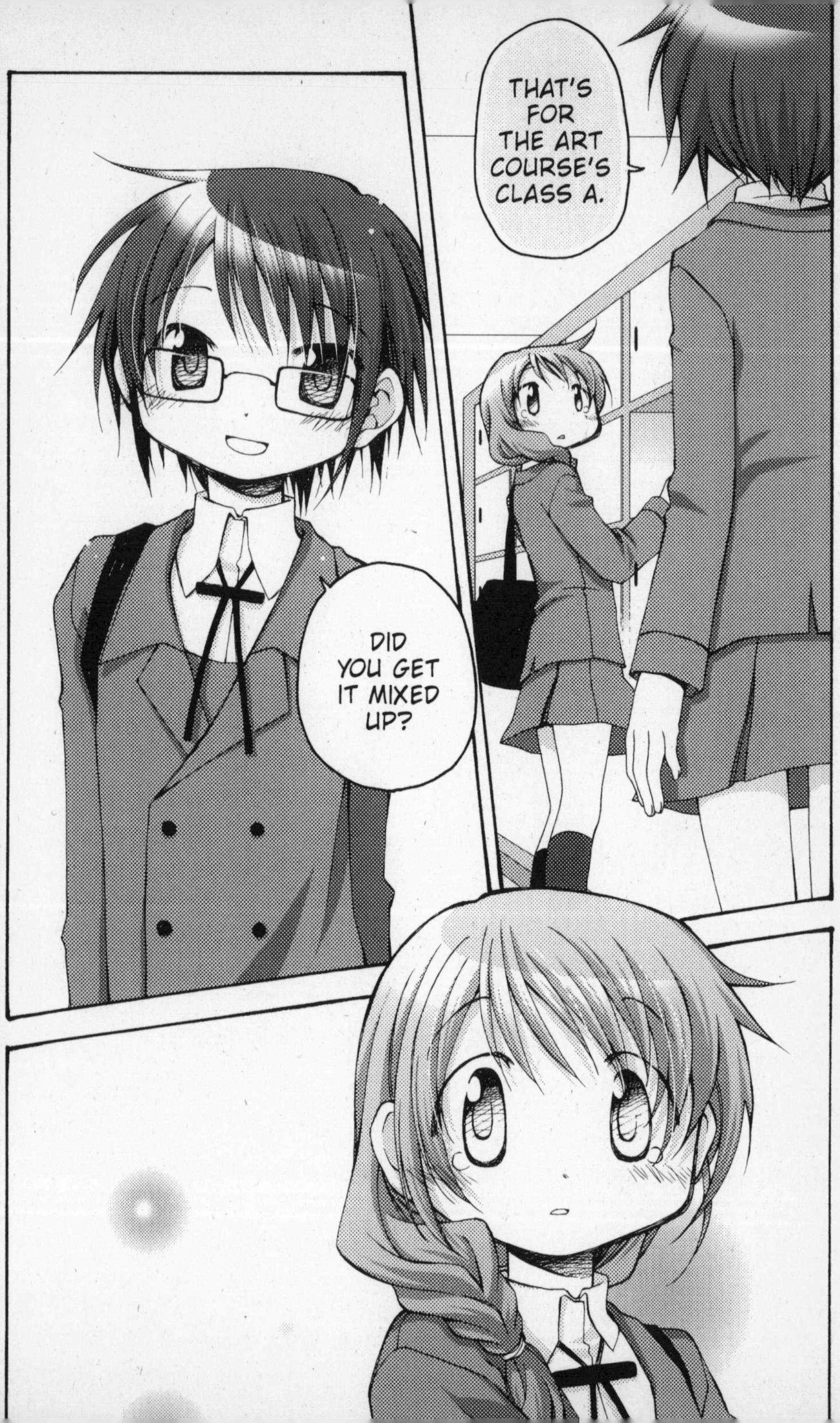
THAT'S FOR THE ART COURSE'S CLASS A.
DID YOU GET IT MIXED UP?

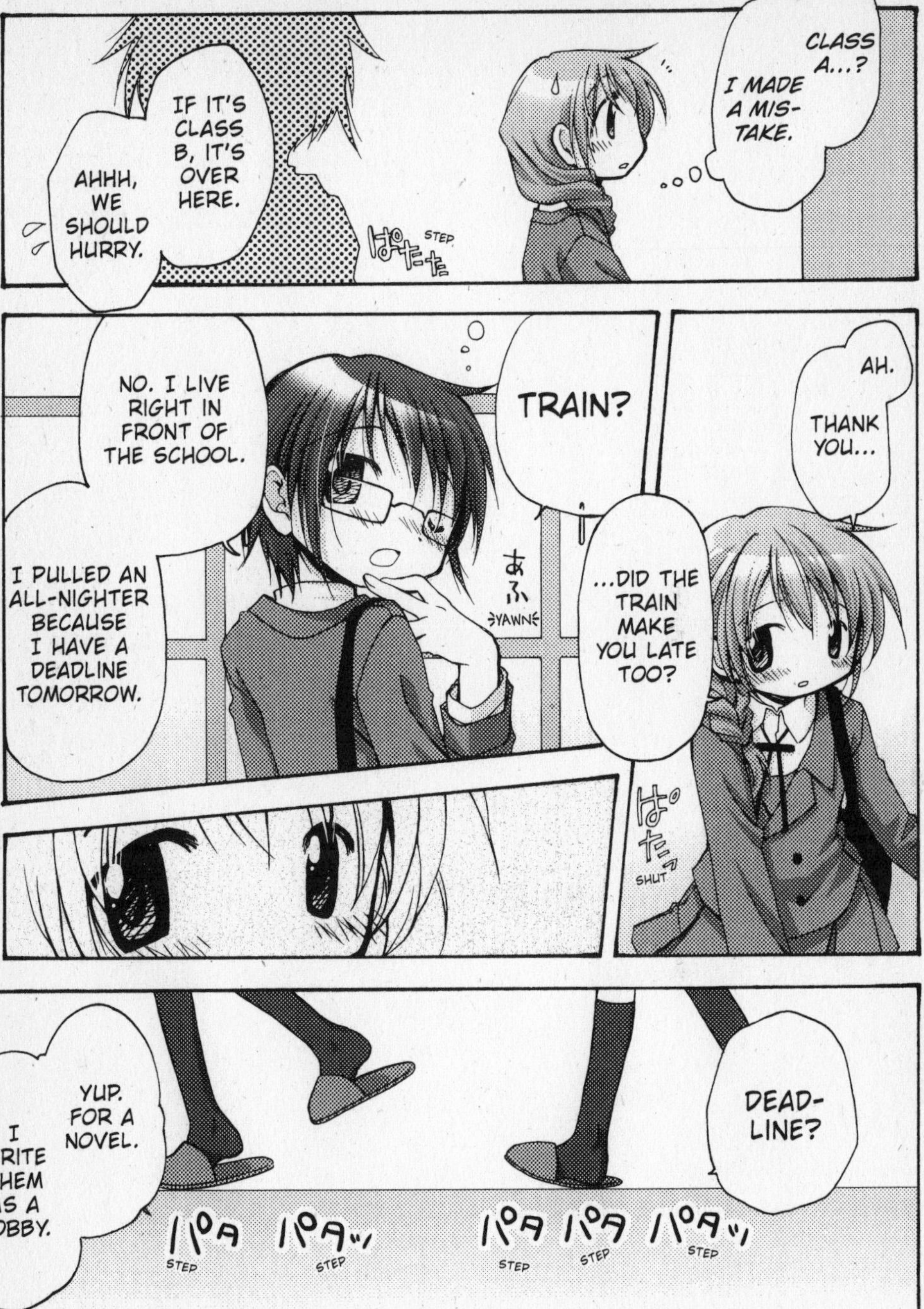
CLASS A...? I MADE A MIS-TAKE.
IF IT'S CLASS B, IT'S OVER HERE.
AHHH, WE SHOULD HURRY.
ぱたた STEP
AH. THANK YOU...
...DID THE TRAIN MAKE YOU LATE TOO?
ぱたっ SHUT
TRAIN?
NO. I LIVE RIGHT IN FRONT OF THE SCHOOL.
I PULLED AN ALL-NIGHTER BECAUSE I HAVE A DEADLINE TOMORROW.
あふ YAWN
DEAD-LINE?
YUP. FOR A NOVEL.
I WRITE THEM AS A HOBBY.
パタ パタ パタッ STEP STEP STEP
パタ パタッ STEP STEP

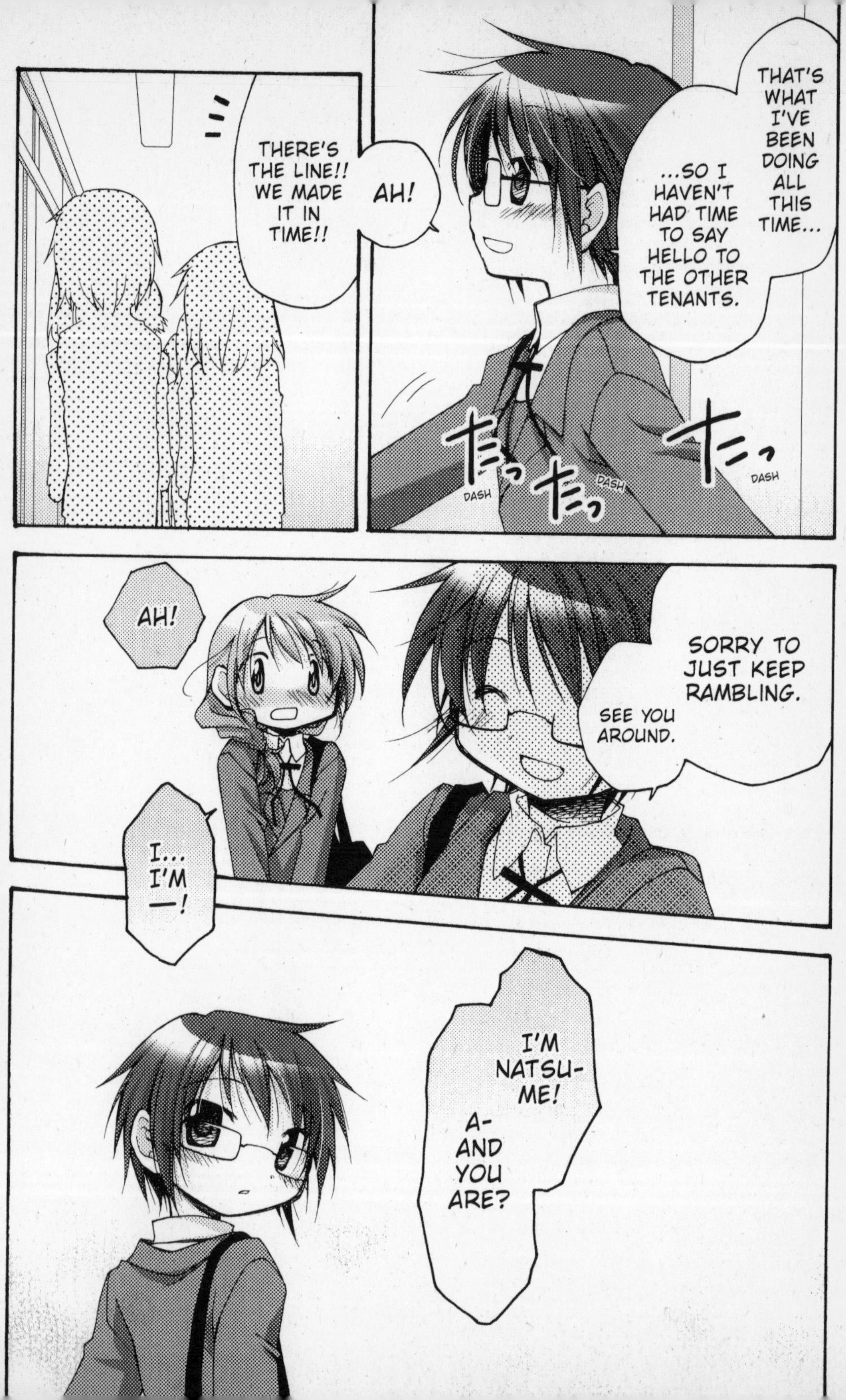
THAT'S WHAT I'VE BEEN DOING ALL THIS TIME...
...SO I HAVEN'T HAD TIME TO SAY HELLO TO THE OTHER TENANTS.
DASH
DASH
DASH
AH!
THERE'S THE LINE!! WE MADE IT IN TIME!!
SORRY TO JUST KEEP RAMBLING.
SEE YOU AROUND.
AH!
I... I'M —!
I'M NATSUME!
A- AND YOU ARE?

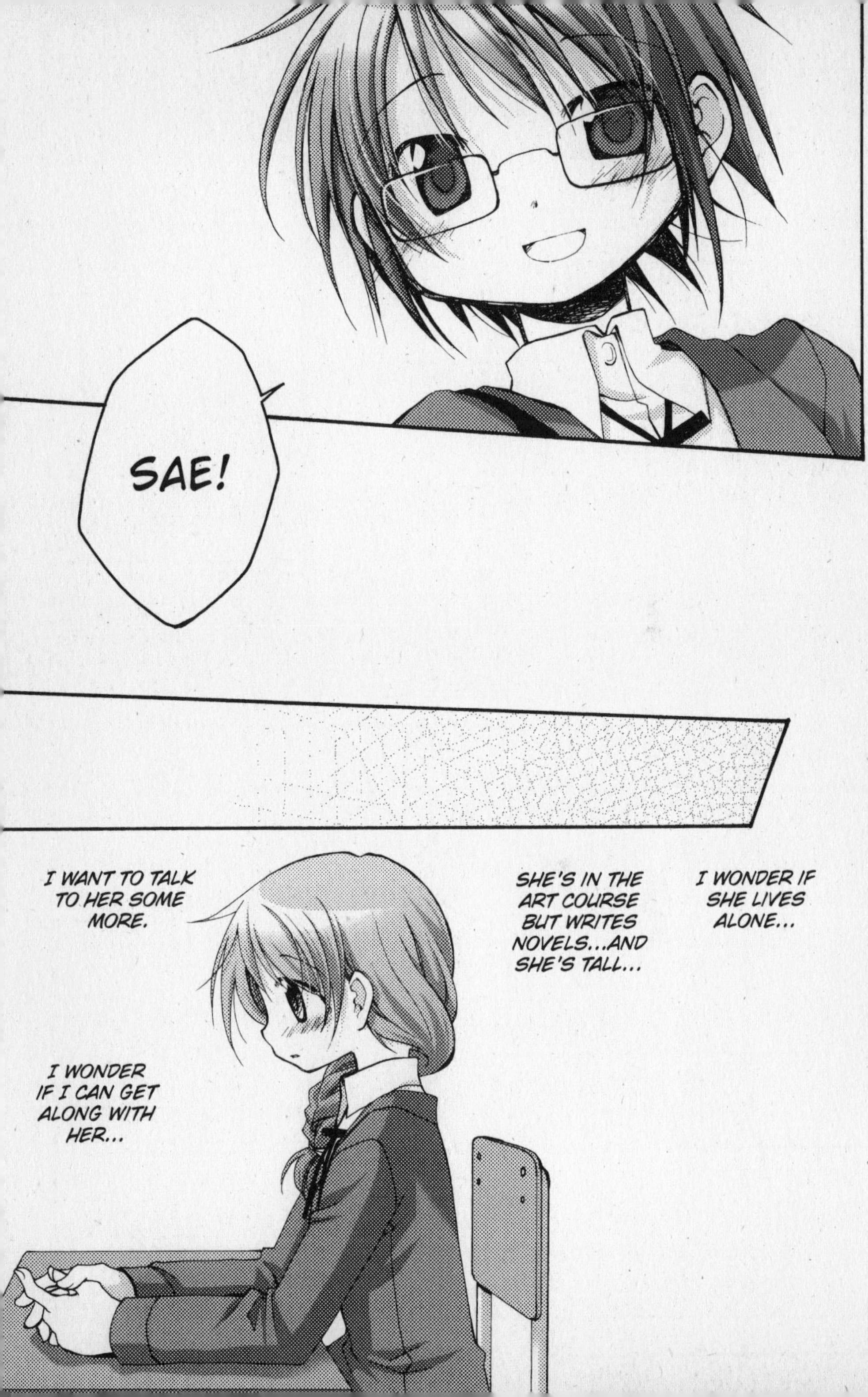
SAE!
I WONDER IF SHE LIVES ALONE...
SHE'S IN THE ART COURSE BUT WRITES NOVELS...AND SHE'S TALL...
I WANT TO TALK TO HER SOME MORE.
I WONDER IF I CAN GET ALONG WITH HER...

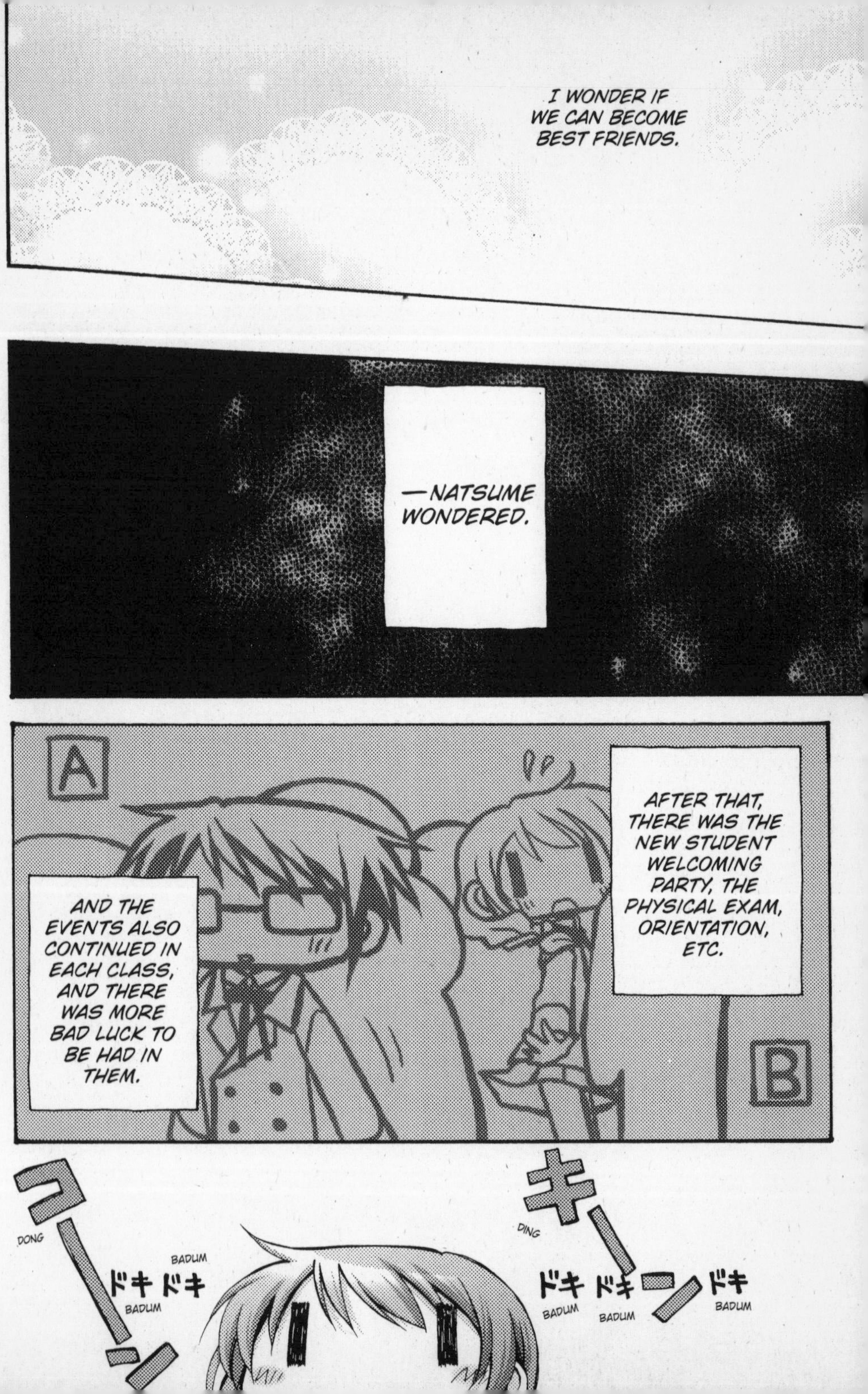
I WONDER IF WE CAN BECOME BEST FRIENDS.
—NATSUME WONDERED.
B
AFTER THAT, THERE WAS THE NEW STUDENT WELCOMING PARTY, THE PHYSICAL EXAM, ORIENTATION, ETC.
A
AND THE EVENTS ALSO CONTINUED IN EACH CLASS, AND THERE WAS MORE BAD LUCK TO BE HAD IN THEM.
キーン
DING
ドキ
BADUM
ドキ
BADUM
ドキ
BADUM
コーン
DONG
ドキドキ
BADUM
BADUM

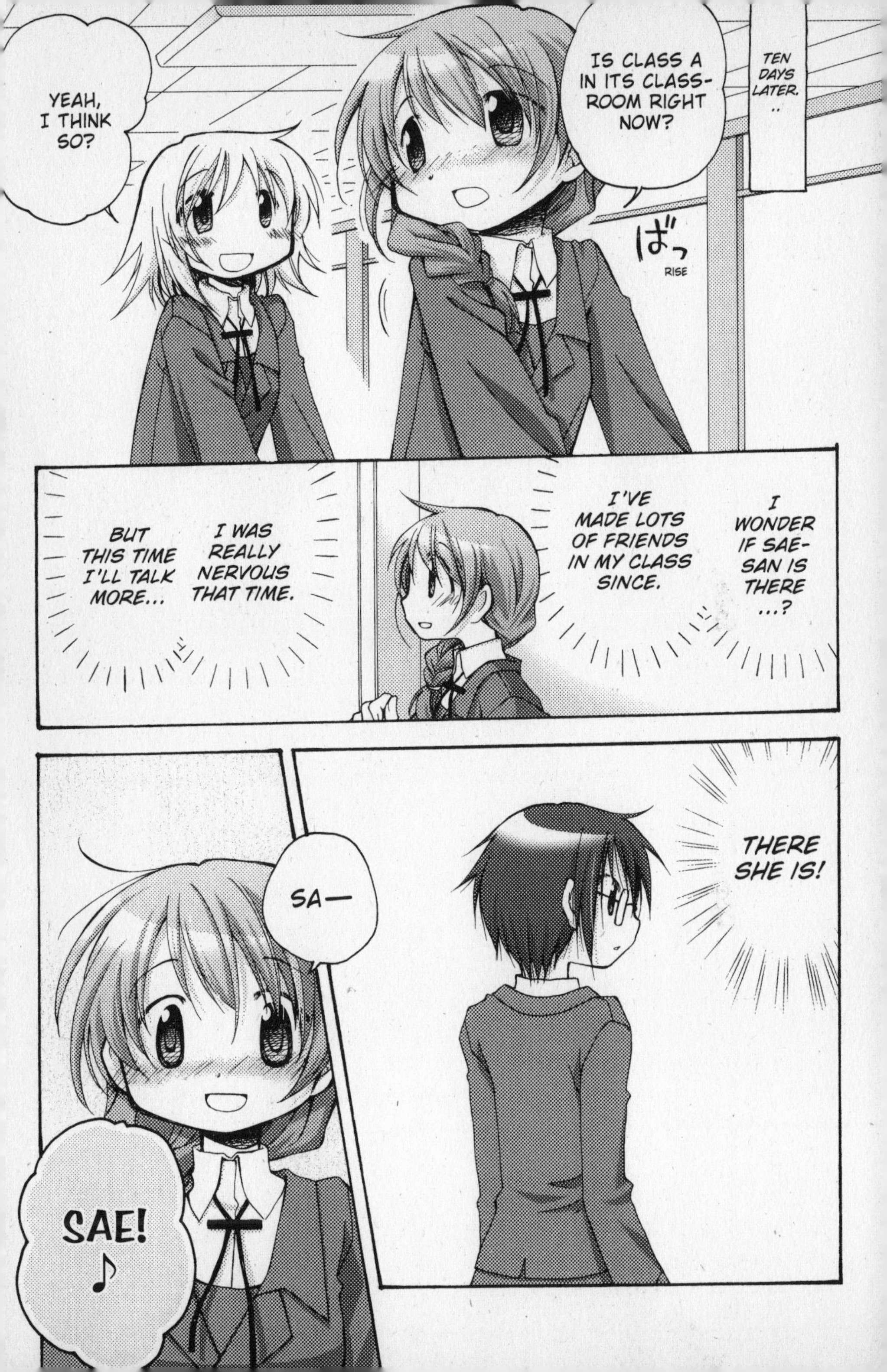
TEN DAYS LATER. ..
IS CLASS A IN ITS CLASS-ROOM RIGHT NOW?
ばっ
RISE
YEAH, I THINK SO?
I WONDER IF SAE-SAN IS THERE ...?
I'VE MADE LOTS OF FRIENDS IN MY CLASS SINCE.
I WAS REALLY NERVOUS THAT TIME.
BUT THIS TIME I'LL TALK MORE...
THERE SHE IS!
SA—
SAE! ♪

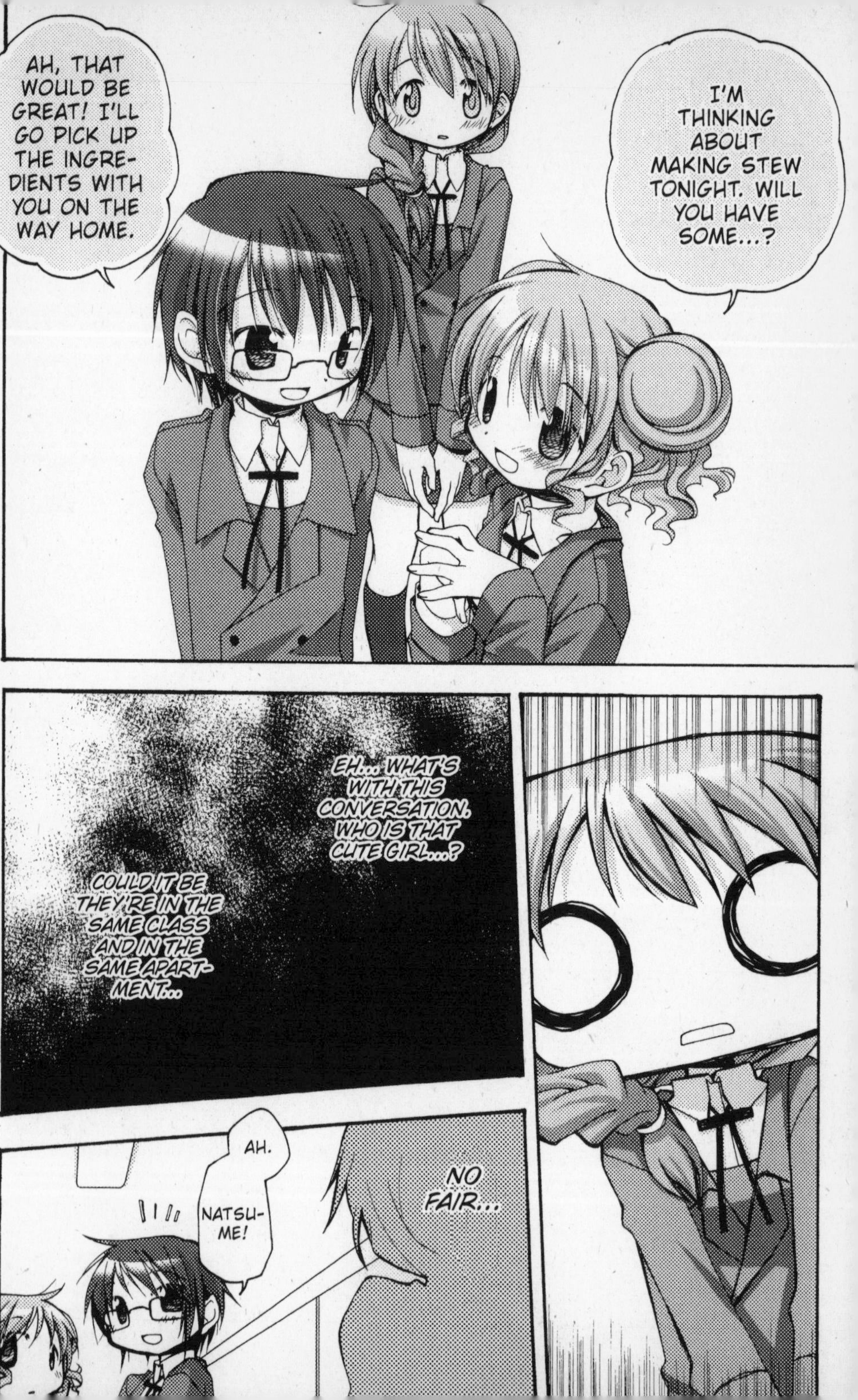
I'M THINKING ABOUT MAKING STEW TONIGHT. WILL YOU HAVE SOME...?
AH, THAT WOULD BE GREAT! I'LL GO PICK UP THE INGRE-DIENTS WITH YOU ON THE WAY HOME.
EH... WHAT'S WITH THIS CONVERSATION. WHO IS THAT CUTE GIRL...?
COULD IT BE THEY'RE IN THE SAME CLASS AND IN THE SAME APART-MENT...
NO FAIR...
AH.
NATSU-ME!

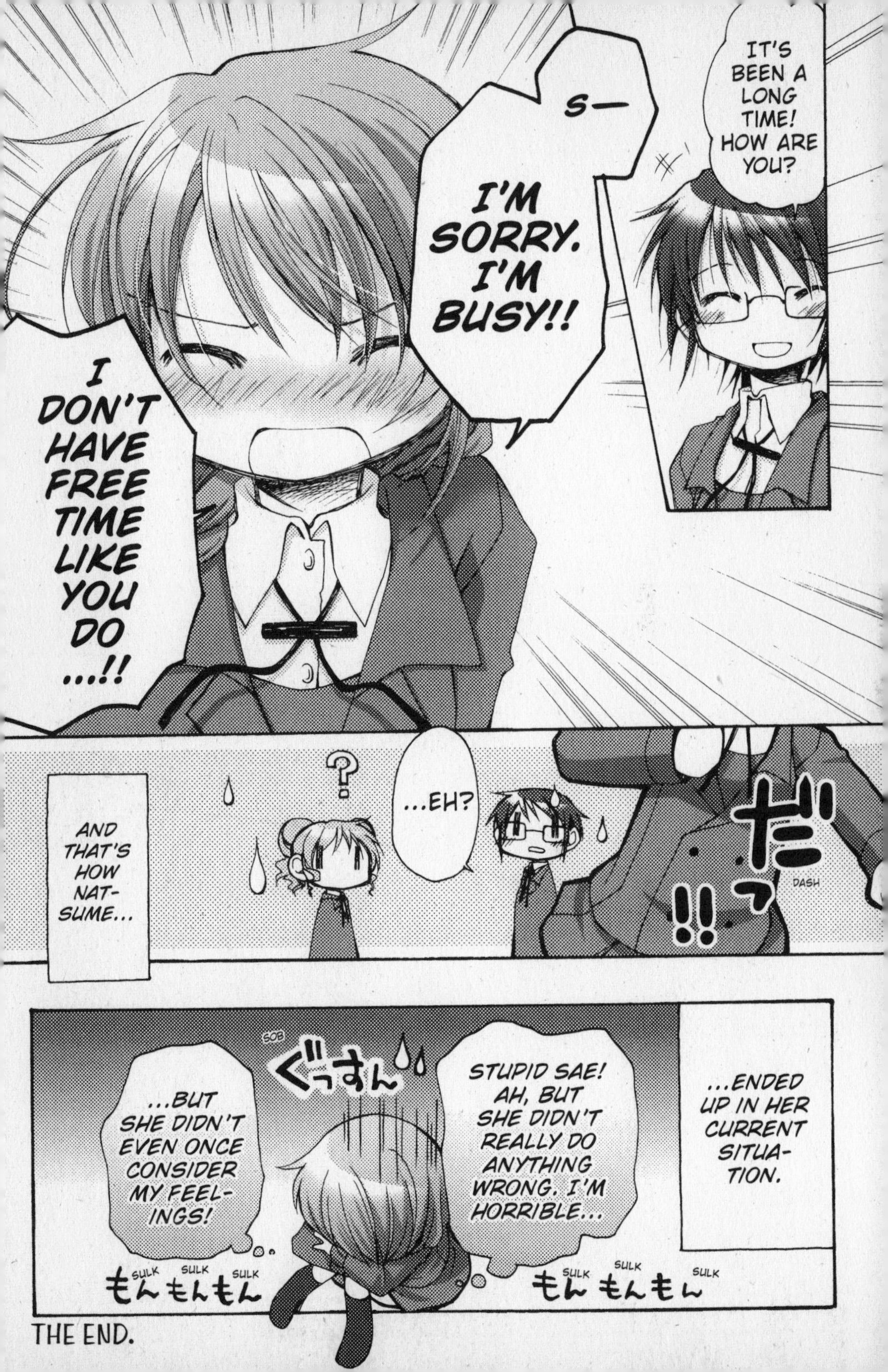
IT'S BEEN A LONG TIME! HOW ARE YOU?
S—
I'M SORRY. I'M BUSY!!
I DON'T HAVE FREE TIME LIKE YOU DO ...!!
だっ!!
DASH
...EH?
?
AND THAT'S HOW NATSUME...
...ENDED UP IN HER CURRENT SITUATION.
STUPID SAE! AH, BUT SHE DIDN'T REALLY DO ANYTHING WRONG. I'M HORRIBLE...
ぐっすん
SOB
...BUT SHE DIDN'T EVEN ONCE CONSIDER MY FEEL-INGS!
もんもんもん
SULK SULK SULK
もんもんもん
SULK SULK SULK

THE END.

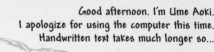

Good afternoon. I'm Ume Aoki.
I apologize for using the computer this time.
Handwritten text takes much longer so...

Thanks to everyone, SUNSHINE SKETCH
is now on its fourth volume.
Thank you very much!!
It's all happening so quickly...

The fourth volume was pretty surprising.
I thought about a lot of things for this volume,
like when should I promote Yuno and company,
what kind of girls should the first-years be, etc.
For now they have safely enrolled and been promoted,
I think?

Oh, and I can't forget Arisawa-san.
She was a favorite, so I had her exchange e-mail
addresses with Yuno (*laugh*).
Maybe she'll show up again??

And Natsume.
The episode where she meets Sae
was planned way in advance
and I wanted to release it,
but it was very difficult to have it as a 4-koma comic.
So I decided to draw it this way.
But as I write this, I haven't even
finished drawing it yet!
I wonder if it'll make it safely into Volume 4...
(*laugh*)

If it turns into a volume that can be placed with the
rest of the volumes, that would make me very happy.

Well, let's meet again. ♪
Thank you very much!

2008.
蒼樹うめ
ありがと〜♡

Special Thanks
Matsuda98, K-bayashi-sama, Komeworks-sama
Dad, mom, grandparents, and I guess my older brother too
Everyone at Houbunsha
Everyone on the anime staff, the voice actors

And of course, you ♡ ♡ ♡

TRANSLATOR'S NOTES

PAGE 4
Okou
Translated as "incense."

PAGE 28
"Gram. Grammar. Glamorous."
Think something along the lines of "funny (gram), funnier (grammar), funniest (glamorous)." In Japanese, "glamorous" is pronounced "gramorous," which is why Miya-chan comes up with this string of thought.

PAGE 30
Kamaboko
Known as "fish cake" in English, *kamaboko* is made of processed seafood products, such as pureed white fish. It is a popular ingredient for udon.

PAGE 47
Shouchuu
A distilled Japanese spirit that is usually around 25% alcohol. Sweet potato *shouchuu* is distilled from sweet potatoes and retains their characteristic taste.

PAGE 55
Bullseye
In the art, the word on Miya-chan's die is *atarime*. When spoken, it can be a homonym for both "bullseye" and "dried cuttlefish," the latter being a popular Asian snack, hence the joke.

PAGE 56
Hikari
Hikari means "light." In this case, Nori is talking about fiber-optic lines for internet. Hikari is also the name of one of the bullet trains in Japan.

PAGE 71
Jimotti
Jimotti is slang for someone who is local. It is taken from the word *jimoto* which means "local."

PAGE 78
Norisuke-san
-suke is a common ending for Japanese boys' names. Miya-chan is being silly by adding it to Nori-chan's name here.

PAGE 83
Juubei Yagyuu and Dokuganryuu Masamune
Famous Japanese samurai who are traditionally represented as having only one eye. Juubei Yagyuu is often portrayed as wearing an eyepatch, while Dokuganryuu ("One-eyed Dragon") Masamune is a nickname for Masamune Date, who is said to have plucked out his own infected eye to stop a deadly bout of smallpox from claiming his life.

PAGE 87
Floral egg crab
In Japanese, this toxic crab is called *subesube-manjuugani*, which is what Miya-chan shouts out here. *Subesube* can also mean "smooth" or "silky," which explains Yuno's reaction.

SUNSHINE SKETCH ④

UME AOKI

Translation: Satsuki Yamashita

Lettering: Keiran O'Leary

HIDAMARI SKETCH © 2009 Ume Aoki. All rights reserved. First published in Japan in 2009 by HOUBUNSHA CO., LTD.,Tokyo. English translation rights in United States, Canada and United Kingdom arranged with HOUBUNSHA CO., LTD through Tuttle-Mori Agency, Inc.,Tokyo.

Translation © 2010 by Hachette Book Group, Inc.

Yen Press
Hachette Book Group
237 Park Avenue, New York, NY 10017

www.HachetteBookGroup.com
www.YenPress.com

Yen Press is an imprint of Hachette Book Group, Inc. The Yen Press name and logo are trademarks of Hachette Book Group, Inc.

First Yen Press Edition: January 2010

ISBN: 978-0-316-08112-2

10 9 8 7 6 5 4 3 2

OPM

Printed in the United States of America